Games User Research Cookbook

This book offers a comprehensive and practical guide to games user research (GUR). Blending theory and hands-on experience, it walks readers through methods, tools, and techniques tailored to the real-world constraints of small- and medium-sized game development studios to support them in delivering better player experiences.

This book is divided into three parts. Part 1 introduces core concepts to game development and explores gameplay experience, together with factors that influence player behaviour and decisions. This part ends by exploring the games user researcher's role and its common challenges. Next, Part 2 presents readers with a ten-step end-to-end research process for a single study. From understanding stakeholders and designing methods, through recruiting participants, moderating sessions, and analyzing results, to delivering actionable insights, this section provides guidance, real-life examples, and templates for integrating research in game development practices, even when the budget and timeline are tight. Finally, Part 3 provides readers with ready-to-use "recipes" for ten research methods covering every phase of the game production cycle. Each recipe includes practical tips, pitfalls to avoid, and actual report excerpts.

Whether you're an indie developer wanting to better understand your players, or a UX designer or researcher moving from application software to the world of games, this book will provide you with all the information on how to use research to gain the insights needed to create better player experiences.

Michał Mycka is a games user researcher both by education and practice. His educational background is in psychology (master's) and economics (PhD). Since 2012, he has provided insights for over 40 games and game-related R&D projects, covering a wide range of genres and platforms. He has worked with developers and publishers ranging from indie to triple-A, such as Gamedust, Klabater, Game Operators, and Ubisoft Reflections, among others. He teaches games user research at Collegium Da Vinci (Poland) and acts as an expert in the Creative Europe Programme.

Games User Research Cookbook

Cookbook
Tools and Techniques for Better Player Experience

Michał Mycka

CRC Press
Taylor & Francis Group
Boca Raton London New York

CRC Press is an imprint of the
Taylor & Francis Group, an **informa** business

Designed cover image: Łukasz Bazela

First edition published 2026
by CRC Press
2385 NW Executive Center Drive, Suite 320, Boca Raton FL 33431

and by CRC Press
4 Park Square, Milton Park, Abingdon, Oxon, OX14 4RN

CRC Press is an imprint of Taylor & Francis Group, LLC

ISBN: 9781032818955 (hbk)
ISBN: 9781032820637 (pbk)
ISBN: 9781003501909 (ebk)

DOI: 10.1201/9781003501909

Typeset in Times
by codeMantra

Access the Support Material: www.routledge.com/9781032820637

Dedication

To Wiśnia, Majka, and Tymon for the fact that you are
and your loving support in all my endeavours.

Contents

Acknowledgements

I wholeheartedly thank my industry friends who took the time to read parts of the book draft and shared their feedback, which helped me improve its content, especially Ula Karpińska, Jakub Matuszczak, Krzysztof Miotk, Łukasz Skubek, Krzysztof Zandecki, and Janusz Bossy. I send special thanks to Łukasz Bazela, who designed the cover image. Warm thanks are also due to Paweł Flieger, who gave me permission to share excerpts from the actual research I conducted at Gamedust, and to Natalia Flieger, who, as a junior user researcher at the time, supported studies presented as examples in Chapters 14, 15, and 22. Report excerpts included in this book were translated and revised for clarity.

Introduction

This book is based on a simple premise: there is no one way to cook properly. It depends not only on variations in a single recipe but also on what you need and what you can afford in terms of both money and time. Sometimes you have time to mingle and may want to prepare something special, and sometimes you are in a rush, and some quick chips will do the trick to save the day. Basically, this book is a run-through of my user research kitchen – how I organize it, and what recipes and utensils I use for various occasions. I have had the opportunity to work for bigger establishments having well-equipped kitchens, which I'm grateful about, but in this book, I focus more on the perspective of smaller and less recognizable restaurants, because apart from their charm, they pose specific challenges and prove to be wonderful learning grounds. When it comes to book structure, it is a kind similar to the one you can find in... a cookbook! First, you have the part most of us tend to omit, where the author's general philosophy, approach to cooking, and the idea behind the recipes are outlined. In Part 1, I go through the definitions, theories, and processes of games and how they are made, taking on three perspectives: the team that is making the game, the players who have to engage with the game, and the game user researchers (that's us!) who have to bridge these two perspectives. The aim is to provide us with the necessary vocabulary and context for the reading: Parts 2 and 3. I wrote Part 1 of this book with the honest hope that you will read it, but if you are here only for recipes – I'm ready for it, as that is what the cookbooks are for. In Part 2, I share the ten-step basic recipe for a study that can be adapted to specific needs and occasions. It's the core of the book where an overview of methods selected to fit small studio capabilities is provided, followed by gathering requirements and laying out the study purpose. Then, I'll go through gathering assets, fleshing out methods and tools, and recruiting participants to finally conduct research sessions and analyze results, to end the whole process with a report preparation and debrief. On the book's website (www.routledge.com/9781032820637), you will find the templates I refer to in Part 2, which can serve as a starting point for taking selected steps in the research process without having to reinvent the wheel. I didn't call Part 2 "basic recipe" for no reason, as it will lay the foundation to what's ahead in Part 3, where I share a list of ten selected recipes and sample effects I got while using them. My aim was twofold: to make the list both affordable and doable in various organizational settings, especially smaller ones. To avoid paying lip service, for this book, I selected examples that come from my experience working with game teams of five to a maximum of less than 20 people. The focus on the small- and medium-sized studios perspective stems both from my personal experiences working in various organizational settings and from my intention to make the book's content approachable for people such as:

- Non-gaming UX specialists (e.g. UX researchers and UX designers) who would like to gain perspective on conducting user research in games.
- Gaming UX specialists working in small- and medium-sized studios or acting as a "one-person research team".
- Small- and medium-sized game developers who are looking to evaluate their players' experience in a more structured and predictable way, while also tailoring the research process to their organizational capabilities.

As with many endeavours that bear some scent of creativity, throughout the book, I relied on three specific core pillars.

I   APPROACHABILITY WITHOUT PREACHING

I use the form "we" a lot in the book. It's a habit I got from interacting with students during academic classes, and it comes from a sense of community and a belief that maybe we'll both learn something new in the situation we're in – in this case, me while writing and you while reading. On the contrary, I want to avoid a stereotypical teacherly tone that judges how things should be done, what is correct, and how important the role of research is. Sure, I believe it's important, but there's just a thin line between conveying a moral and moralizing I didn't want to cross (it's for you to judge, if I managed), so let's not treat this book as a normative document. I decided to use real-life examples throughout the book, which are simply imperfect in objectively depicting reality, as they come from a specific context and limitations of the moment. At the same time, I believe they add texture and realism to topics covered in this book, showing how research often unfolds in practice and can act as a nudge for your own endeavours. While writing, I also assumed that as adults we can take each other seriously without using overly conceited or complicated language, and framing games user research in a cooking metaphor shouldn't take away from the seriousness of the craft.

II   INFORMED SELECTIVENESS

I tried to stay away from the "backpack philosophy" approach by providing an exhaustive review of methods, approaches, and theories behind them. Generally, one can be overwhelmed with a number of things to keep in mind while conducting research. As they say, if two psychologists look at any behaviour, they will come up with at least three competing theories that try to explain it. Certainly, there is nothing as practical as good theory, but I rather focused on providing scaffolding, so you can start doing research and learn additional things as you go. Another thing is that the book focuses on methods, most of which are relatively easy to conduct on your own in smaller organizational settings; hence, I placed less emphasis on statistical inference and research relying on a large number of participants. However, this doesn't mean that I have totally neglected the topic of statistics, because even when we examine small samples, we can use descriptive statistics and perhaps even apply selected tests to support our efforts.

III   OUTCOME ABOVE OUTPUT

In most cases, imperfect research is still a hundred times better than no research at all. Of course, it makes sense if we follow certain rules and know the limitations of the different methods and the context in which to apply them – we simply cannot have great outcomes out of the crappy output. However, we will rarely have occasions to afford time and money to prepare and conduct a study by the book and get a near-perfect result in return. Such an environment is more likely to be met in academia, where, by definition, we are looking for results that will expand our general understanding of some phenomenon or part of reality and will stand the test of time (until some better explanation is found). In this book, we will focus on conducting research in the wild, where results must be delivered on time, are related to a specific product (game), have to be actionable, and most of the time have a short expiry date. In user research practice, as in many other specialties, we will have to make some trade-offs, as at the end of the day, it doesn't matter how hard we chopped, mixed, baked, or how beautiful or perfect the garnishes were, what matters is if we didn't end up hungry.

Alright, enough talk – let's cook up some research!

Part 1

User Research for Games

This part will introduce us to the topic of games, their creation, and playing them. The aim is to grasp key concepts for games user research, understand both the subject and context of our work, as well as equip us with a basic vocabulary to communicate effectively with the development team. We will start by examining the game itself, its components, and the production cycle. Next, we will explore key concepts that shape the player experience, with a focus on the factors that influence player behaviour and decision-making. Finally, we will discuss the role of games user researchers and how to navigate between the perspectives of the development team and the players.

DOI: 10.1201/9781003501909-1

1 What Is a Game, Actually?

We'll start by discussing the game itself and how it differs from application software, together with looking at various criteria, we can divide games into different types. We'll then look at typical game components and the disciplines involved in their creation, both those we aim to support and those that can support us. We'll conclude by examining typical phases in the game production cycle, together with key questions we help to answer at each of them, and the assets we'll have at our disposal for research purposes.

Topics covered in this chapter:

- Coining a working definition and typology of video games relevant to user research purposes.
- Identifying the main disciplines involved in video game creation and their typical questions.
- Exploring game design frameworks, such as MDA (Mechanics – Dynamics – Aesthetics) and RGD (Rational Game Design).
- Gaining an overview of the game production cycle, with a focus on common challenges, research questions, and assets in each phase.

1.1 YET ANOTHER DEFINITION

Certainly, all of us have an idea of what a game is, and we know when we spot one. You may ask, why bother about the definition then? When it comes to communicating outside of a casual chat about a game we played last night, one of the crucial reasons for building definitions for basic terms is to structure reality and improve communication within the discipline and with our stakeholders. Simply, when you call something by name, it is not only obviously easier to spot it, but also to methodically analyze it. Certainly, we could spend a long time listing all the definitions and trying to distil the ultimate one. But it's not my aim, and generally such endeavours, although instructive, can be quite long and futile. In a practical context, we just need the definition to provide us with a solid frame we are willing to agree on and use for a given purpose and time – may it be a short design discussion, running a series of research studies, or just reading this book. So, I'll refer us to a few definitions, which I find usable on a daily basis while running research. It's not about that other definitions are not or are less valuable – nothing could be more wrong. It's just that the mere fact of listing multiple definitions wouldn't structure reality better for us, as each subsequent one will add less and less informational value. So, without further ado, let's start with the definition coined by Bernard Suits [2005, p. 43]:

the voluntary attempt to overcome unnecessary obstacles.

Let's dissect it. The game as an activity is a voluntary one (i.e. I engage in it because I want to). No one has to drag me to do it, it's just a goal in itself. It's just one thing that sets video games apart from application software, where you have an outside goal you have to realize (e.g. you have to work in software to earn money, so you can pay your bills in another software, so you have where to live and you can order your food in yet another software). Another thing is that the obstacles are the things that all of the application software wants to avoid at all costs, and it does it for a good reason. While I work in a spreadsheet, I don't want to overcome any obstacles; I want to be as efficient as possible and get the job done. If I would take the same approach to designing a game, I would end up with the "hit to win" button available just after clicking the "new game". Let us take, for example, sports games like volleyball. Lines constrain the playing field, and we have this annoying net hanging in

DOI: 10.1201/9781003501909-2

the middle. Those are obviously some of the unnecessary obstacles we have to overcome to earn points and ultimately win this game. Although we can easily eliminate them. Let's take off the net and make the playing field bigger. Certainly, now it is much easier to play as we have eliminated obstacles, but the game has lost all its sense. That sets Games User Research apart from mainstream User Research (e.g. done for banking apps, e-commerce, and so on) – we deal with a product that is used, just for the sake of using it.

Let's move on to another definition that I find fit for purpose is one coined by Chris Crawford [1984, 2003]. He defines game as:

> *a closed formal system that subjectively represents a subset of reality.*

The term "system" means that the game is a set of elements that interact with each other in complex ways. This system is "formal" as it contains rules for the interaction of elements, and "closed", that is, it does not allow for the interaction of elements that aren't described by the rules. And it holds especially true for video games, as in board games, players sometimes make up rules on the fly, as their specific situation wasn't described in the manual (or they misinterpreted the rules and play the game in a different way than intended). Video games don't have or allow that, leaving little room for improvisation in the basic mechanics. Although at times, players may find consequences unforeseen or unintended by the designers while interacting with some of the game systems (e.g. playing law-abiding citizens in *GTA* or locking Sims in rooms without doors). However, if it's not a bug, it's still within the system.

What is interesting and valuable in Crawford's proposition from the user research perspective is separating games from other activities based on the complexity of the interactions. We have activities such as immersing ourselves in various types of storytelling, e.g. in the form of books, movies, or TV series. They aren't interactive by nature, because we cannot influence the course of events (there are, of course, interactive books or movies, but these are isolated cases). Certainly, each of us can experience a story differently, and while returning after some time, we can see different or additional meanings in them, but we cannot change them as such; they're objectively the same all the time. But toys are interactive! When we look at how children play, we can easily realize that we can tell many stories with just one toy. Taking a doll for example, we can interact with it by arranging its legs and arms in different poses, we can dress it up and tell all kinds of stories about the fact that it went on a trip, fought a dragon, ate something, fixed something, talked to someone and argued with someone... we just can tell 152 or more stories with this one doll. Okay, toys allow us to tell stories and are interactive, but what do toys not have? They do not have a correct solution – we can't play with them wrong. Of course, we can break a toy or hurt ourselves or someone with it, and in this sense, we can play with it in the wrong way, but as a rule, from the perspective of telling a story or interacting with it, there is nothing we could do wrong here. There is no predetermined goal built into playing with toys. But hey! Puzzles have a goal – finding the correct solution. Let's take a Rubik's cube. I can tell stories about my millionth attempt at this puzzle. I can interact with it by turning the walls and even play with it just to occupy my hands during a phone call. Finally, I can direct my actions towards finding the correct solution (i.e. arranging single-colour walls). However, I cannot lose in this whole process. Of course, I can say that this cube defeated me, but I cannot lose at it. This leads us to the fact that although puzzles are interactive and have a goal in the form of finding the correct solution, there is no conflict inherent in achieving this goal. However, you can definitely lose the game, as there is a conflict that ends up in an unequal result (i.e. someone is losing a game). We can summarize these relationships in Figure 1.1.

What could this mean for us? In games user research (maybe even in game development in general), in addition to playing games, it's helpful to have other interests. Being well-read or watching (and analyzing) movies helps to spot various meanings in participants' statements or some constructions used in the game itself (e.g. narrative tropes). Solving various types of physical puzzles or just watching others do it helps understand what constitutes desirable difficulty in a challenge and what is undesirable, which can be quite a challenge itself during research and analyzing results.

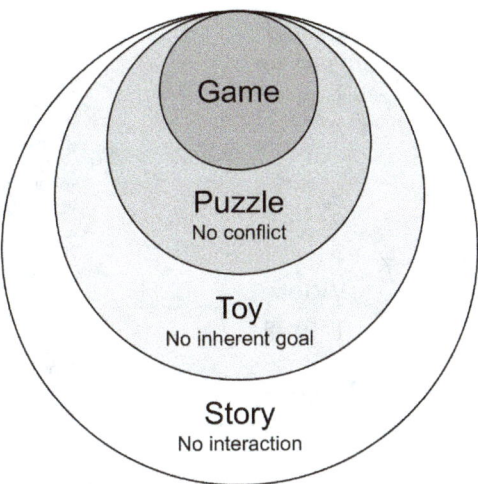

FIGURE 1.1 Relationship between game, puzzle, toy and story. (Own elaboration based on Crawford (1984)).

Pure gold are children while they play and engage with toys – this is a festival of joy and imagination. Another thing I draw from this division for myself is a solution to the apparent dichotomy between gameplay and narrative, which lingers in some development teams. It doesn't matter which of these dimensions we start from, and it's not about which one is more important, as it can vary from game to game (e.g. chess can be seen as a story about two kingdoms at war). We might be more focused on one or the other for sure, but at the end of the day, they both build the experience and should reinforce each other. Just to sum it all up, we can use the definition coined by Fullerton et al. [2008], who describe games as:

> a closed, formal system that engages players in a structured conflict and resolves its uncertainty in an unequal outcome.

Although we may add cautiously that this unequal outcome is not only a win, but a win or a loss. After all, some games are impossible to lose (e.g. *Animal Crossing: New Horizons*), but also some are impossible to win (e.g. endless runners like *Temple Run*) in a strict sense.

Okay, we have a working definition of a game. So, let's take a closer look at the types of video games. Video games are an internally diverse group that doesn't have one unified classification. The topic is important to running efficient and effective research, because the division of games adopted by the researcher often determines the efficacy in recruiting research participants reflecting the intended target audience. There have already been "quite a few" attempts to address this subject [Wolf 2001; Aarseth et al. 2003; Whalen 2004; Elverdam & Aarseth 2007; Clearwater 2011; Lee et al. 2014; Osathanunkul 2015]. In general, attempts to classify or create typologies of games are based on systematizing video games by assigning them categories based on various dimensions, including:

- type,
- genre,
- number of players,
- purpose,
- age category,
- hardware platform,
- distribution model,
- artistic style,
- method of presentation,
- temporal aspect,

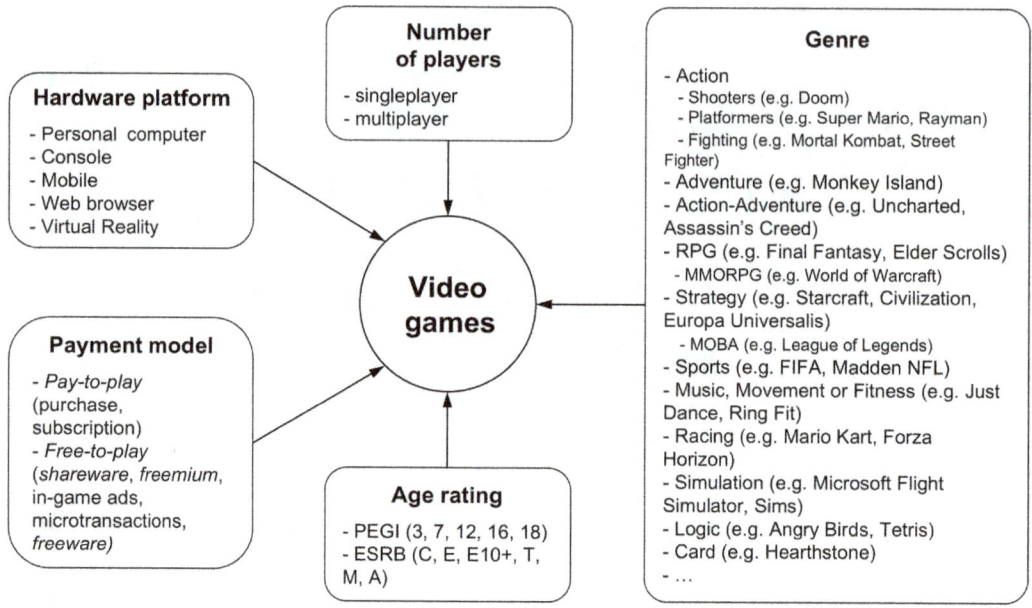

FIGURE 1.2　Typology of video games. (Own elaboration.)

- perspective,
- theme,
- world presented,
- mood,
- type of ending,
- … (you can just add another dimension here)

Some academic researchers focused on creating information systems that enable games to be searched for by diverse groups of people, proposing game classifications spanning multiple categories and hundreds of concepts to describe them [Aarseth et al. 2003; Elverdam & Aarseth 2007; Lee et al. 2014]. However, we will stay down to earth and focus on the frequent divisions by genre, hardware platform, number of players, and payment model, because this is what players most often come into contact with, e.g. via press outlets and video game distribution platforms. Figure 1.2 presents a working typology of video games, based on the review of literature, press outlets, and distribution platforms (e.g. Valve's Steam). It can act for us as a framework for deriving typical variables that are worth considering while recruiting participants for our studies.

1.2　STRUCTURE AND COMPONENTS

As we mentioned already, the game is a closed formal system, and as such, it consists of various elements such as gameplay systems, mechanics, aesthetics, narrative, and controls, among many others. Obviously, making all of those elements and integrating them into a coherent whole we call a game is an interdisciplinary effort. In small-scale productions, members have to wear multiple hats to make things happen, but in large-scale productions, we meet people coming from various disciplines who are involved in the process, each with their own goals and challenges. With a dose of naivety, we can have a look at the credits of the selected triple-A title, and based on the people involved in the creation process, we could try to reconstruct what are some of the game components and disciplines we will be dealing with. Certainly, some of the disciplines can be genre, feature, or game type specific, so we will keep them in larger categories to keep a clear view of who we can meet down the road and on some examples of the questions we may help to answer. What is equally important, we will also have a look at some of the disciplines that can help us.

1.2.1 WE SUPPORT…

- Design – People who oversee the creative process from initial concept all the way to game release. This discipline is responsible for shaping the gameplay, narrative and defining the rules governing the game world. It includes a diverse set of competencies and skill sets, which in larger projects are the basis for separating a number of specific roles.
  - Who we can potentially meet: Game Designer, Systems Designer, Level Designer, Quest/Mission Designer, Narrative Designer, Writer, Technical Designer, UI Designer, UX Designer, Economy Designer, Monetization Designer.
  - Some of the questions we help to answer:
    - Do players feel the intended emotions or reactions to the game?
    - What are the most memorable moments in the experience?
    - Do players understand what they have to do and how to do it?
    - Does the game (its level or fragment) have appropriate pacing, difficulty, and length?
    - Do players understand the characters' intentions and motivations?
    - Do players understand what is happening within the story?
- Art – People who oversee and create the visual layer of the game from 2D concept art to 3D models for characters, items, creatures, and whole environments.
  - Who we can potentially meet: 2D Artist, 3D Artist, Technical Artist, Concept Artist, UI Artist, Environmental Artist, Character Artist, Weapon Artist, VFX Artist.
  - Some of the questions we help to answer:
    - Do players like what they see?
    - Are players able to read key information about the game elements and their state?
    - Does the form of the various elements communicate their functions well?
- Animation – This discipline includes making the game world alive, from animating characters and elements of the environment to creating cinematics.
  - Who we can potentially meet: Gameplay Animator, Cinematic Animator, Motion Capture Specialist, Technical Animator.
  - Some of the questions we help to answer:
    - Do the animations have the right feel?
    - Do the animations communicate the intentions of the characters (e.g. enemies/ NPCs) well?
- Audio – People designing and creating the game soundscape. Discipline encompasses both those who record and implement sounds and music in-game, but also voice-actors.
  - Who we can potentially meet: Sound Designer, Music Designer, Composer.
  - Some of the questions we help to answer:
    - Are the sounds appropriately matched to the environment/items/characters?
    - Does the sounds/music adequately communicate the state of various elements in the game world?
    - Can the player differentiate the sounds of different weapons/items?
    - Does the music help build the intended mood or pacing?
- Production – This discipline is focused on planning, organizing, and monitoring the creation of the game throughout its development. People in this discipline strive to ensure that a game is delivered on time, with the intended quality, and within the budget, given the available resources and potential risks.
  - Who we can potentially meet: Producer, Associate Producer, Project Manager, Release Manager, Live Ops Manager, Project Closer.

- Some of the questions we help to answer:
  - What are the most significant risks to the game reception from the player experience perspective?
  - Is the gameplay experience of individual elements and the game as a whole of an expected quality level?
  - Do players expect other (previously undefined) mechanics or functionalities?

1.2.2 WHILE COOPERATING WITH...

- Programming – This discipline is substantial in the development process, as they write code in order to bring the game to life in the form of playable game builds.
  - Who we can potentially meet – Gameplay Programmer, Graphics Programmer, Audio Programmer, Engine Programmer, Tools Programmer, among many others.
  - How we can cooperate – This discipline is substantial in the development process, and we may support them in better understanding players' wants and needs. In turn, they can help us better understand technical constraints, which allows us to deliver more feasible suggestions. More directly, we cooperate with them to have the required game builds ready for research or we request additional features that help us run studies more efficiently (e.g. asking for various debug options like an option to skip various sections of the game).
- Quality assurance – People who focus on the quality, ensuring that the game is properly tested, and bugs and errors are tracked down and squashed throughout development. This discipline is faced with a range of tasks, from checking functional errors (Functional QA), through checking the correctness of translations and adaptations (Localization QA), to ensuring that the game is compliant with platform requirements (Certification QA).
  - Who we can potentially meet – QA Specialist, QA Engineer, Tester.
  - How we can cooperate – We can learn what is and what isn't working as intended, what are the current functional problems and typical workarounds. Basically, we can be better prepared to run efficient research without unexpected problems with game builds.
- Marketing – This discipline ensures that players will hear about the game through reviews, ads, social media, various communities, platforms and websites, and even face-to-face events.
  - Who we can potentially meet – Brand Specialist, Marketing Specialist, PR Specialist, Community Manager, User Acquisition Manager.
  - How we can cooperate – They help us to understand how the game will be communicated to players via various assets (e.g. trailers, store fronts, product packaging) and channels (e.g. social media, press outlets). In exchange, we can be instrumental in assessing whether the marketing assets are experienced by the players as intended, and whether expectations built by marketing activities are in line with actual experience with the game.
- Analytics – People who focus on collecting and interpreting player and gameplay data to guide decision-making.
  - Who we can potentially meet – Data Scientist, Data Analyst, Business Intelligence Specialist.
  - How we can cooperate – Generally, cooperation between user research and analytics can provide a complete picture of player behaviours, making room for better focus in research on actual problem areas, providing better insights and a base for decision-making. Simply put, data analytics can deliver an answer to "what" is happening in the game, precisely pointing to "where" and to "what extent" this happens (e.g. 42% of players abandon the game on the third section of the tutorial, spending there on average 20 out of 48 minutes of their play session). While we can provide support to pinpoint "what" is happening with the player and "why" this is happening (e.g. study participants highlighted that the tutorial was too long and boring for them,

because new mechanics were introduced at a slow pace. Additionally, in the third section, some of the participants got stuck and didn't know what to do next, because they didn't notice the tutorial prompts placed in the environment).

1.2.3 GUIDED BY...

Certainly, all those people could toss the elements they're working on to the wall to see what sticks and goes well together, but it could be a really tiresome and resource-intensive endeavour (which actually may happen to some extent). All in all, the whole game isn't just the sum of its parts. Fortunately enough, knowledge about what the effect of combining different elements should be, which of them should come to the foreground and which should constitute a background is encapsulated in creative vision, core pillars, and player fantasy. Depending on the team we work with, we can find all those things or just some of them, and they can be more or less formalized. For user researchers, knowing and understanding them is useful, because they set the frame against which we will usually test various assets provided by the team (e.g. game builds, concept arts, narrative beats).

1.2.3.1 Creative Vision

Creative vision refers to the overall concept and unique artistic direction that encompasses ideas around gameplay, narrative, visual, and auditory aesthetics of the game. Creative vision is crucial for guiding the creative process and ensuring that all elements of a game align with the intended experience.

1.2.3.2 Player Fantasy

Simply put, the player fantasy is the answer to the question "Who am I playing as?". It conveys emotions and thoughts that the team wants the player to experience while playing in the world they created.

1.2.3.3 Core Pillars

Core pillars are basic definitions of parameters that are fundamental to realizing creative vision. They set direction and focus areas for the team and guide people from different disciplines involved in the production process, helping them make cohesive design decisions that support the vision. In smaller teams, we most often will find "Gameplay pillars" or "Game Design pillars". However, in bigger teams, core pillars for other components are not an uncommon thing to define (e.g. Narrative pillars).

When we look at the things mentioned above, they already show us some of the things we will be looking for during research throughout the game's production cycle. At least at the high level. Depending on the team and the game we're working on, we can find many other information both in explicit (e.g. documents like Game Design Document) and implicit form (e.g. team members' knowledge on the project). This will be a truism, but creative endeavours can be chaotic and hectic, and the road to realizing the creative vision – which itself can change in the process – most of the time isn't readily available. **The part of the user researchers' job in such circumstances is to structure the reality and deliver insights on it for the team so they can better understand player experience "as is" and navigate it to the "to be" state**. In this endeavour, it's worth relying on existing scaffolds used by designers that will provide us with yet another perspective on what we will be looking for during research.

1.2.4 GAME DESIGN FRAMEWORKS AND APPROACHES

Our goal is not to become game designers, but to understand the problem space they're navigating to support them better. My father used to say that a good engineer wants to understand why and how something is done before making any improvements. Certainly, I am no engineer, but my informed guess is that selected game design frameworks and approaches should give us some basis to structure what we observe during research, a better grasp of its parts, and how those parts interact with each other to create the whole experience. Whether intentionally or not, specific designers or even whole teams make assumptions about how the elements of the game should be structured to create the intended experience.

1.2.4.1 Top-Down and Bottom-Up Approaches

Ideas for a new game may come from various sources. Someone got an idea for a cool mechanic, technological advancements provided for novel interaction or artistic presentation, market research localized some niche in the current landscape, or someone has a new story to tell or a new way of telling an old story. When game creation begins with novel game mechanics, interaction, or other elements, the team has to build a larger system around it, for which suiting player fantasy needs to be crafted. This is a bottom-up approach. On the contrary, the top-down approach starts with the player fantasy for which a general gameplay concept is developed and then goes all the way down through designing systems, to the creation of suitable mechanics and elements (see Figure 1.3).

So much for the division at the conceptual level. When the team uses the top-down approach, it might be hard to decide on which elements to choose on the lower level. And when the team is focused on the bottom-up approach, it may be hard to combine various elements into a coherent player fantasy. What might seem already obvious is that both approaches are complementary, and most of the time, team members have to switch between them depending on the current needs.

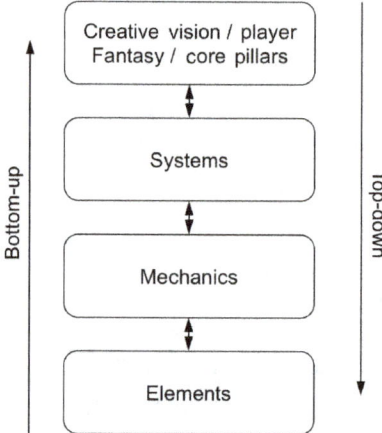

FIGURE 1.3 Top-down and bottom-up approaches to game design. (Own elaboration.)

BOX 1.1   THE POINT OF VIEW DEPENDS ON THE POINT OF SITTING

Do not mistake top-down and bottom-up approaches for hierarchy in the team and the focus of various team members. In the smaller teams, people usually have to wear many hats, but when we look at more structured teams or large-scale productions, we can more easily observe some differences in typical work focus:

- High-level focus – generally on the director level, people focus on a bird's-eye view of the game and provide goals and guidelines to inspire the whole team, ensuring that various gameplay systems and elements are creating a coherent player experience.
- Mid-level focus – team leaders' focus is to translate high-level vision and goals into more specific actions and tasks needed to be performed within the game component to ensure it adds to the intended experience.

- Low-level focus – specialists focused on actually designing and implementing specific elements, mechanics, or systems within the game.

Certainly, there are roles that, with their work, break those divisions to prevent information siloing and communication noise, and user researchers many times can aim to be one of such roles in the team.

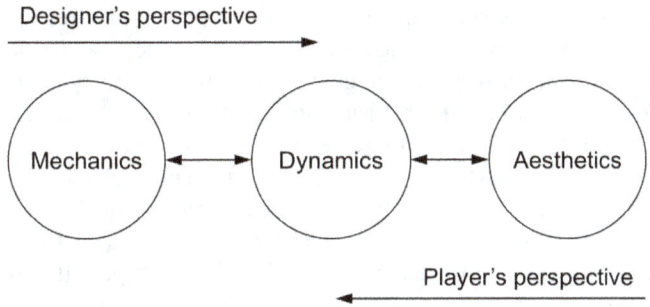

FIGURE 1.4 Player's and game designer's perspectives within the MDA framework. (Own elaboration based on Hunicke et al. (2004)).

1.2.4.2 MDA Framework

The MDA Framework proposed by Hunicke et al. [2004] can be used to understand how various layers of the game create engaging experiences. It focuses on three game components: Mechanics, Dynamics, and Aesthetics (hence the MDA). Mechanics refers to the essential rules and systems built on those rules that govern the game world. This encompasses elements such as goals, actions needed to achieve those goals, controls we need to perform the actions, feedback loops that inform us of the effect of our actions, but also any other systems that build the game. Just to provide us with an example, in a game like the *Witcher* series, mechanics would include the character's ability to walk, run, fight, cast signs, use inventory items, and interact with NPCs, among many others. The interactions emerging from various mechanics put into motion are what constitute Dynamics. It is when the game is played by the players that we can observe how the rules form various patterns and influence flow, pacing, and behaviour of the game. In games like *Anno* series, the Dynamics would include how players manage various resources, units, and trade routes, city planning, strategy for reaching new population and influence levels, and managing the increasing complexity and relations as the game progresses. The way Dynamics are presented through audiovisual and narrative design, together with actual player reactions and responses, is what refers to Aesthetics. For example, in *Stray*, Aesthetics can refer to artistic style, mood, and emotions connected to exploration and finding a way home as a cat living in a dystopian future.

To briefly summarize, we can say that Mechanics are the core of the game. Dynamics come from how players interact with the Mechanics. Aesthetics are the emotional and psychological responses that players experience as a result of the Dynamics. What is important to notice is that game designers in this model start with the Mechanics to create Dynamics that should have an intended Aesthetic effect. Players start the other way around (see Figure 1.4).

We, as user researchers, want to combine those two perspectives. We will observe the effect of the designer's work in the form of players' reactions to Aesthetic, and if it is not as expected, we will try to work our way to assess what potential issues they face with the Dynamics, and what are the underlying problems with specific Mechanics.

1.2.4.3 Rational Game Design

The Rational Game Design (RGD) coined at Ubisoft [McEntee 2012; Herold 2018; Ubisoft 2018] is a framework that integrates game design with knowledge from fields such as psychology and architecture. The main aim is to support the creation of meaningful, memorable, and intuitive gameplay experiences by controlling the complexity of various gameplay situations, providing clear and readable ways of presenting game elements, keeping balanced difficulty, while taking into account player skills and motivations. RGD deconstructs games into a set of elements and proposes processes and tools to combine them to get the intended effect on the gameplay experience [McEntee 2012; Herold 2018].

We will focus on the perspective RGD provides on analyzing games for user researchers. I happened to conduct research on a racing game in which an RGD-inspired approach in analyzing gameplay systems proved useful in proposing specific research topics and developing research questions. We will break down the most important gameplay system in this type of game, namely driving. Driving provides a means to fulfil the basic game goal, which is "to win at races". Driving as a gameplay system contains a set of interconnected mechanics like accelerating, using brakes, and keeping the intended direction. In RGD, mechanics are defined as "a challenge that can evolve from easy to hard" [Herold 2018]. If there is no challenge present, we are dealing with action (e.g. clicking the button in the menu). The challenge to be overcome requires skills from the player (whether mental, physical, or social) that are translated to required inputs (e.g. button or thumb stick). The effectiveness and ease of this process is modified by the use of atomic parameters, which can be defined as difficulty factors. Each mechanic has at least one atomic parameter, which, depending on the value, will impact the difficulty of the challenge associated with the mechanic within a given situation in the game. We can summarize it in a graph below (Figure 1.5).

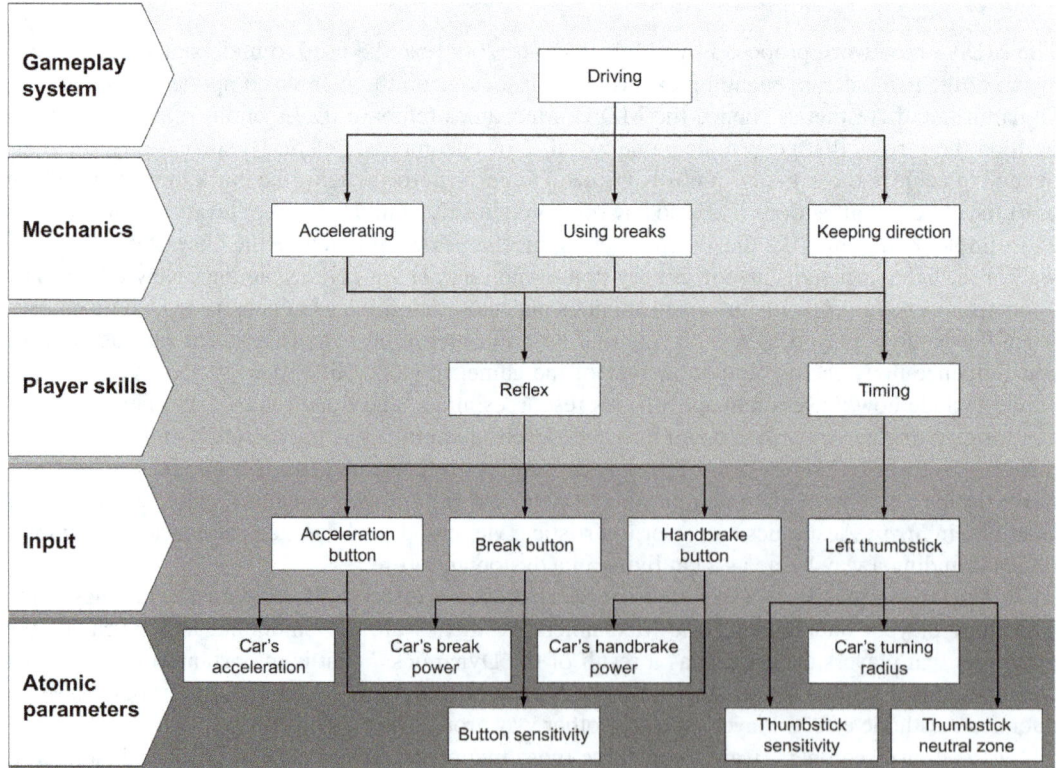

FIGURE 1.5   Driving gameplay system analysis within Rational Game Design. (Own elaboration.)

The aim of RGD is to make various game elements and situations clear and readable for the player with the use of signs and feedback. If we focus on a single mechanic like "using breaks", we can take a closer look at the signs & feedback it can provide for the players:

- Visual effects – black tire marks on the road.
- Audio effects – tire squeal; change in engine sound related to the drop in RPM.
- Animation – white smoke rising from the tires; depending on the input, the tires spin noticeably slower or stop.
- HUD – speed and RPM pointers move proportionally to the input signal.
- Camera – gets closer to the car as the speed decreases.

However, making the mechanics clear and readable does not prevent boredom from occurring when used repeatedly. In addition to changes in the atomic parameters themselves, RGD also proposes to modify the context in which the mechanics occur in the game. This context consists of the pace and space of the game:

- Pace modifiers – time limit, forced move (e.g. the last one in a lap loses).
- Space modifiers – variable visibility, changes in terrain elevation, variable FOV (tunnel vs. open space).

Analyzing pace & space modifiers is one of the first steps in exploring how diverse the experience offered by the game is. In this context, RGD also outlines elements subject to modification to provide players with variety in experience, such as:

- Game ingredients – basic game elements and their parameters, e.g. various car models with differing parameters such as max speed, acceleration, gear shift, and weight.
- Aesthetic & context – elements introducing a new context for using the systems present in the game or elements introducing diversity to the artistic layer, e.g. introducing different environments in which the race takes place (mountains, beach, desert, swamps, etc.), but also different conditions that affect the reception of the experience (driving the same race at different times of a day).
- Exotic gameplay – using existing systems in an unusual or unique way from the perspective of the rest of the gameplay, e.g. racing on ice.

Based on the above and taking into account player skills and motivations, designers can build a varied gameplay experience with a defined set of elements in a predictable way. Certainly, we will leave it to game designers to decide whether RGD can act as a magic formula for creating games or not. For us, it provides one of many ways for structuring the game elements, and a useful set of tools for analyzing them and spotting some of the potential issues, even before research is done to formulate some of the questions and hypotheses.

Certainly, this selective review is not exhaustive, and various disciplines other than game design have their own specific frameworks and processes. It does not mean we have to learn all of them, but understanding how various people in our team work and the perspectives they apply should make communicating research results a whole lot easier.

1.3 PRODUCTION CYCLE

My friend, who is a game producer, used to say that creating every game is, in fact, an R&D project, because of the unpredictable nature of the matter and constant risk management. In fact, many of us are familiar with titles pushed back multiple times or not living up to the expectations, whether financial, artistic, or just ours as players and team members. Certainly, it's not an easy feat to deliver a game on time with expected quality, scope, and within budget, as design and creative vision can change in the process, and there may be technical and licensing issues, together with financial pressures. Those are just some instances of a typical bread and butter in the industry. Organizing the game's creation in the production process allows for a more predictable environment with better budget estimations and higher chances of delivering the intended creative vision on time. What is equally important, especially for user research, is that the **production plan acts as a reference for planning research efforts in the mid- and long-term perspective, so we can prioritize accordingly and allocate the time and resources where they're most needed by the team**.

The game production cycle is a process that can be divided into distinctive phases, gates to pass, and milestones to reach, each of them with specific design and business goals. Games vary in scope, budget, and time, so a single phase can span from weeks or months, depending on the scale and quality assumptions of the project. However big or small a game is, research should aim to assess, bring up, and help to mitigate at least part of the risks during the production cycle. Each game studio can have its own specific way of how the production cycle looks, and there will be some variability in assets at our disposal. Without doubt, there are even teams working in YOLO ("You Only Live Once") mode all the way without any stated or lived process, but for the sake of the presentation clarity, we will focus on the more structured way of seeing things. In general, there is a typical set of phases that a game should go through before it sees the light of day. We will take the wider approach to describing challenges of each phase, just to have a better understanding of the context in which research can take place and understanding that our activities, however important, will not always be of top priority for the team.

1.3.1 CONCEPTION (A.K.A. IDEATION) – WHAT DO WE WANT TO MAKE?

As we already mentioned, there are multiple ways ideas are born, and the thing is that the sole idea most of the time is not enough. Some even say that "ideas are the cheapest thing in the process". In the conception phase, ideas are elaborated on to distil a creative vision for the game. The initial team is relatively small and dedicates time to explore various themes for the game, develop prototypes exploring potential mechanics, elements, or parts of the gameplay. Drafts of the player fantasy, game world, narrative, and gameplay systems are created. It may start with a high concept document (i.e. a 1–2 page long document stating what the game is about and what it wants to achieve artistically and business-wise) and ends with a concept document or game pitch accompanied by the prototyped content (e.g. gameplay demo, art demo) which are presented to internal or external stakeholders (e.g. publisher) to secure further funding. If the team is working on a sequel, it may outline elements that can be reused from previous entries and that can be improved or changed. Generally, the team tries to answer a tone of basic questions to understand if the game idea is worth further exploration. And the good news is that we can support them in this endeavour! At least to some extent and if we stay proactive, as many teams at this stage don't have an idea what questions we could help them with or may be reluctant to turn to user research support. Some of the questions we may help find answers for:

- What feelings and thoughts do this game (or concept) evoke in players?
- Is the player's fantasy interesting for the players? What would it have to be, to be engaging?
- What other games come to the player's mind when they approach this game or concept?
- What opportunities do we find for this game in the context of other games available in the market?

Main assets we should be able to use during the conception phase may include, but are not limited to:

- Pitch deck and/or concept document
- Prototype(s) or demo

- Concept arts
- Narrative beats
- Other documentation underlying team's assumptions (e.g. competitor and reference titles selected by the team, Unique Selling Points list)

Worth mentioning is that there are other vital topics in this phase where we as user researchers have little to no influence on (those other vital topics), but those topics can or will influence us. The team is also focused on delivering first drafts of:

- Project budget and revenue assumptions, together with revenue streams
- Business model assumptions
- Target platforms
- Marketing strategy outline

In the end, if the team was successful in pitching the game to internal or external stakeholders and secured funding, they can proceed to the next phase. If not, they will have to either go back and iterate on their initial idea or the game can be simply cancelled or shelved.

1.3.2   PRE-PRODUCTION – HOW SHOULD WE MAKE IT?

At this stage, the team focuses on exploring and defining the scope of the game, budget, time, and resources that will be needed to deliver it. During this phase, most of the crucial design and technical decisions are about to be made, and much of the vital project documentation is also created, including the Game Design Document and its derivatives (e.g. Narrative Design Document, Art Bible, Level Design Document). The expected tangible effect of this phase is a game build in the form of first playable and/or vertical slice, which aims to showcase the game's creative vision, artistic intentions, main gameplay mechanics, and at least part of the game's planned content (e.g. quests, levels, or maps) in the target quality. Both the first playable and vertical slice are created to present a functional expression of the creative vision in playable form. In general, a vertical slice can be seen as a slice of a cake, which can be very small, but contains all the ingredients, and the team builds it to understand if they can, want, or should create the whole cake (game). Certainly, it can vary from studio to studio what the vertical slice should consist of, so we will not get ourselves into a discussion about whether the cheesecake should have raisins or not. With a vertical slice built near the end of the pre-production, we should be able to assess what is at the heart of the game experience and how well the creative vision is realized. When it comes to the first playable, its scope is smaller than that of vertical slice (e.g. it can showcase only selected core pillars for the creative vision), and if it does appear, it precedes the vertical slice as a gate during the pre-production phase. Besides using vertical slice to get buy-in from stakeholders, it is not uncommon practice to use it as a base for teaser trailers or to present a game to the press. **Early in the pre-production, some teams may still be reluctant to ask us to run user research studies, as many things in the game "aren't ready", so there is a belief that players won't provide reliable answers. The basic answer to this doubt is "if it's ready, it's too late".** Certainly, not all the questions could be answered at this stage, but it doesn't limit our capacity in providing answers for vital questions like:

- Do players understand the game's vision, and does it resonate with them?
- What feelings and thoughts do this game or its component evoke in players?
- What experiences do players need or expect?
- What experiences would players want to reject or not see in this type of game?

Some of the assets which should be available at our disposal during the pre-production phase may include:

- First playable or vertical slice build
- So-called "gyms" (i.e. separate scenes/builds used to test specific mechanics and gameplay systems)
- Game Design Document and, depending on the project scale, other more focused documents may accompany it (e.g. Art bible, Narrative Design Document, Level Design Document, but also player journey maps depicting minute-to-minute gameplay)
- Teaser trailers (not necessarily available to the public)

As always, there are other things going around. The team is focused on planning the production, scoping, and prioritizing features, figuring out how long it would take to deliver the game, and how much money it would cost. Businesswise, the team usually has to deliver things like:

- Game revenue expectations
- Detailed project budget
- Marketing strategy outline

If stakeholders decide they want to proceed with making the whole cake, I mean, the game, the actual production can start. If not, there is still a high risk of cancelling the game or giving the team additional time to refine it.

1.3.3 PRODUCTION – ARE WE MAKING IT RIGHT?

In the production phase, with the creative vision firmly set, the team focuses on actually making a game, i.e. creating production-quality code, art assets, and all the planned content. At this stage, the team typically grows in size, the scope is usually quite well defined, and budgets, together with deadlines, are set. However, the team still has to constantly manage risks, as there might be the urge to add new elements or features to the game, which might end in scope creep or pivot, and the initial ideas won't always easily translate well into the desired gameplay experience. The production phase is usually the longest in the production cycle, ranging from several months to several years, and it typically consists of a few milestones to pass:

- Alpha – reaching this milestone means that the game is feature-complete – it has all crucial features in place and is fully playable from start to finish. Although the quality of the game will be far from final – many assets will need to be added or improved, various gameplay improvements still need to be made, and bugs await to be fixed.
- Beta – game now represents a content-complete version, which means that all of the planned content is now ready, with changes limited to bug fixes, balancing, and polishing. Some studios conduct beta tests that are either open to everyone or closed (invitational).
- Gold (a.k.a. release candidate) – When all the critical issues have been tackled, the game is balanced, and bugs hopefully resolved, a game build called a release candidate is ready for distribution. The gold status dates back to the days when developers signed off on a version of the game they considered final, which was sent to a publisher for manufacturing.
- Release – This is basically the day the game comes out to the world. Brace yourself and celebrate!

Production is the phase where, often, direct requests to run user research studies are made by the team, as they want to refine the experience. At the same time, the further the game is into the production phase, the harder it becomes to make substantial changes in design. However, some of the typical questions we may ask include:

- Do players understand and know how to perform what is expected from them by the game?
- Do players feel the game is balanced, well-paced, and long enough?
- Does the game progression meet players' expectations and encourage them to stay or return to the game?

Typical assets which should be available at our disposal during the production phase, may include:

- Various game builds ranging from the mentioned earlier gyms, through specific quests/missions/maps, to the whole game
- Project documentation (including mentioned earlier, but now refined Game Design Documents and its derivatives)
- Marketing assets, including, but not limited to, trailers, product page.

On the business end, the team monitors and updates previously outlined approaches to budget, revenues, and marketing strategy. Most of the time, there are things not working as intended, some of the risks materialize in a nasty way, and there are lots of iterations before delivering actual increments. If the process is going outside the boundaries defined by stakeholders (whether it be time, scope, quality, or budget), team actions may need additional approvals and adjustments or the game can be cancelled. In many games, production is the most costly and time-consuming phase of the production cycle, and it is why it is also more prone to external influences over which we have little to no control (e.g. investor withdrawal, release of a similar competitor game).

1.3.4 Post-Production (a.k.a. Post-Release) – How Could We Make It Better?

Well, the game is out in the wild and now we have to live with it. Depending on how well a game was received and sold in a given time-frame and what were the plans to support it post-release, the team's focus may go from squashing bugs they didn't have time for before the release or new ones discovered by the players, through preparing game-balancing patches, delivering additional content that had been cut to meet deadlines, to just bringing new content and improvements in the form of downloadable content or expansions. For games distributed as GaaS (game as a service), post-production might actually be the start of a journey, where the team improves the experience and delivers new content to both keep the existing player base and develop it further for a prolonged time. In this phase, many teams may rely strongly on analytics, which is a good sign, but as we mentioned earlier, there is still a lot of space for fruitful cooperation with user research. Some of the questions we ask in post-production include:

- What are the main pain points players encounter?
- What do players expect from future updates?

When it comes to the assets available at our disposal in the post-production phase, to those we have already mentioned in the production phase, we can add those naturally occurring after release (e.g. customer support tickets, user and expert reviews).

Business-wise, as we already hinted, post-release is the time of comparing a game's market performance to the expectations made before the release, measuring the effectiveness of marketing efforts, and making necessary adjustments. If the game lived up to the expectations placed in it, the team can support it longer after release with various fixes and additional content. If not, the game may be briefly supported based on the budgeting done in the earlier phases or support may be suspended.

With this accent, we went through the whole production cycle. Now, let us summarize it in Table 1.1.

TABLE 1.1

Summary of Goals, Assets, and Research Questions within the Production Cycle

	Conception	Pre-Production	Production	Post-Production
Main question	What do we want to make?	How should we make it?	Are we making it right?	How could we make it better?
Team goal	Funding the next phase Defining creative vision	Funding the next phase Defining scope, time, budget, quality, resources, risk	Monitoring and staying within the defined ranges for scope, time, budget, quality, resources, risk	Adjusting scope, time, budget, quality, resources depending on the outcomes (e.g. reviews, revenue)
Typical assets at our disposal	Prototype(s) Project documentation	First playable and/or vertical slice Project documentation Marketing assets	Game builds Project documentation Marketing assets	Game builds Project documentation Marketing assets User and expert reviews
Research questions	What feelings and thoughts do this game (or concept) evoke in players? Is the player's fantasy interesting for the players? What would it have to be, to be engaging? What other games come to the player's mind when they approach this game or concept? What opportunities do we find for this game in the context of these other games?	Do players understand the game's vision and does it resonate with them? What feelings and thoughts do this game or its component evoke in players? What experiences do players need or expect? What experiences would players want to reject or not see in this type of game?	Do players understand and know how to perform what is expected from them by the game? Do players feel the game is balanced, well-paced, and long enough? Does the game progression meet players' expectations and encourage them to stay or return to the game?	What are the main pain points players encounter? What do players expect from future updates?

Annotation. (Own elaboration).

Certainly, looking at the game through the eyes of the team that creates it is crucial to properly understand their needs and pains inherent to the production cycle, but it doesn't provide us with the whole picture. In the next chapter, we'll see what the players' perspective looks like.

1.4   CHAPTER SUMMARY

In this chapter, to establish a solid foundation, we began with a working definition of a game: a voluntary activity designed to overcome unnecessary obstacles within a closed system, leading to a win or loss. We also discussed game typologies and came up with one that can be useful for us during participant recruitment in user research.

Game development is an interdisciplinary process involving design, art, animation, sound, production, and programming, with each discipline having distinct goals and questions. Additionally, we can cooperate with QA, marketing, and analytics to support each other's efforts. The creation process requires collaboration to integrate these elements cohesively, guided by creative vision, core pillars, and player fantasy. We support it by assessing player experience, helping to refine the game, and ensuring it aligns with the intended design. We explored frameworks like MDA and RGD, which can help us structure and analyze gameplay, as well as provide us with a basic vocabulary to communicate with our team.

We also examined the game production cycle, which consists of conception, pre-production, production, and post-production phases. Each phase comes with its own set of goals, challenges, and assets. Our role is to assess risks and support decision-making at each phase, helping the team to understand players and ensuring that actual player experience aligns with the creative vision.

REFERENCES

Aarseth, E., Smedstad, S. M., & Sunnanå, L. (2003). A multi-dimensional typology of games. In *Digital Games Research Conference (DiGRA)*.

Clearwater, D. A. (2011). What defines video game genre? Thinking about genre study after the great divide. *Loading...*, 5(8), 29–49.

Crawford, C. (1984). *The Art of Computer Game Design by Chris Crawford*. Osborne/McGraw-Hill.

Crawford, C. (2003). *Chris Crawford on Game Design*. New Riders Publishing.

Elverdam, C., & Aarseth, E. (2007). Game classification and game design: Construction through critical analysis. *Games and Culture*, 2(1), 3–22.

Fullerton, T., Swain, C., & Hoffman, S. S. (2008). *Gamedesign Workshop A Playcentric Approach to Creating Innovative Games* (2nd ed.). Elsevier.

Herold, D. (2018). *RGD Workshop : Rational Game and Level Design*. YouTube. https://www.youtube.com/watch?v=xqHAjwrNp70

Hunicke, R., Leblanc, M., & Zubek, R. (2004). MDA: A formal approach to game design and game research. In *Proceedings of the AAAI Workshop on Challenges in Game AI* (vol. 4, no. 1).

Lee, J. H., Karlova, N., Clarke, R. I., Thornton, K., & Perti, A. (2014). Facet analysis of video game genres. In *IConference 2014 Proceedings* (pp. 125–139).

McEntee, C. (2012). *Rational Design: The Core of Rayman Origins*. https://www.gamedeveloper.com/design/rational-design-the-core-of-i-rayman-origins-i-

Osathanunkul, C. (2015). A classification of business models in video game industry. *International Journal of Management Cases*, 17(1), 35–44.

Suits, B. (2005). *The Grasshopper: Games, Life and Utopia*. Broadview Press.

Ubisoft. (2018). *Game Creators Odyssey*. https://gamecreatorodyssey.com/.

Whalen, Z. (2004). Game/Genre: A critique of generic formulas in video games in the context of "the real." *Works and Days* 43/44, 22(1 & 2), 289–303.

Wolf, M. J. P. (2001). Genre and the video game. In M. J. P. Wolf (Ed.), *The Medium of the Video Game* (pp. 113–136). University of Texas Press.

2 Player Experience

In this chapter, our focus shifts from the game and team making it to key concepts shaping the gameplay experience and player experience, with a focus on the factors that influence player behaviour and decision-making.

Topics covered in this chapter:

- Exploring key concepts that describe the gameplay experience, like (game)flow, fun, and immersion, together with usability and accessibility as essential elements of experience.
- Understanding the broader concept of player experience, and how economic, socio-demographic, and psychological factors influence player behaviour and decision-making.
- Examining the player consumer decision-making process to provide context for understanding gameplay experiences.

2.1 SOME DEFINITIONS AGAIN

We already used the term "experience" in various forms and variations. To not rely on the notion of what it is, let us define how we will understand it throughout this book. We will start with **gameplay experience, which can be defined as a state consisting of the player's thoughts, emotions, and actions** [Ermi & Mäyrä 2005; Takatalo et al. 2010]. **However, it doesn't result from the properties of the video game or the player's characteristics alone, but appears during the interaction between the game and the player** (Figure 2.1).

Experience understood in this way is usually described using various terms, such as (game)flow, fun, or immersion. We will take some time to better understand those terms, as they are often used in existing literature, materials available on the Internet, and sometimes within the team discussions.

2.1.1 (GAME)FLOW

Research into what makes various experiences pleasurable for people, conducted by psychologist Csikszentmihalyi [1975; Nakamura & Csikszentmihalyi 2002], led to the description of the flow phenomenon. It is defined as a state of optimal experience that occurs during various activities, associated with the occurrence of intense engagement, strong motivation, and distorted perception of the passage of time. This state occurs in situations when the activity is characterized by a clearly defined goal, is a challenge requiring skills, provides frequent feedback on progress, requires concentration, and performing the activity is a reward in itself. In our context, it's worth noting that an important condition for the occurrence of flow is an appropriate match between the skills of the person and the difficulty of the challenge they face (Figure 2.2).

Another condition for an optimal experience is that the challenge should have a clear goal, be limited by certain rules, and require the person to make an effort. When we compare it to the game definitions that we discussed earlier, it's not surprising that Csikszentmihalyi's theory resulted in attempts to determine how flow elements manifest in video games. Sweetser and Wyeth [2005] proposed a model of gameflow, which consists of eight main elements that are equivalent to those identified earlier by Csikszentmihalyi and one additionally identified by the authors. The first element is the game itself, which is a necessary but insufficient element for the occurrence of flow. The game should focus the player's attention by posing appropriately difficult challenges. These challenges, in order to engage the player, must have a clearly defined goal that the player can fulfil. On the way to achieving this goal, the game should provide the player with feedback on the progress made. The player himself

DOI: 10.1201/9781003501909-3

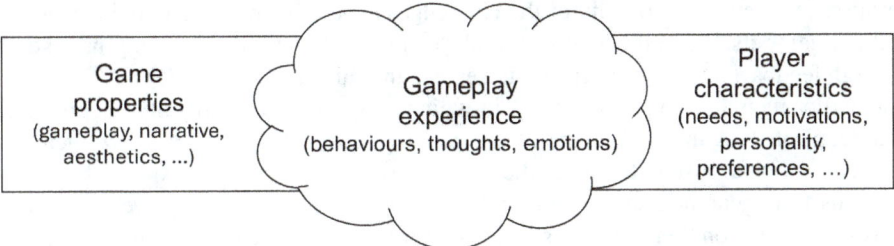

FIGURE 2.1 Gameplay experience as a result of the player's interaction with the game. (Own elaboration based on Ermi and Mäyrä [2005, p. 8] and Takatalo et al. [2010, p. 26].)

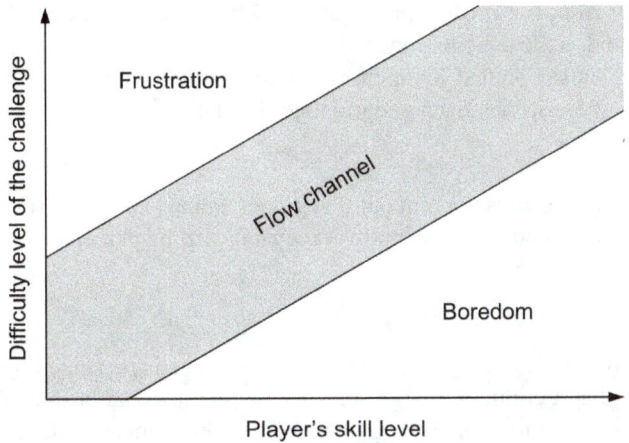

FIGURE 2.2 Relationship between player skill and challenge difficulty. (Own elaboration based on Csikszentmihalyi [1975].)

must have the appropriate skills to meet these challenges and be able to experience a sense of control. After meeting these conditions, the player can experience immersion manifested by the loss of the sense of passing time. The last of the elements mentioned by the authors – social interaction – found its place in the model because games provide opportunities for interaction with other people, which in themselves can be highly enjoyable, even when people are not interested in the game itself. To measure the flow experience in video games, the authors proposed a set of heuristics for assessing games, which can be used during expert analysis [Sweetser & Wyeth 2005].

2.1.2 TYPES OF FUN

Another attempt to describe the experience associated with the use of video games, also based on the theory of Csikszentmihalyi [1975], was undertaken by Nicole Lazzaro [2004b]. In her opinion, the experience offered by games consists primarily of the emotions they evoke in players, which lead to deriving pleasure from the game. Based on her own observations and interviews conducted among gamers and non-gamers, the author [Lazzaro 2004a, 2004b] identified four paths through which video games evoke desired emotions in players. These paths were defined as the "four keys" to fun [Lazzaro 2004a]:

- The first is "hard fun", in which the game, by posing increasingly difficult challenges and puzzles, supports the evocation of emotions such as frustration or *fiero* (i.e. personal triumph over adversity) in the player. In order for the game to effectively evoke these emotions, the level of difficulty of the challenges should be matched to the player's skills, and the game itself should support the player in developing and applying new strategies through feedback on their progress, successes, and failures.

- The author then mentions "easy fun", in which, thanks to the ambiguity, incompleteness, and detail of the game world, the player can experience emotions of amazement, horror and fear, which arouse in them not the desire to win, but for further exploration.
- "Serious fun" generates excitement and emotions such as relief in players, focusing the player's attention on their internal state. Games of this type focus not so much on entertainment itself, but on additional pedagogical value, where by raising serious topics (e.g. death) they encourage the players to reflect later.
- "People fun" is based on the game offering opportunities for cooperation or competition between many players. The emotions experienced by players include amazement, *schadenfreude* (i.e. joy from the misfortunes that befall a rival), and *naches* (i.e. joy or pride in the progress and achievements made by the mentee). It is worth noting that the video game becomes only a pretext for spending time together with other people, as well as an opportunity to share stories from playing together. This "key" to fun is most often used by multiplayer games.

A contribution of this proposal is to point out that games can evoke very different and extreme emotional states, both positive and negative, and yet they can still be perceived by players as enjoyable.

2.1.3 IMMERSION

A different perspective on describing the gameplay experience is presented by Jennett et al. [2008]. The authors believe that a common feature of all video games that have achieved broadly understood success is their ability to strongly engage players in the game, and the experience that accompanies it is called immersion. Immersion is a dynamic state consisting of the player's attention and cognitive assessment related to the challenges posed by the game, accompanied by strong and often extreme emotions [McMahan 2003; Jennett et al. 2008]. Immersion has three basic features [Jennett et al. 2008]:

- Lack of awareness of the passage of time;
- Lack of awareness of the real world;
- A sense of being in the game environment and involvement.

Immersion as a state of involvement in the game, however, is not a uniform experience, but rather a gradual and time-varying one, which depends on players overcoming emerging barriers on the way to being completely immersed in the game. Brown and Cairns [2004], based on in-depth interviews with players, list three successive levels of immersion. The first one is called "engagement", which requires the player to overcome a barrier related to preferences for the game genre. In order to become "engaged", the player must put in some effort and invest time to learn the game controls and its rules. Then, the player can reach the next level of immersion, i.e. "engrossment", which in turn requires overcoming a barrier related to the game's design. At this level, the player should no longer pay attention to how to control the game, and various elements of the game should connect with each other in such a way as to influence the emotions experienced by the player. The last level of immersion is "total immersion", which requires overcoming barriers related to empathy for the game world and resonance with the atmosphere prevailing in the game. The state of total immersion is described as a sense of presence in the game world and of being cut off from reality to such an extent that the game becomes the only thing that matters to the player. Achieving total immersion requires a great deal of effort and attention from the player and is therefore a rare and fleeting experience, whereas experiences of "engagement" and "engrossment" are more frequent and lasting

[Brown & Cairns 2004; Jennett et al. 2008]. Immersion is positively correlated with the desire to continue playing [Strojny & Strojny 2014], and this experience is accompanied by both positive and negative emotions [Jennett et al. 2008].

From a theoretical perspective, immersion overlaps with the flow experience in that it assumes a distorted sense of the passage of time and in that the game presents the player with a series of challenges. However, according to Jennett et al. [2008], although immersion is a precursor to the flow experience, it is also a qualitatively distinct experience during the gameplay. Immersion as a gradual experience rarely reaches the intensity of the flow experience and in this sense, the flow experience can be considered an extreme version of immersion. An additional distinguishing feature is that there are video games that do not meet all the criteria for the occurrence of flow and are, at the same time, highly immersive. It is worth noting here the observation made by Takatalo et al. [2010] that narrowing the experience of flow to only the "optimal experience" and thus limiting it exclusively to extreme situations does not reduce its usefulness for the analysis of players' experience, even in cases where some of the criteria have not been met by the game. For our needs, we can assume that immersion occurs before the occurrence of flow and is a less intense experience that is more frequently noted by players. The experience of flow also requires, in addition to meeting the criteria of immersion, the presence of a number of additional elements, such as the presence of a clearly defined goal and immediate feedback from the game, so flow can be considered a special case of immersion.

2.1.4 Usability

In the approaches to the gameplay experience we discussed so far, it has only been signalled that the player should know the rules and be able to control the game in order to get involved in it. In this context, let's take a closer look at the concept of usability. Usability can be seen as a factor determining how easy it is for the player to understand and use various game elements. The common terms related to usability include "user friendliness", "intuitivity", "ease of use", and some call it even a

---

BOX 2.1   SHOULD FISH RIDE A BIKE?

Researchers working on some of the theories discussed in this book provide us with ready-made tools for measuring player state and impressions, mainly in the form of checklists and questionnaires. However, questionnaires designed in academia can be seen as too general to be directly applicable to practical contexts. We could ask what good is it for a game to score high on a questionnaire, if we cannot tell what specific elements of it should be improved to get a better score. And in fact, many of those questionnaires were not created with an aim to evaluate products, but to measure theoretical constructs, so let us not judge a fish by how well it rides a bike. We can still find a lot of inspiration in them for our own tools that we will create for more practical purposes. The way the questions are constructed so that they are not judgmental or suggesting, or the answer formats available, can be quite useful, especially when we are not familiar with questionnaire design and psychometry.

Some of the questionnaires you may want to explore:

- IEQ (Immersion Experience Questionnaire) by Jennett et al. [2008]
- GEQ (Game Engagement Questionnaire) by Brockmyer et al. [2009]
- GEQ (Game Experience Questionnaire) by Ijsselsteijn et al. [2013]
- UPEQ (Ubisoft Perceived Experience Questionnaire) by Azadvar and Canossa [2018]

"golden gate" to the gameplay experience. According to Jakob Nielsen (2012), usability consists of five elements that can be defined in the form of questions:

- Learnability – How easy is it for players to learn the controls and the rules of the game when they play the game for the first time?
- Efficiency – When players have learned the controls and rules, how quickly can they perform required actions?
- Memorability – When players return to the game after some break, how easy is it for them to get back to performing the required actions with the same efficiency?
- Errors – How many errors or mistakes do players make while performing actions, how severe are these errors, and how easily can players find work-arounds?
- Satisfaction – How pleasant is it to perform actions in the game?

One thing I have to admit is that I used "actions" instead of the word "design" suggested by Nielsen. Why's that? We borrowed the definition of usability from application software, which, as we already said, has different goals than games. While we want individual actions players need to perform (e.g. clicking a button in the menu; managing inventory), to meet usability criteria, when it comes to challenges, we don't always want players to overcome them on their first try or for their solutions to be obvious.

The other thing we have to mention while discussing usability is the context of use. Simply, the game can be played at various places and times, which may have specific requirements or pose specific challenges. While working on games for specific platforms (e.g. mobile or VR) or in specific genres (e.g. fitness games or party games), it may be one of the considerations while planning or conducting research. Mobile games do not require a special space and can be played practically anywhere, but this requires taking into account the fact that players will often have to mute the sound (e.g. on a bus, in a queue). On the other hand, VR games may require a relatively large physical space to play, which availability may vary greatly among players. On platforms such as PC and consoles, we may have some implicit assumptions about the context of use, but it still remains important. After all, there can be many contexts of use, for example, if our players also play at night, it may be necessary for them to mute the sound during the game because a small person is sleeping in the next room. With this last example, we touched on a topic related to accessibility, which is worth at least some attention.

2.1.5 ACCESSIBILITY

Accessibility, as defined in ISO 9241-11:2018, can be seen as: "extent to which products, systems, services, environments and facilities can be used by people from a population with the widest range of user needs, characteristics and capabilities to achieve identified goals in identified contexts of use". Accessibility is often viewed through the prism of disability, understood as certain characteristics of groups of players. In this approach, we can consider disability in terms of impairment types: vision, motor skills, hearing, speech, cognitive, and emotional. However, it is worth noting that efforts at accessibility can allow a much wider group of players to fully enjoy the experience than it might seem at first glance. This becomes obvious when we look at disability as something that occurs when players encounter barriers that prevent them from participating in the game, not solely because of their impairment or difference. In this approach, called the social model of disability, we think in terms of the barriers that players encounter. These barriers can be permanent (e.g. player didn't hear the sound, because of permanent hearing loss or being deaf), temporary (e.g. player didn't hear the sound, because of hearing loss resulting from an ear infection), or be the result of situational factors (e.g. player didn't hear the sound, because of muting it, as they wanted to hear child in the next room).

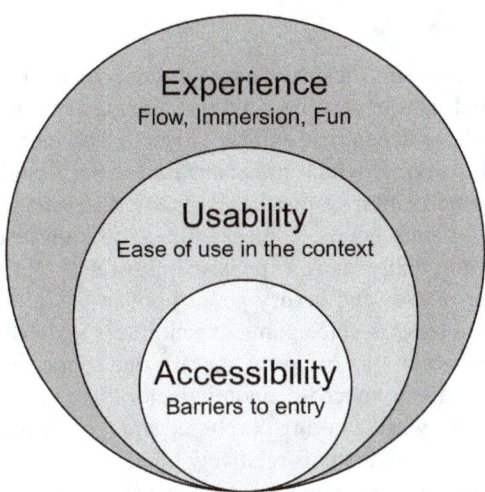

FIGURE 2.3 Relationship between accessibility, usability, and experience. (Own elaboration.)

Accessibility and usability are commonly used concepts and the relationship between them may be difficult to clearly examine. Thatcher et al. [2006] suggest that accessibility can be seen as a subset of usability, as usability issues affect most of the users equally, irrespective of the barriers they face. On the other hand, usability focuses on ease of use, and with accessibility in mind, we aim to expand it to the widest group of players possible. Whichever way we will look at the distinction between accessibility and usability, **first we need to remove potential barriers to entry for players so that they can efficiently learn the rules of the game and use them to finally get engaged in it**. If we want to sum it all up, we can come up with another diagram, showing us relations between experience, usability, and accessibility (Figure 2.3).

2.2 REASONS FOR PLAYER BEHAVIOUR AND DECISIONS

In user research, we focus on how the game is experienced by the actual players. We live with the assumption that the better the gameplay experience, the greater the chance that someone will buy the game, play it, and leave a good review. While this holds true, playing a game does not happen in a vacuum. I believe that it is worth considering other factors that shape player decisions and behaviours, so I invite you to think about the player as a consumer for a while, and to explore how that shapes the way we will look at **player experience** throughout the rest of this book (i.e. **the general experience that the player has with the game including those before, during and after gameplay**). Some might say that this is the playing field of consumer research. However, my approach is that this type of excursion can give us a wider perspective on gameplay experience and user research. First, knowing other perspectives does not hurt and shouldn't derail our focus on gameplay experience. Second, outside of academia and large-scale projects, we rarely have the comfort of working in narrowly defined disciplines. Third, even if we have the comfort to work solely in our discipline, it is good to have some basis for cooperation with others and a higher chance of providing more applicable insights.

We will first focus on the factors shaping player's experience, and for our purposes, we will divide them into three major groups:

- Economical;
- Socio-demographic;
- Psychological ones.

2.2.1 Economical Determinants

Economic factors are those that significantly shape player consumer behaviour. Basic economic factors include income, which is a necessary condition for meeting needs, and its limited nature forces the player to choose those needs that will be satisfied. The income a player has at their disposal affects their standard of living, which translates into the size and structure of expenditures. A person with a small income primarily purchases goods that satisfy the most basic needs. As income increases, demand for such goods increases to a saturation level, and then begins to flatten as the consumer begins to choose more expensive substitutes. With income, the consumption of higher-order goods also increases and luxury goods appear (e.g. a collector's edition of a video game). Many of the statistical reports place game expenditures under the "recreation and culture" category. And what we know about this category, that it's one of the first to cut when people's disposable income is at risk (e.g. due to macro-economic factors like inflation rates). Another thing is that people are more risk-averse while making purchases when the level of their disposable income is endangered and/or the price of the game is relatively high.

Generally, purchasing a game is accompanied by the risk of making an incorrect decision. As in the case of books, movies, and other experience-based goods, players are only able to accurately assess the value of a video game after actually playing it, so they cannot fully predict the various consequences of their purchase decision. When making a decision to buy a game, the player may consider various types of risks, which are accompanied by specific doubts:

- Functional risk – concerns about whether the game actually fulfils declared function, e.g. doubts about whether the game offers gameplay for a sufficiently long time, whether the features work as described, and whether the gameplay actually provides the experience described by the game distributor.
- Economic risk – doubts related to the price of the game itself, as well as the expenses that the player must incur in order to play it, e.g. need to invest in an additional controller enabling effective control of the game.
- Time loss risk – concerns related to the amount of time that must be devoted to actually assess the experience offered by a game. Basically, after installing and running the game, the player must first understand the basic rules governing the game world, then learn to use the interface effectively in order to be able to benefit from the game and evaluate it, and this process requires time that could be spent on other things (e.g. watching a movie on VOD).
- Psychological risk – concerns about whether the game will allow the player to satisfy their needs or express their own identity. Let us note here that psychological risk is related to functional risk, e.g. concerns about whether the game will provide the desired experience are related to whether it has features that work as described by the distributor (e.g. on the product page).
- Social risk – concerns about the group reaction. It can be both the judgements made by the people in the player's environment and unwanted behaviours by other players in-game (e.g. toxic behaviours).
- Physical risk – concerns about safety when using the game, e.g. player considering whether they have adequate space and will not hit anything during a movement game that requires waving hand-held controllers, or whether undesirable symptoms such as headaches or nausea will occur during a VR game.

In order to reduce the perceived risk accompanying the decision, the player uses various strategies and means of action:

- using available information about the game, e.g. its genre or the age category;
- being guided by the good reputation of the game, e.g. industry awards, recommendations from other people and reviewers;

- basing a decision on previous positive experience with other games from the same developer or publisher;
- purchasing games from a reputable developer or publisher;
- purchasing a sequel or another entry in the franchise they positively experienced;
- using safeguards against an unsuccessful purchase, e.g. returning the purchased game.
- using games distributed in a subscription or free-to-play model, e.g. freemium, but also demo versions.

In the classic pay-to-play model, the price of a game is another of the key elements in building the player's expectations of the experience offered. In the case of triple-A titles, smaller details can change the rating from positive to negative as the expectations are higher. On the other hand, when a title is cheaper, relatively more can be forgiven. Although players may differ in their sensitivity to prices, generally, if players have money to spend, those are just obvious observations for us. However, things can get "interesting" when players' disposable income lowers, and players become more risk-averse while making purchases. Players may gravitate toward titles that carry a lower risk, although they may be relatively expensive (e.g. an award-winning AAA title from a reputable developer/publisher) and limit their spending on mid-priced titles that carry a much higher risk for them. Additionally, switching from classic purchase to subscription and free-to-play models can be much more prevalent. This description may partly resemble the situation in the industry in recent years, but for us, more interesting conclusions are that:

- The price of the game provides context in which the player assesses the experience.
- The price of the game is an important basis for player expectations. It is not the user researcher's role to set prices, but it is worth checking whether there is no dissonance in the player's mind between the actual experience offered by the game and the price it will have.
- The price together with the way the game is marketed (e.g. through trailers, product page, advertisements) builds expectations through which players can evaluate the experience. Therefore, it may be worth checking whether there is no dissonance between what we say about the game and what the player will actually experience in it.

BOX 2.2   HOW MUCH FUN FOR A DOLLAR?

The price of a game can trigger considerations in players' minds. For us, at least two of them are interesting, which can be summarized as follows: "How many hours of entertainment will I get for a dollar?" and "Is the price fair for the experience the game offers?". Even though the game can provide a great gameplay experience, and have proper exposure, it can still be prone to lower sales or negative reviews as the experience itself was too short for a given price or did not meet expectations built on it and marketing materials (e.g. trailers or product page). As user researchers, we can probe for this by adding simple modifications to studies focused on other topics and monitor them throughout the production cycle.

Sometimes we may want to take an even broader look at the price topic. In many free-to-play games, instead of spending time during gameplay to acquire selected items, players can spend in-game currencies or real money to get them in the in-game store. This puts players in a time vs. money choice situation that can be perceived as unfair (e.g. "This game is forcing me to spend money because I can't get this item in any reasonable amount of time without paying" or "This game is pay to win! I don't want to pay, but those who pay have an unjust advantage over me"). To see how different items available in the in-game store are perceived, we can ask players about two things:

- Impact on gameplay – The level of impact of the item on gameplay (e.g. skins, although they may emphasize the player's status, have no real impact on gameplay; a permanent or temporary boost for a character can give the player a significant advantage). The example question: "What effect does this item have on gameplay?"
- Additional effort required – How much additional effort or money is required to get the item, which can be perceived as negligible or insignificant, through lesser or greater grinding (i.e. engaging in repetitive activities to earn rewards such as experience points, but also in-game currency), to the need to spend real money. The example question: "Does obtaining this item require any additional effort on your part outside of your typical gameplay?"

What we do know is that the answers to these two questions inversely affect the perceived fairness of the game. For example, skins that require players to put in a lot of effort or money to get them, but have no impact on gameplay, are usually seen as fair. Similarly, a powerful weapon (high impact on gameplay) obtained during the boss fight at the end of the level (low additional effort required). On the other hand, a set of equipment that expands the abilities of our character and makes it easier to win the mentioned boss fight (high impact on gameplay), which is only available for real money (high additional effort required), may be more often seen as unfair.

It is worth noting that while the price of the game itself influences the expectations on gameplay experience and purchasing decision, the player must also have the appropriate equipment to be able to run and play the game. According to Scherer and Naab [2009], for this reason, other types of expenses are taken into account by players when making decisions:

- Investment costs – an expense determining whether a given game will be considered as a potential purchase option at all. Such an expense is the purchase of the appropriate equipment needed to run the game, e.g. a dedicated console, new PC components, or a controller.
- Exposure costs – the expense intended for the purchase of the actual game.
- Usage costs – the expense intended for using the product, in the case of games using a subscription or micropayments.

As newer generations of computer components and consoles, as well as more hardware-demanding games appear, investment costs in certain periods can have a strong influence on players' purchasing decisions. It is also worth noting that some games are distributed only for a single hardware platform (so-called "exclusive"), so due to potential investment costs, the player can choose substitute products available for the platform they own, despite the satisfactory price of the game itself. From the game creator's perspective, this is when ideas like "Let's make *Legend of Zelda*, but for PC" can come into play.

We can have the notion that, based on the economic determinants player's purchase decision is solely the result of assessing risks for a given price. On the contrary, economists are tricky beasts, and they provide us with other factors we can take into account. One of such factors is the consumption set [Rassuli & Harrell 1990], which in our context can be described as games that players already own (or have access to), as well as other substitute products and services (e.g. access to VOD) that fulfil the same need (e.g. for entertainment). Player's existing consumption set sets

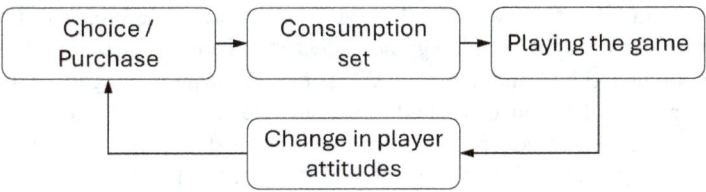

FIGURE 2.4   Player's consumption set. (Own elaboration based on Rassuli and Harrell [1990].)

a reference point for the purchase decision (e.g. Do I need another game?), which later sets context for post-purchase behaviour (e.g. Do I want to play a game or rather watch a movie? Which of the games I have access to will be best for today's evening?). Basically, starting with the first game, the player fills in an empty consumption set over time, which results in each subsequent choice being dependent to some extent on the previous ones. This process is continuous, because the existing consumption set is constantly updated (created, supplemented, or reduced) by the player's subsequent choices. After playing a specific game, things such as the player's attitudes are changed and then taken into account in the next decision to purchase or play the same or another game. We can summarize it in Figure 2.4.

Okay, players have their game libraries, but what is in it for us? We can point to at least three useful takeaways:

- It's worth knowing what the study participants have been playing recently, to better understand their reference points.
- Comparing research results from different periods can be difficult because the players we talked to a few months ago can have different reference points than the players we talk to today.
- At some periods, a single game can have a significant impact on the player's expectations, e.g. *Half Life: Alyx* served this function for a while, being a reference point for many players when forming expectations for playtested VR games.

2.2.2   SOCIO-DEMOGRAPHIC DETERMINANTS

The demographic factors that influence player consumer behaviour most often include those that describe the player (sex and age) and those that describe their household (household composition). As these variables are largely related to socio-cultural factors, such as culture, education, and ways of spending leisure time, we will look at both groups altogether.

There is a notion that a player's sex determines certain preferences related to gameplay. Various researchers noted that males tend to show stronger preferences for competitive games, such as action games, sports games, and strategy games [Lucas & Sherry 2004; Heeter et al. 2008; Tekofsky et al. 2016]. On the other hand, females are more likely to prefer story-oriented games that allow for building social relationships, such as action-adventure games, MMORPGs, and simulators [Lucas & Sherry 2004; Carr 2005; Dawson et al. 2007; Tekofsky et al. 2016]. Some genres in which the influence of sex on preferences was less evident were adventure games and RPGs [Tekofsky et al. 2016; Terlecki et al. 2011].

While there can be differences between males and females in preferences for video game genres and hardware platforms, the gaming population in Europe and the United States is characterized by almost an equal share of both sexes, which corresponds to data presented in the industry reports [see ESA 2024; GGIA 2024]. It is worth noting that men play much more often and spend more time playing, are more confident in their skills during the game, and are more likely to share information about their gaming experiences with others [Dawson et al. 2007; Ogletree & Drake 2007; Terlecki et al. 2011], which may partly explain the still popular stereotype that video games are mainly played by them. However, we have to note that different preferences of women and men regarding the experiences sought in video games may result from cultural influences. Based on the results of a study conducted by [Ratan et al. 2022] simultaneously in Singapore, Germany, and the United States, the cultural differences related to gender roles may better explain genre preferences than sex. Authors noted that in general, in more masculinized cultures, such as the United States and Germany, there is greater social pressure for women not to play. In comparison, the culture of Singapore, which is less masculine, does not discourage women from playing to the same extent, so female and male genre choices are much more similar. What does this mean for us? Due to cultural norms (including those related to gender) in various countries, we may encounter specific challenges at different stages of conducting research, e.g. from the more difficult and resource-intensive recruitment of female participants to the more frequent belief among male participants in their own abilities to overcome difficulties with the game (despite no observable differences in skill).

As with other products and services, the age of players can be a general source of information about their current and future needs. In the case of video games, this variable is of particular importance, as it allows probing not only the amount of spending on games, but also how much time players will be able to spend on playing video games. For our purposes, we can define age categories that reflect changes in the way players use games and make purchasing decisions based on two criteria. For groups under 18, we could use periods of mental development, as it better captures cognitive abilities. On the other hand, when dividing older groups, it is worth taking into account typical changes of a professional and family nature, as they better explain purchasing decisions and the amount of time spent on playing. It is worth noting here that the player as a member of a household does not make decisions in a social vacuum. The purchasing decisions made by the player are greatly influenced not only by their age, but also by the age of other people in their household. We could think of the presence of children, as even if they do not have their own funds to purchase the game and have limited legal capacity, they have an influence on the choice of family activities in free time, e.g. playing a specific video game. Table 2.1 contains the general characteristics of the player age groups.

TABLE 2.1

Characteristics of Players' Age Groups

Age [Years]	Separation Criteria	Group Characteristics
Below 3	Socio-cognitive development	Children in this age group are keenly interested in playful activities, but the complexity of the rules and the presence of puzzles make the gameplay offered by video games too cognitively demanding for them. Although video games arouse interest in this group due to the multitude of colours, animations, and graphic effects, they are treated as toys – the ability to manipulate objects (e.g. a character) is more important than solving a puzzle or achieving a defined goal.
3–6	Socio-cognitive development	Children show interest in the gameplay offered by video games, and games created for this group are often based on relatively simple puzzles or have a luck-based character. At this age, children are already able to distinguish the real world from the one offered by the game, and the game itself can become an opportunity to activate the imagination. However, the choice and possible purchase of games is made by parents, with whom children usually play, and who help overcome more difficult challenges or bend the rules to make the game enjoyable and interesting.
7–12	Socio-cognitive development	In this age group, children start to use the rules of logic in their thinking, which helps them understand cause-effect relationships, so they are more willing to take on more difficult challenges in games. During joint games, it becomes important for all participants to follow the rules of the game. At this age, preferences related to video games start to come to the fore, and children express their opinions about which ones they like (or dislike), no longer easily accepting what their parents choose for them.

(Continued)

TABLE 2.1 (*Continued*)

Characteristics of Players' Age Groups

Age [Years]	Separation Criteria	Group Characteristics
13–17	Socio-cognitive development	At this age, due to biological and socio-cultural factors, there may be noticeable differences between the interests of boys and girls. At this time of life, individuals are focused on defining their own identity, so teenagers of both sexes are interested in experimenting with new types of experiences. For this reason, opportunities to build one's own character, make choices (including moral ones), or question generally accepted social rules become important in the game.
18–24	Professional and family changes	Due to continuing their education or taking up employment, people from this group play less than children. Most adult players at this point, thanks to previous experimentation, already have some established preferences for gameplay. This is also the first age group to have their own money to buy games.
25–34	Professional and family changes	Due to professional activity, entering into permanent relationships or building a family, most adults in this age group are people who play less often or with their young children. On the other hand, this group also includes people whose primary way of spending free time is playing video games. These people constitute one of the most important market segments, because they buy many games and often share information and opinions about games, potentially influencing the purchasing decisions of people around them.
35–54	Professional and family changes	Adults in this age group are mostly involved in work and/or family obligations, so they spend less time playing. However, as children grow up, they look for video games that offer entertainment for the whole family. Among people who treat video games as their main way of spending their free time, this group includes buyers who spend the largest amounts of money on buying individual games.
55 and more	Professional and family changes	Players in this age group have more free time again. Their children are often independent enough, and they themselves will retire relatively soon. Some people return to video games they played when they were younger. Others reach for new gaming experiences. People in this age group often treat video games not only as a form of entertainment, but as a way to provide themselves with adequate stimulation and maintain good mental condition.

Annotation. (Own elaboration based on literature).

What we can note here is that spending 5 hours weekly on games is something different for players in their mid-40s than for players in their early 20s, which is worth taking into account during selecting participants for research (we will look at this topic more in Chapter 10). Another thing is that, depending on age, players may have different gaming and life experiences, expectations, and consumption sets. On a more general level, when looking at different typologies (like the one presented above), it is good to keep in mind that they are not perfect or written in stone. They are useful in illustrating how a particular variable works (in this case, age), but they are only relevant in a limited way, e.g. life does not end at 55, and in late adulthood, we could find other specific groups. They are also valid for a limited time as different societies and their norms change, e.g. in Western societies, fewer people are choosing to have children [U.S. Census Bureau 2023; OECD 2024], more people are playing games (both overall and across age groups), and the average age of players is increasing [see ESA 2024; GGIA 2024]. Last but not least, it is worth for us to keep in mind that **typologies (or industry and market reports) give us a good overview of various contexts influencing players, but are no substitute for us actually asking players about their needs, experiences, and habits**.

When considering demographic and social factors, we couldn't ignore the role of education level. The education level is one of the most reliable determinants of financial possibilities and the structure of consumer expenditure. Consumers with higher education earn higher incomes on average, and therefore have a greater ability to satisfy their needs (and buy games!). Equally important, education is also related to the player's sensitivity to marketing information, as well as to the choice of activities in their spare time. Researchers note that people with secondary and higher education travel and read more often, and are also more interested in cultural and social life [Hoyer & MacInnis 2008]. As a side note, we have to take those statements cautiously, as we describe some correlations, which do not imply causation. We do not judge here if having a higher education level leads to traveling, reading, or is the opposite, or whether both are caused by something different (e.g. openness to new experiences).

While it is worth monitoring various socio-demographic variables during participant recruitment, they are usually not the main recruitment criteria for us, but only additional information that helps us invite a diversified group of players.

2.2.3 PSYCHOLOGICAL DETERMINANTS

When we analyze player's consumer behaviour, we certainly have to pay attention to psychological factors. We will start with player needs. Need can be defined as a state of lack of something and at the same time, a factor activating the functions of a motive to act towards changing this state. This state of lacking something creates tension that dynamizes player behaviour towards its reduction, i.e. satisfying the need.

One of the most well-known models describing player needs is the one proposed by Ryan, Rigby, and Przybylski based on Self-Determination Theory, which includes three basic needs motivating the players [Ryan et al. 2006; Przybylski et al. 2010; Rigby & Ryan 2011]. The first of these is the need for competence, which is defined as a sense of being effective when performing a selected activity. In order to satisfy this need, a game should have a clearly defined goal, the description of which includes criteria for success and/or failure. The challenge of achieving the goal should be optimal, i.e. it cannot overwhelm the player with its level of difficulty, and the player himself should believe that at some point they will achieve success, even if they experience a series of failures along the way. During the completion of the challenge, the player should also receive clear, useful, and non-judgmental feedback from the game about the progress made. Due to the frequency with which feedback is provided by the game, we can distinguish three types of feedback [Rigby & Ryan 2011]:

- Granular – the game responds to individual actions performed by the player, e.g. the number of damage dealt displayed after dealing a blow to an opponent.
- Sustained – the game signals an uninterrupted series of successes for the player, e.g. immediately after dealing an uninterrupted series of blows to an opponent, the player receives additional experience points for effectiveness.
- Cumulative – this type of information gives the player a more lasting sense of the overall level of effectiveness achieved throughout the game, e.g. the total number of points obtained during the game level or the level of the player's character.

What we can note is that a factor that has a significant impact on how well the need for competence is satisfied is usability. In research conducted by Ryan, Rigby, and Przybylski [2006], the ease with which players controlled the game significantly moderated how the satisfaction of the need for competence affected the desire to continue playing. In other studies, it turned out that while a game may have a clearly defined goal, have an appropriate level of difficulty, and provide feedback, if the player is unable to learn to control it, this will lower their overall sense of competence and thus lead to a lack of desire to continue playing [Przybylski et al. 2014].

Another player need is the need for autonomy, which can be defined as the player's desire to have the freedom to make choices that are interesting and have an impact on the gameplay. This need is satisfied in three basic ways [Rigby & Ryan 2011]:

- Identity – this is the ability to choose a player character in the game world (e.g. selecting a leader in *Civilization* series) or create a player's own character by choosing features such as but not limited to gender, race, and appearance (e.g. character creation in *Sims*).
- A multitude of available activities – games based on satisfying the need for autonomy give players the ability to choose from a wide range of available activities, e.g. in *The Legend of Zelda: Breath of the Wild*, apart from discovering the world and the game's narrative in any order, the player has the opportunity to complete many side challenges, fight monsters, solve puzzles, cook, or hunt.
- A variety of available strategies – this is the provision of choices regarding solutions and tactics in overcoming the challenges posed by the game, e.g. in *Civilization VI* the players can win in several ways: military (by defeating other players), scientific (by being the first to establish a base on the moon), cultural (by attracting a certain number of tourists), or points (by gaining a certain number of victory points).

The last is the need for connectedness, which can be defined as the desire to have valuable relationships with others [Ryan et al. 2006]. This need is satisfied within games offering a multiplayer mode, because it is generally satisfied by other players. Players are more willing to engage in activities that provide the opportunity to experience the game world with other people. As in the case of the previous needs, specific ways of satisfying need for connectedness have also been defined:

- Acknowledgement – is letting the player know that the game world and/or other players have noticed their presence.
- Support – in addition to noticing the player's presence, it is important to provide them with support appropriate to the circumstances, e.g. in multiplayer games medic class provides healing or revives other players, thanks to which they can rejoin the game.
- Impact – is allowing the player to influence the game world and other players. Often, the support provided to one player is the influence that another player has.

The better a game satisfies these needs, the more players are likely to return to it, experience greater enjoyment from the game, and are more likely to recommend the game to their friends. Ryan et al. [2006] note that satisfying players' needs leads to the broadly understood experience of immersion, and that the conditions necessary for full satisfaction of the need for competence overlap with those required to achieve the state of flow. Rigby and Ryan [2011] also note that while some researchers suggest that the experience of immersion may be influenced by such features of a video game as the realism of graphics, animation, special effects, and sound, research indicates that the satisfaction of the player's needs can be a stronger predictor of the immersion.

BOX 2.3   MAYBE THE PLAYER'S MIND IS A BLACK BOX?

Self-Determination Theory grew in opposition to the behavioural view of motivation. In this view, in order not to worry about subjective internal states such as motivation, we can treat what happens in the player's mind as a black box and focus on things that we can objectively observe and predictably modify – inputs to the box in the form of stimuli provided by the game and outputs in the form of the player's reactions. The behavioural view of motivation is based on the law of effect formulated by Edward Thorndike, which states that a person is more likely to repeat those actions that have positive consequences, and will avoid behaviours that bring negative or unpleasant effects. Sounds common sense, and based on Skinner's research results, we can learn that if we want to encourage players' behaviour, we can give them something pleasant for the right action (positive reinforcement, e.g. getting reward for completing a quest) or take away some unpleasant elements associated with the action (negative reinforcement, e.g. getting rid of the debuff, which is an effect that weakens the player character). We may also want to discourage the player's behaviour by delivering them something unpleasant for specific actions (positive punishment, e.g. player character death after leaving the play area) or taking away something pleasant for specific actions (negative punishment, e.g. reduced speed of the player character when injured). As you may already have noticed, words like positive and negative are used differently than in the common language. Reinforcement is about encouraging behaviour, and punishment is about discouraging behaviour, which can be done in a "positive" (giving something to the player) or "negative" way (by taking something from the player). All types of reinforcements and punishments can be delivered on a varied basis (e.g. number of actions and/or time), which lead to varied behavioural patterns.

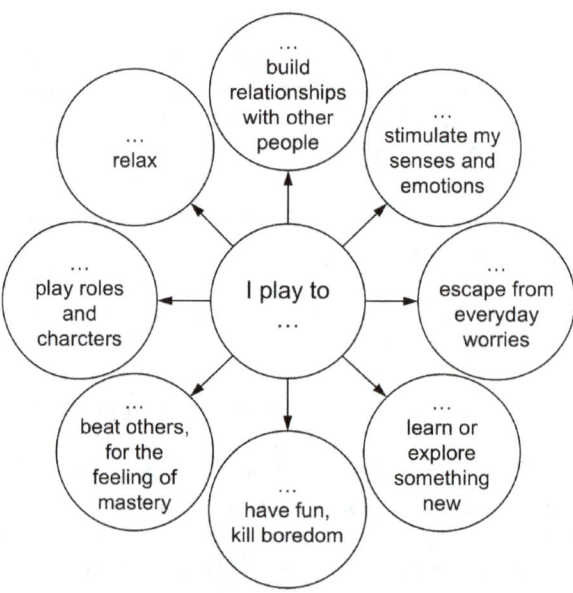

FIGURE 2.5 Some of the common motives for playing games. (Own elaboration.)

The way in which specific needs are satisfied among players can be varied. As we mentioned already, the unsatisfied need activates the function of motive. Motives are the reasons for player actions and determine their specific behaviours. Figure 2.5 summarizes some of the motives that guide players when choosing video games.

The above-mentioned motivations may result from the needs, demographic and social characteristics of the player, but also differences at the characterological level.

Another factor that shapes a player's consumer behaviour is personality. Personality can be defined as "specific psychological traits that characterize a given person, which lead to relatively logical and lasting ways of reacting to the environment" [Kotler 1999, p. 170]. Players differ in the intensity of individual personality traits, which allows for predicting differences in their behaviour. Certainly, one can find many personality theories. In our case, the OCEAN model by Costa and McCrae [1976; McCrae & John 1992] is worth noting, as it defines personality dimensions such as extraversion (a tendency to seek sensory stimulation and sociability), neuroticism (hypersensitivity, shyness, and impulsivity), openness to experience (curiosity, aesthetic sensitivity and a tendency to search for new ideas), conscientiousness (consideration, reliability and perseverance in pursuing a goal), and agreeableness (trust, altruism and straightforwardness). Research conducted by Nick Yee [2016] shows that individual motivations of players are manifestations of different personality traits. The desire to compete and establish relationships with other people is associated with the intensity of extraversion, while the desire to achieve mastery results from the intensity of conscientiousness. On the other hand, players with a high level of openness to experience seek opportunities to play roles and characters, discover stories, and learn new things in games.

A bit older, yet still popular perspective on describing player characteristics was proposed by Richard Bartle [1996]. Based on observing and analyzing the behaviour of people participating in multiplayer video games, Bartle proposed a typology in which four basic types of players can be distinguished:

- Achiever – A player who strives to achieve the best possible results during gameplay (e.g., the fastest time in a racing game, or the best kill-to-death ratio in a shooter). This is a player who focuses on collecting visible signs of mastery (e.g. achievement badges, trophies) by overcoming the challenges posed by the game, within the rules.
- Explorer – A player focused on discovering the game world and its story. This type of player focuses on collecting unique information about the game and discovering places in the game world that other players have not been. They derive satisfaction from solving puzzles and experimenting with the rules that govern the game world.
- Killer – A player who strives to win against other players in the game, using any means available to them in the game. Like the Achiever, the Killer is focused on winning, not so much by overcoming the challenges the game presents, but by eliminating other participants.
- Socializer – A player who views the game as an opportunity to build relationships with other players. This type of player focuses on helping others in the game more than on their own achievements.

However descriptive, from our perspective, we have to note that Bartle's proposal describes some of the playstyles rather than personality traits. What is worth remembering, though, is that in some cases, a differently defined playstyle can be one of the important recruitment criteria (e.g. when we are dealing with a game that allows for various approaches to overcoming a single challenge or a level, whether it be by brute force, stealth, rhetoric).

BOX 2.4   A PLAYER WITH AN ATTITUDE

Another variable that depends to some extent on personality, and which also influences the player's consumer decisions, is attitudes. Attitudes are learned or acquired predispositions to a certain evaluation of things, which are expressed in the behaviours, affect (motivation and emotions), and thoughts. Attitudes result from the interaction of external influences (e.g. marketing activities; information received from other people) and the player's own experiences (e.g. the game played). A characteristic feature of an attitude is its strength, which is expressed in the level of the player's negative or positive opinion on the game. The most commonly accepted hypothesis is that attitudes determine behaviours in such a way that the more positive attitudes a player has towards a game, the greater the probability of purchase. However, apart from extreme cases (e.g. franchise fans), players' attitudes are subject to change over time. More precisely, if we asked a player today whether "they would play our game in six months" their actual behaviour may have little to do with the declaration they made. This is one of the many reasons why we put more emphasis on observed behaviour than what our participants say about their future behaviour.

Certainly, we cannot do without describing the role of emotions. Considering this dimension of experience, but also the decision-making process, is supported by classic works in the field of neurobiology [LeDoux 2000; Damasio 2006]. Bechara and Damasio [2005], based on research involving patients with damage to the areas of the brain responsible for processing emotions, showed that compared to fully healthy people, they make more risky and maladaptive decisions. Emotions play an important role at every stage of the decision-making process, although with varying intensity.

Emotion can be defined as "a subjective mental state that triggers a priority for the related program of action. Its experience is usually accompanied by somatic changes, facial expressions and behaviours" [Doliński 2008, p. 322]. In the description of emotions, we can distinguish their three basic dimensions:

- Sign (valence) – emotions can be perceived as positive (e.g. joy, surprise) or as negative (e.g. sadness, disgust);
- Intensity – expressed as changes in the level of body activation, especially the activity of the autonomic nervous system, but also changes in cognitive processes (e.g. slowing down or accelerating the course of thought);
- Content – defining the significance of the stimulus that triggered the emotion and stimulates the person to act (e.g. approaching or avoiding something).

Let us note a still popular view that experiencing a positive emotion is associated with seeking contact with the thing that elicited it, while experiencing a negative emotion leads to avoiding the thing that elicited it. This rule applies to positive emotions, such as joy or surprise, and negative emotions, such as sadness, fear, or disgust. However, anger as a negative emotion still leads to an approach reaction, belonging in terms of content to the same group as surprise and joy [Harmon-Jones 2004]. Some answers to how emotions affect players' behaviour is provided by Poels et al. [2012], who measured two dimensions of emotions that appear during the use of video games: sign (positive vs. negative) and intensity (strong vs. weak). It turned out that positive emotions during the game predict whether the player will want to continue playing, and a higher intensity of emotions during the game results in a longer time spent in the game and a greater willingness to recommend the game to friends. An interesting aspect is that the study also compared self-report methods, such as Self-Assessment Manikin (SAM) [Bradley & Lang 1994], with psychophysiological methods such as galvanic skin response (GSR) and electromyography (EMG). Both types of methods proved effective in measuring players' emotions [Poels et al. 2012].

If we have highlighted the role of emotions, we have to mention factors related to cognition. What comes to our aid in analyzing gameplay experience and player behaviour in general are concepts of perception, attention, and memory. We can assume that:

- Perception is the grasp of objects and events in the environment through the senses (sight, hearing, touch, smell). It is the recognition of the properties of things, organizing them, understanding, and giving them meaning. In our context, we try to answer the question: Is the player able to recognize what the game communicates to them at a given moment (e.g. dangerous elements in the environment)?
- Attention is a process that is responsible for selecting information and focusing the player perception and thinking on an object or event. Attention is the player's ability to separate signals from noise in their environment. In our context, we would ask: Is the player able to efficiently and effectively capture crucial information about the game and/or what is happening in the game (e.g. In the heat of battle, can a player notice that their character is about to run out of health points)?
- Memory is the ability to record and recall various pieces of information, associations, or sensory impressions. Here, we try to answer the question: Can a player easily remember and recall given information, and are there any things they need to be reminded of (e.g. Is the player able to use different systems effectively after a long absence from the game)?

BOX 2.5   MENTAL EFFORT SETS EMOTIONS IN MOTION

When players engage in a game, they typically need to process information, make decisions, and overcome various challenges. This cognitive load (i.e. the mental effort required to perform actions or overcome challenges) can also directly affect how they feel. At the same time, games are often designed to evoke specific emotional responses, which in turn can influence how players process information. For example, when players experience fear during a game, their attention may narrow, making it harder for them to process more complex information. Typically, our goal is to determine whether the cognitive load and emotional experiences of players align with the design intention. Below are some questionnaires you may want to explore in this regard:

Cognitive Load:

- NASA-TLX (NASA Task Load Index) by Hart and Staveland [1988]

Emotions:

- PANAS (Positive And Negative Affect Schedule) by Watson et al. [1988]
- SAM (Self-Assessment Manikin) by Bradley and Lang [1994]
- GEW (Geneva Emotion Wheel) by Scherer [2005]
- DEQ (Discrete Emotions Questionnaire) by Harmon-Jones et al. [2016]

Above mentioned cognitive processes can be treated as resources that are limited (e.g. it can be hard to focus on a few things happening at once on the screen), can be distracted (e.g. by the loud noise coming from the next room), and are prone to various biases. When it comes to biases, we can consider them both in the context of the player and ourselves as user researchers. Although perception, memory, and attention are usually considered in the context of gameplay experience, we have to remember an obvious thing, that players use them all the time, e.g. also while processing information delivered in the trailers or product pages. The information a player extracts and remembers about a game can have an impact on both their purchasing decision and how they evaluate gameplay experience. In the study conducted by Livingston et al. [2011], participants were asked to read a game review and then play it. One group of participants read a negative review, while the other group read a positive review prior to playing. As we might expect, participants who read negative reviews gave the game a lower rating. While the impact of reviews on sales is obvious, it turns out that who wrote the review does not matter – players can be influenced by both professional game reviews and other players' comments.

2.3   WHERE DOES THE EXPERIENCE START?

When it comes to the gameplay experience, while it can be influenced by various factors, it is something that happens during the game itself. Player experience also includes the experience before and after playing. However, if we start thinking about it more broadly, one of the common questions we can ask ourselves is: Where does the experience actually begin? When is the game launched? When is it installed? When is a player visiting a product page? When is a trailer watched? The answer is important for us because it allows us to define our playfield and our relationship with other specialties (e.g. marketing). Personally, while I focus on the gameplay experience as a user researcher, I take it as a vital part of player experience, which I view through the lens of the player's consumer decision process, as it better structures the outcomes we are striving for (i.e. better reviews, specific playtime, lower return rates, higher sales). For this reason, in Part 3, you will find case studies in which participants watched a trailer before starting the actual game and then read the product page - especially for studies done at later stages of the production cycle, when these kinds of marketing materials are already available to the public. Having this in mind, let's look at how we can structure the process of how the player's consumer decision is formed, while keeping a keen eye on gameplay experience.

The classic model for the consumer decision-making process assumes that a player goes through a series of stages in a linear fashion. From recognizing a need ("I have some time tonight, should I play something?"), through searching for information ("What could I play?"), evaluating options ("Do I prefer *Civilization VI* or *Anno 1800*?"), making a purchase decision ("Is *Anno 1800* worth buying?"), and feelings after the purchase ("Was it fun to play?"). This process is presented in a simplified way in Figure 2.6.

This approach to the player's consumer decision-making process gives us a view of the process's structure and course. However, when we take a closer look, certain gaps appear that, as user researchers, we may want to fill in:

- It brings the player's experience down to the feeling of satisfaction or dissatisfaction after playing, which makes this model too simplified for us to be useful;
- In reality, not every player goes through all the steps in the established order, and the process itself is characterized by varying pace, returning to earlier stages and even skipping some of them, depending on the characteristics of the player and situation;
- Players engage in unconscious behaviour and the use of heuristics that are not taken into account in the rational approach to the decision-making process [Kahneman & Tversky 1979; Erasmus et al. 2001];
- Players do not always have clear and stable preferences, but they build and constantly update them during the decision-making process [Bettman et al. 1998];
- There are some observations that escape such a description of the decision-making process, e.g. players can play games without having to make a purchase in the first place; players buy games that they don't play at all.

If we want to use an example, it could look like this: A player heard from his friend about a great game he spent yesterday evening playing, which he highly recommends. Our player has not been disappointed so far with the recommendations from his friend, so he decides to check out the title in the demo version to see if he would actually like to buy it. We can schematically present this process in Figure 2.7.

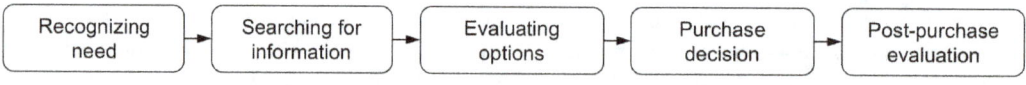

FIGURE 2.6   The classical approach to making a purchase decision. (Own elaboration.)

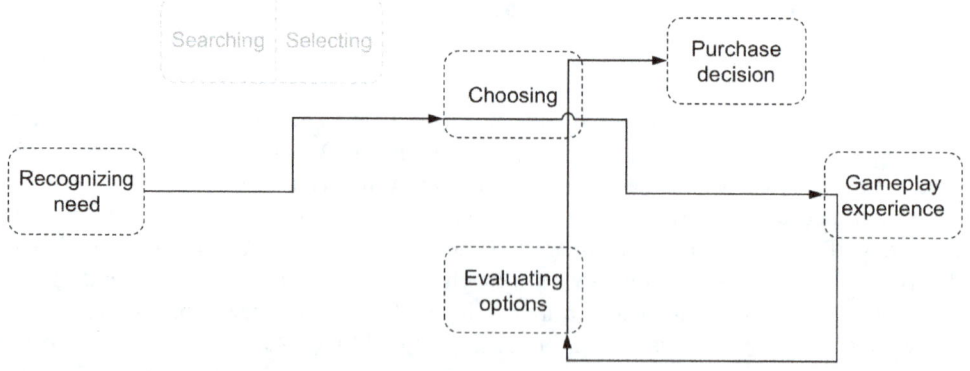

FIGURE 2.7   Example of making a decision to purchase a game. (Own elaboration.)

This and many other examples bothered me so much that I tried to structure the player's decision-making process in a different way [Mycka 2022], (see Figure 2.8).

Things just got a little bit more complex, so we will digest this diagram bit by bit. Let us first note that the model takes into account the course of the consumer decision process known from the classical model (player recognizes the need, searches for information and selects options, which they then evaluate and choose one, which they buy and play – such a course can be considered typical for games distributed in the pay-to-play model). What has changed here is the separation of the choice itself from the decision to purchase a game into separate elements. This is due to two reasons. First, in the case of video games distributed in the free-to-play model (including demo versions), players have the opportunity to experience the game before making any purchase (moving from point X3 directly to gameplay experience in the model). Second, the player can choose a specific game but not decide to buy it (feedback loops existing in the model departing from point X3) or can postpone this purchase (occurrence of a delay after making the choice). We have to note here that after making a purchase, the player may not play the game (feedback loops leading from point X5 through points X7 and X8) or postpone playing it (delay after the purchase decision). We also take into account that video games can be used multiple times before making a purchase (after the experience, there is another delay). We also take into account the breaks and delays that may occur during decision-making. Delays result from the fact that different elements of the process may occur simultaneously, which may involve waiting for further actions if their outcomes are related. Breaks in decision-making may be internal (X9, e.g. when there is no agreement among household members on which activity to choose for the afternoon). External breaks occur due to changes in factors that are criteria for choosing (X11, e.g. the price of the game has changed). On the other hand, breaks related to the appearance of a new option (X10) result from the possibility of learning about another game, but also another thing that might consume players' time, like a movie or a book.

We could end on a note that "It's only a model", and in fact – it is! As with any theoretical model, it provides us with a map of a territory, not the territory itself. In other words, however simplified, it can be useful in structuring our view of player experience, allowing us to make various assumptions and hypotheses about its causes and consequences, all of which we can (and some of them have to) check and study as user researchers.

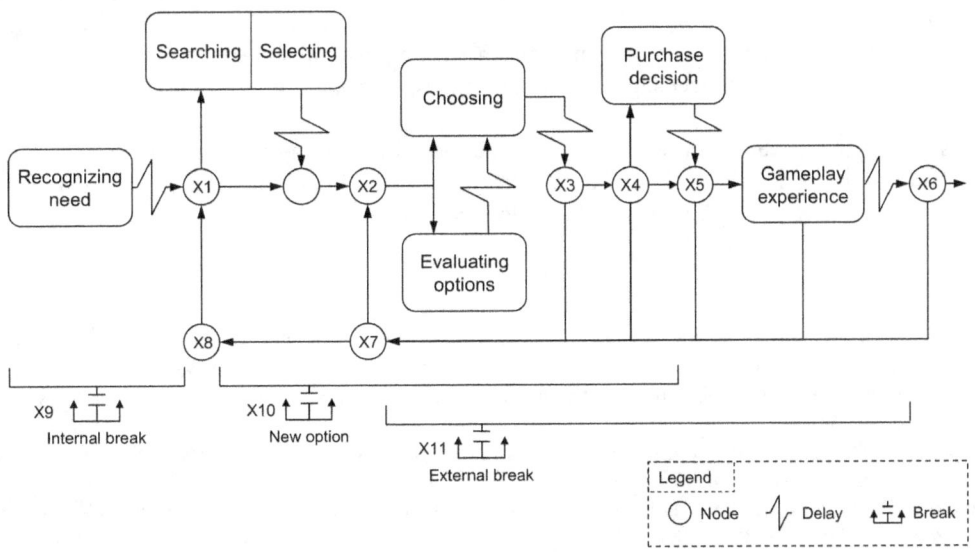

FIGURE 2.8   Overview of the player's decision-making process. (Own elaboration.)

BOX 2.6   EXERCISE: MEDITERRANEAN SNACK

Bread provides texture, fills, and serves as a good base, but is rather dry on its own and can make us thirsty. Olive oil, on the other hand, is full of flavour, flexible in its applications, but can be difficult to grasp due to its liquid nature. When we combine them, they create a simple yet nourishing snack. We can look at theory and practice the same way.

To avoid being too dry in our overview of theories and models, let's give it a more practical flavour. I encourage you to try a simple exercise. Choose a game and analyze it using one of the theories we discussed in this chapter. For instance, consider in what ways the game support needs for competence, autonomy, and relatedness (e.g. Are goals clearly defined? What types of feedback are provided and what is missing?) or examine how players' expectations for gameplay experience change through each stage of the decision-making process. As you draw your conclusions, deliberately omit elements that a given theory doesn't cover to better capture what the theory allows you to understand and what isn't considered. Repeat the exercise with other games, each time changing theory to not over-rely on a single perspective on experience.

2.4   CHAPTER SUMMARY

We started with the gameplay experience that can be seen as a state that emerges from the interaction between the player and the game, involving thoughts, emotions, and actions. We discussed key concepts like flow, immersion, and fun to highlight different aspects of gameplay experiences. We took a look at usability and accessibility as crucial elements in creating gameplay experience by stating that: first, we need to remove potential barriers to entry for players (accessibility) so that they can efficiently learn the rules of the game and use them (usability) to finally get engaged in it (experience).

We then broaden our perspective and look at player experience (i.e. the general experience that the player has with the game, including those before, during, and after gameplay), and look at player behaviour and decisions through factors that influence it:

- Economic factors: income, price, purchasing risk, consumption set, investment, and usage costs.
- Socio-demographic factors: age, sex, household composition, and education.
- Psychological factors: needs, personality, attitudes, emotions, and cognition.

Understanding the player experience as a consumer decision-making process, which often unfolds in a non-linear manner with breaks and delays down the line, allows us to form better research questions and examine gameplay experience in a wider context.

REFERENCES

Azadvar, A., & Canossa, A. (2018). UPEQ: Ubisoft perceived experience questionnaire: A self-determination evaluation tool for video games. In *ACM International Conference Proceeding Series* (vol. 5, pp. 1–7).

Bartle, R. (1996). Hearts, clubs, diamonds, spades: Players who suit MUDs. In *Proceedings of the iConference 2014*.

Bechara, A., & Damasio, A. R. (2005). The somatic marker hypothesis: A neural theory of economic decision. *Games and Economic Behavior,* 52(2), 336–372.

Bettman, J. R., Luce, M. F., & Payne, J. W. (1998). Constructive consumer choice processes. *Journal of Consumer Research*, 25(3), 187–217.

Bradley, M. M., & Lang, P. J. (1994). Measuring emotion: The self-assessment manikin and the semantic differential. *Journal of Behavior Therapy and Experimental Psychiatry*, 25(1), 49–59.

Brockmyer, J. H., Fox, C. M., Curtiss, K. A., McBroom, E., Burkhart, K. M., & Pidruzny, J. N. (2009). The development of the game engagement questionnaire: A measure of engagement in video game-playing. *Journal of Experimental Social Psychology*, 45(4), 624–634.

Brown, E., & Cairns, P. (2004). A grounded investigation of game immersion. In *CHI'04 Extended Abstracts on Human Factors in Computing Systems* (pp. 1297–1300).

Carr, D. (2005). Contexts, gaming pleasures, and gendered preferences. *Simulation and Gaming*, 36(4), 464–482.

Costa, P. T., & McCrae, R. R. (1976). Age differences in personality structure: A cluster analytic approach. *Journal of Gerontology*, 31(5), 564–570.

Csikszentmihalyi, M. (1975). *Beyond Boredom and Anxiety*. Jossey-Bass Publishers.

Damasio, A. R. (2006). *Descartes' Error. Emotion, Reason and the Human Brain*. Vintage Books.

Dawson, C. R., Cragg, A., Taylor, C., & Toombs, B. (2007). *Video Games: Research to Improve Understanding of What Players Enjoy about Video Games, and to Explain Their Preferences for Particular Games*. London, UK: British Board of Film Classification.

Doliński, D. (2008). Mechanizmy wzbudzania emocji. In J. Strelau (Ed.), *Psychologia. Podręcznik akademicki. Tom 2: Psychologia ogólna* (pp. 319–349). GWP.

Entertainment Software Association (2024). 2024 Essential Facts about the U.S. Video Game Industry.

Erasmus, A. C., Boshoff, E., & Rousseau, G. G. (2001). Consumer decision-making models within the discipline of consumer science: A critical approach. *Journal of Family Ecology and Consumer Sciences*, 29, 82–90.

Ermi, L., & Mäyrä, F. (2005). Changing views: Worlds in play fundamental components of the gameplay experience: Analyzing immersion. In *Proceedings of the 2005 DiGRA International Conference: Changing Views: Worlds in Play*.

GGIA (2024). *Annual Report of the German Games Industry*. https://www.game.de/en/publications/annual-report-of-the-german-games-industry-2024/

Harmon-Jones, C., Bastian, B., & Harmon-Jones, E. (2016). The discrete emotions questionnaire: A new tool for measuring state self-reported emotions. *PLoS ONE*, 11(8), e0159915.

Harmon-Jones, E. (2004). On the relationship of frontal brain activity and anger: Examining the role of attitude toward anger. *Cognition & Emotion*, 18(3), 337–361.

Hart, S. G., & Staveland, L. E. (1988). Development of NASA-TLX (task load index): Results of empirical and theoretical research. *Advances in Psychology*, 52(C), 139–183.

Heeter, C., Egidio, R., Mishra, P., Winn, B., & Winn, J. (2008). Alien games: do girls prefer games designed by girls? *Games and Culture*, 4(1), 74–100.

Hoyer, W. D., & MacInnis, D. J. (2008). *Consumer Behavior* (5th ed.). Cengage Learning Inc.

Ijsselsteijn, W. A., Kort De, Y. A. W., & Poels, K. (2013). *The Game Experience Questionnaire*. Technische Universiteit Eindhoven.

Jennett, C., Cox, A. L., Cairns, P., Dhoparee, S., Epps, A., Tijs, T., & Walton, A. (2008). Measuring and defining the experience of immersion in games. *International Journal of Human Computer Studies*, 66(9), 641–661.

Kahneman, D., & Tversky, A. (1979). Prospect theory: An analysis of decision under risk. *Econometrica*, 47(2), 263–291.

Kotler, P. (1999). *Marketing. Analiza, planowanie, wdrażanie i kontrola*. Felberg SJA.

Lazzaro, N. (2004a). *The 4 Keys 2 Fun*. https://nicolelazzaro.com/wp-content/uploads/2012/03/4_keys_poster3.jpg

Lazzaro, N. (2004b). *Why We Play Games: Four Keys to More Emotion Without Story*. https://xeodesign.com/xeodesign_whyweplaygames.pdf

LeDoux, J. (2000). *Mózg emocjonalny. Tajemnicze podstawy życia emocjonalnego*. Media i Rodzina.

Livingston, I. J., Nacke, L. E., & Mandryk, R. L. (2011). Influencing experience: The effects of reading game reviews on player experience. In J. Anacleto, S. Fels, N. Graham, B. Kapralos, M. S. El-Nasr, & K. Stanley (Eds.), *Entertainment Computing - ICEC 2011* (pp. 89–100). Springer.

Lucas, K., & Sherry, J. L. (2004). Sex differences in video game play: A communication-based explanation. *Communication Research*, 31(5), 499–523.

McCrae, R. R., & John, O. P. (1992). An introduction to the five-factor model and its applications. *Journal of Personality*, 60(2), 175–215.

McMahan, A. (2003). Immersion, engagement, and presence: A method for analyzing 3-D video games. In M. J. P. Wolf & B. Perron (Eds.), *The Video Game Theory Reader* (pp. 67–86). Routledge.

Mycka, M. (2022). *Wpływ doświadczenia związanego z korzystaniem z gier wideo na decyzje konsumenckie graczy/Impact of gameplay experience on video game players' consumer decisions*. [Doctoral thesis, Poznań University of Economics and Business]. https://bip.ue.poznan.pl/501/mgr-michal-mycka.html

Nakamura, J., & Csikszentmihalyi, M. (2002). The concept of flow. In C. R. Snyder & S. J. Lopez (Eds.), *Handbook of Positive Psychology* (pp. 89–105). Oxford University Press.

Nielsen, J. (2012). Usability 101: Introduction to usability. Nielsen Norman Group. https://www.nngroup.com/articles/usability-101-introduction-to-usability/

OECD (2024). *Society at a Glance 2024: OECD Social Indicators*. OECD Publishing.

Ogletree, S. M., & Drake, R. (2007). College students' video game participation and perceptions: Gender differences and implications. *Sex Roles*, 56, 537–542.

Poels, K., Van den Hoogen, W., IJsselsteijn, W., & de Kort, Y. (2012). Pleasure to play, arousal to stay: The effect of player emotions on digital game preferences and playing time. *Cyberpsychology, Behavior, and Social Networking*, 15(1), 1–6.

Przybylski, A., Deci, E., Rigby, S., & Ryan, R. (2014). Competence-impeding electronic games and players' aggressive feelings, thoughts, and behaviors. *Journal of Personality and Social Psychology*, 106(3), 441–457.

Przybylski, A., Rigby, S., & Ryan, R. (2010). A motivational model of video game engagement. *Review of General Psychology*, 14(2), 154–166.

Rassuli, K. M., & Harrell, G. D. (1990). A new perspective on choice. *Advances in Consumer Research*, 17(1), 737–744.

Ratan, R., Chen, V., De Grove, F., Breuer, J., Quandt, T., & Williams, P. (2022). Gender, gaming motives, and genre: Comparing Singaporean, German, and American players. *IEEE Transactions on Games*, *14*(3), 456–465.

Rigby, S., & Ryan, R. (2011). *Glued to Games: How Video Games Draw Us in and Hold Us Spellbound*. ABC-CLIO.

Ryan, R., Rigby, S., & Przybylski, A. (2006). The motivational pull of video games: A self-determination theory approach. *Motivation and Emotion*, 30(4), 347–363.

Scherer, H., & Naab, T. K. (2009). Money does matter. In T. Hartmann (Ed.), *Media Choice: A Theoretical and Empirical Overview* (pp. 70–83). Routledge.

Scherer, K. R. (2005). *The Geneva Emotion Wheel*. Social Science Information.

Strojny, P., & Strojny, A. (2014). Kwestionariusz immersji – polska adaptacja i empiryczna weryfikacja narzędzia/The Immersion Questionnaire – Polish adaptation. *Homo Ludens*, 1(6), 171–185.

Sweetser, P., & Wyeth, P. (2005). GameFlow: A model for evaluating player enjoyment in games. *Computers in Entertainment*, 3(3), 3–3.

Takatalo, J., Häkkinen, J., Kaistinen, J., & Nyman, G. (2010). Presence, involvement, and flow in digital games. In R. Bernhaupt (Ed.), *Evaluating User Experience in Games* (pp. 23–46). Springer.

Tekofsky, S., Miller, P., Spronck, P., & Slavin, K. (2016). The effect of gender, native English speaking, and age on game genre preference and gaming motivations. In *International Conference on Intelligent Technologies for Interactive Entertainment* (pp. 178–183).

Terlecki, M., Brown, J., Harner-Steciw, L., Irvin-Hannum, J., Marchetto-Ryan, N., Ruhl, L., & Wiggins, J. (2011). Sex differences and similarities in video game experience, preferences, and self-efficacy: Implications for the gaming industry. *Current Psychology*, 30(1), 22–33.

Thatcher, J., Burks, M. R., Heilmann, C., Lawton Henry, S., Kirkpatrick, A., Lauke, P. H., Lawson, B., Regan, B., Rutter, R., & Urban, M. (2006). Web Accessibility: *Web Standards and Regulatory Compliance*. Springer-Verlag.

U.S. Census Bureau. (2023). *An Aging U.S. Population with Fewer Children in 2020*. https://www.census.gov/library/stories/2023/05/aging-united-states-population-fewer-children-in-2020.html

Watson, D., Clark, L. A., & Tellegan, A. (1988). Worksheet 3.1 the positive and negative affect schedule (PANAS; Watson et al., 1988) PANAS questionnaire. *Journal of Personality and Social Psychology*, 54, 1063–1070.

Yee, N. (2016). *Gaming motivations align with personality traits*. Quantic Foundry. https://quanticfoundry.com/2016/01/05/personality-correlates/

3 What Is Our Role Then?

In this chapter, we will discuss our role as games user researchers and how to navigate between the perspectives of the development team and the players.

Topics covered in this chapter:

- Defining the role of games user researchers.
- Understanding the factors and attitudes substantial in building a trusting and effective relationship with the production team.
- Recognizing the challenges and conditions that affect user research, including organizational maturity and the placement of user research within the studio structure.
- Addressing common misconceptions about the role of user research in game development.

3.1 SUPPORTING THE TEAM

Now that we have defined what a game is, how it is produced, what the typical disciplines are involved in the process, and what the player experience is, we can summarize our role:

> *The Games User Researcher's role is to support game development teams in delivering the best player experience possible according to the intended vision, within given business objectives and technical constraints.*

When we think about providing support, we can start with the trivial fact that **our primary task is to do actionable research, and consider how to do it in a valid and reliable way**. We will have plenty of time for that in Parts 2 and 3, as this is the basis of our work. For now, we will focus less on the methods and tools and take a closer look at the research soft underbelly.

Let's start with the typical advice given to designers to "kill their darlings", or in other words, to let go of ideas that sound neat but don't work. This phrase reflects an emotional attachment to the ideas someone feels particularly proud of, and which can be really hard to part with. Ideas, when elaborated or implemented, may not provide such a great experience as intended, as players lack this maternal attitude towards them. We are one of the disciplines (among other people in and out of the team) to deliver that kind of news, by saying that "those darlings will have an uphill and winding road to school". Certainly, we strive to do this in a more structured and deliberate way not to end up as just another opinion in the crowd. However, in these circumstances of emotional attachment to ideas and a multitude of voices, **no matter how beautiful the research report is or how well it aligns with the facts, if the team doesn't trust it (or us), it limits our impact on design and business decisions**. Do not get me wrong, I firmly believe that well-done research defends itself without us being present in the room, but my common observation is that if the top-notch methodology and proper reasoning were enough to convince someone, there will be much less discussion on the value the research brings to the table.

3.1.1 DOCTOR–PATIENT METAPHOR

When it comes to discussing trust, we may come across the concept of encapsulating researcher-game relationship in a doctor-patient metaphor. And actually, when we get to the methods and tools, we might get the impression that our goal is to accurately diagnose all ailments of the game and objectively indicate the treatment method in accordance with the best available knowledge. This metaphor also sheds light on some of the desirable aspects of our relationship with the team, which are worth being reliable, transparent, communicative, and empathetic.

DOI: 10.1201/9781003501909-4

3.1.1.1   Reliability

Setting clear expectations, and doing what we agreed to do with the team, and not doing what we didn't agree on. Basically, the team is relying on us to perform research that will help them to make specific decisions. We are not asked to give advice on how the game should be designed or our opinions on what would be a fun feature to add (generally, nobody goes to a doctor for advice on what to wear). The other thing is that some of the questions cannot be answered in the form or time proposed by the team. If we know that we can't deliver the answers, because they are not available based on the data we gathered or general knowledge, or we simply do not have time or resources to find them, we have to state it upfront with the team to not end up under-delivering or over-promising.

3.1.1.2   Transparency

Being honest about the challenges with the research and its limitations, and sharing our reasoning behind actions. Even in research, not everything is always going according to plan, and there is no single silver bullet for finding the required answers. The one thing written into our specialty is being open about it, to let the team make informed decisions on how they want to proceed.

3.1.1.3   Communicativeness

Communicating effectively requires us to actively listen to the team's pains and needs, i.e. understand what the team is telling us and ensure that we understand what they want to achieve and what they want to avoid. At the same time, communication is not a one-time act of gathering requirements, so keeping the team in the loop about the progress of research helps to avoid misunderstandings and provide the team with what they actually need. While communicating with the team, we aim to provide actionable feedback, so the one which is:

- Clear – provided in a language that the team understands, and avoids jargon;
- Useful – it should allow for taking action;
- Non-judgmental – we do not evaluate the competence of people in the team, only the game.

However, communication is a two-way road, so we should be ready to ask the team for feedback on our actions and how we could improve in the future to deliver better value.

3.1.1.4   Empathy

Delivering research it's not about making someone feel good or bad about their job. The project and its environment can do enough in this respect, so we don't have to jump on this bandwagon. We want to stimulate action and catalyze informed decision-making on the side of the team, which, besides delivering quality results, requires us to understand the situation they're in, their constraints, and how they perceive it. After all, what's the point of insisting on some design change recommendation if the team is not able to implement it (e.g. based on time or budget, or simply holding to creative vision).

BOX 3.1   BAKING BREAD OR BREAKING BAD?

Ethical considerations are an inevitable part of conducting research (or at least they should be). In this context, our obligations when conducting research include:

- Providing participants with the necessary information and explanations about what awaits them during the study, so that they can give their informed consent to participate.
- Taking care of the privacy of participants (e.g. not sharing their data or image publicly, but also informing them about the purposes for which we will use the collected data).

- Not exposing participants to unnecessary harm, whether mental or physical, e.g. in VR game research, there is always a risk of adverse symptoms, so it is worth sensitizing participants to the possibility of taking a break or interrupting the study if they feel uncomfortable.
- Approaching participants with respect (e.g. respecting the diversity of their backgrounds and perspectives, but also rewarding them for their time).
- Reporting results in a factual manner that reflects the experiences of the participants (e.g. avoiding selective reporting of results or cherry-picking, and clearly indicating the limitations of the study).

While these topics may be obvious to some extent, there may be many less obvious challenges to be aware of when conducting research. One such topic is the identification of conflicts of interest. Conflict of interest is a situation where we are involved in multiple interests, and supporting one of them could thwart another. A common example would be detecting and reporting dark patterns (also known as deceptive patterns) used in free-to-play games, such as time-limited offers (e.g. a special power-up bundle offer today only!) or anchoring (e.g. placing a cheaper item right next to a more expensive one to make it look affordable), which players may not even be aware of. Dark patterns may work to the financial success of the game (which in the end could influence our payroll), but are based on harming or misleading players (which we should avoid).

To share a personal example, I was once asked by a producer to prepare some video clips from research sessions where participants were enjoying the experience or saying positive things about the game. I asked him why he wouldn't use the report, after all, it describes both positive and negative aspects of the experience with links to the recordings, which give a pretty good idea of the state of the game. It turned out that he was preparing for a meeting where the publisher was to share the results of their own evaluation of the game build, based on which a decision was to be made about accepting a milestone (which involved paying cash for further production). I explained that it was understandable that the team wanted to do the best they could at such a meeting, after all, it could have serious consequences for the studio. However, from an ethical perspective, the results should not be presented in a selective or misleading way. Ultimately, after discussion, we managed to reach an agreement that it is worth sharing what we have observed in the research – both positive and negative – and at the same time presenting what we intend to do with it, because in the end these things will most probably come out anyway, so there is no reason to pretend that everything is great. Did we solve it properly? I do not have a simple answer here, because in such situations you can find other good, or maybe even better solutions - the most important thing is to reach an agreement while holding integrity, although it may not be easy.

The requests we get or the research we conduct may raise many questions that do not have obvious and easy answers, but trying to spot such situations and giving them a second thought is a good first step to not end up cooking something that we do not want to.

3.1.2 KINDERGARTEN TEACHER–PARENT METAPHOR

The doctor-patient metaphor seems to accurately reflect certain aspects of research work. On the other hand, the team does not always act like a worried family waiting for a diagnosis and treatment recommendations, and we may not be seen as lifesavers (at least most of the time). It can also build a notion of asymmetry (because it assumes that "we know and they don't, and we have to explain it to them") and false expectations (e.g. that the team will request support or be referred to us, and simply adhere to the things we say). In this context, our perspective can complement the view of the researcher-team relationship as the relationship between parents and the person who looks after their child while they are at work. It is a more down-to-earth metaphor compared to a doctor, but it allows us to better capture the actual dynamics of the relationship we may have with the team:

- Parents have more or less specific beliefs about how they want to raise their child (i.e. creative vision for the game).
- Parents know – or at least believe they know – what's best for their child (i.e. almost everyone in the team has the idea of the perfect gameplay experience).
- Parents can put much more attention to what happens outside the kindergarten (i.e. as we already mentioned, there is tone of work to be done during production cycle, and research is only one of them).
- Kindergarten teacher observes the child and can signal the difficulties to the parents (i.e. we conduct research and write reports on the game for the team).
- Kindergarten teachers have little to no control over how recommendations will be implemented outside the kindergarten (i.e. we are delivering recommendations, but the team has to make actions based on them).
- Parents may get defensive when listening to their child's difficulties (i.e. receiving feedback, especially negative one, even when it is constructive, can be a hard experience in itself).
- Parents may be reluctant to take actions on the child's difficulties, e.g. explaining that it will pass with age (i.e. with multiple priorities, the team may resort to quick, common sense attempts to solve the problem, e.g. if players don't understand, we'll explain it later in the tutorial).
- The child seen a few weeks or months ago may now be a completely different person (i.e. game during production cycle can tremendously change from build to build).
- The child's development is not only about progress, and we can observe periods of regress (i.e. there can be periods where game elements, features, or systems are only partially implemented, and the game has more bugs, which ends in worse evaluations of player experience, even though we are further in the production cycle).
- Predictions about how well the child will cope in life based on kindergarten behaviour alone are prone to error at best (i.e. we are just one of the specialties taking care of the player experience and we may have a limited view of the potential factors of success or failure of the game).

From this perspective, conducting research may sound like quite a challenge, but after all, no one said it would be easy. However, what we can draw from this metaphor is that effectively delivering value to the team may also require us to be proactive, flexible, and patient.

3.1.2.1   Proactivity

Direct requests from the team to conduct research may appear late in the production cycle. This may be due to the team having observed some player experience issue and is now investigating it, or because the team at an earlier stage simply did not know whether and what to ask about, or did not want to conduct research on something that, in their opinion, wasn't ready. Therefore, instead of just waiting for requests, it is worth looking for areas where conducting research could bring value, planning ahead and anticipating upcoming challenges (e.g. based on creative vision, core pillars, and communicated needs and challenges), and discussing it with the team.

3.1.2.2   Flexibility

More often than not, the team may be swamped with work on a game and keeping up with business requirements, and even if they value user research input, their time to consume it or engage in the process can be simply constrained. Another thing is that in periods of multiple iterations and changes in design, user research has to keep up with the pace of the team, as research insights expiration date can be short. Adapting our plans and approach to team constraints and the current situation can save frustrations both for us and them.

3.1.2.3 Patience

Certainly, research methods vary in time needed to perform, and a single study can be a time-consuming endeavour. When we take a bird's-eye view of the production cycle, conducting research in the production phase can be seen as a relatively common practice, while conducting research in pre-production or concept phases more often requires us to do some legwork. When we join the team, we can try the "big bang" approach and try to gain stakeholder acceptance for various research initiatives throughout the production cycle, but this approach rarely has a chance of success, not only due to budget constraints, but also due to the lack of appropriate process and logistical support. More often safer choice is the "evolutionary" approach, where we propose research as an opportunity arises (e.g. we suggest a topic for the next study after performing one requested by the team). It helps the team to get accustomed to the research processes and see value in things we deliver, which can be the basis for discussion on more developed approaches in the future.

Whether we think of ourselves as doctors or kindergarten teachers, where we actually are in this spectrum depends greatly on the organizational setting and the maturity of the team we are cooperating with.

3.2 ORGANIZATIONAL MATURITY AND SETTING

We can safely assume that no single team wants their game to perform poorly, either in terms of sales or reception, and most of the teams are interested in providing the best possible player experience. However, practices that are harnessed to achieve this goal can vary significantly across the studios. Depending on how well-established and developed user research practices are and what place we occupy in the organizational structure, delivering actionable results may require us to overcome more or fewer challenges, and can have varying impacts on the game's success.

3.2.1 ORGANIZATIONAL MATURITY

When it comes to organizational maturity, we can find some useful conceptualizations directly applicable to games user research [McAllister 2018]. The general idea is that our impact on the game's success depends not only on our skills or the mistakes we make, but also on the quality of the environment in which we operate. Typically, organizational maturity models are based on dividing it into separate levels or stages, each of them defined by a state, challenges, and possible means of action to level up, ultimately achieving a defined ideal state. Sampling a studio's organizational maturity in terms of user research allows us to better align our activities with available possibilities, as well as identify blockers that prevent us from improving our practices. While these models aim to be universal across studio sizes, precise positioning at a specific level and checking how much more work lies ahead of us before we reach the end-game makes more sense in larger studios. After all, the situation is more complex to assess, we have more people involved in the process, more interests to satisfy, and the changes themselves may require more time and money to bring the expected effect. Let's make it simpler, because after all, why talk about a tanker when we're in a sailboat? Instead of looking at specific levels, we can boil it down to basic questions worth asking to identify some of the blockers that can prevent us from running studies effectively in smaller organizational settings.

3.2.1.1 Do We Have a Budget?

Whatever activity we undertake, it costs us at least the time that we have to devote to it, which could be spent differently. If we work in a research position, the basic component of the budget will be our salary. If not, we will have to spend additional time or time that we would normally spend on tasks assigned to our role. Other basic costs are the remuneration of research participants (which can take the form of money or in-kind), but also the cost of maintaining the infrastructure needed for research (even if we conduct research in a studio's conference room). Generally, if we do not have a dedicated budget for the basics at our disposal or it is granted on an ad-hoc basis, it makes research planning difficult and requires us to adapt methods to make them within our reach (e.g. running research with friends and family after hours).

3.2.1.2   Do We Have Expertise?

Not everything comes down to money. As we will see in the following chapters, we have a wide range of methods that allow us to answer various questions that arise during the production cycle. While we will take a closer look at some of the methods, there are others that may require more preparation and logistical support. I assume that it is worth earning the necessary experience by conducting research using a given method, but some of the challenges are worth consulting with people who have already done it (e.g. by looking for a mentor or entrusting the research to external partners).

3.2.1.3   Do We Have Team Buy-in?

The team consists of people who are ultimately supposed to implement the recommendations we provide (at least some of them). If there is reluctance or hostility on the part of the team, conducting research can be highly difficult, providing the necessary information and assets will not be a priority, and the recommendations themselves may not be taken into account when making decisions. This can be one of the basic blockers for user research in general, resulting from various factors (e.g. not knowing the role and value of user research, or having misconceptions about it). We have already mentioned some of them in the context of the role that user researchers play in the team, and we will talk more about typical misconceptions later.

3.2.1.4   Do We Have Impact?

The previous three questions touched more on topics related to blockers in preparing and conducting research. However, the mere fact of conducting research, having a budget and support from the team will not translate our actions into a positive impact on sales and reception of the game. A good indicator of how we did can be reviews (from experts or players). We can find in them both things that we missed, but also things that we signalled based on the research, but that were not addressed by the team. Depending on the root cause, we identified (e.g. results were not delivered on time, communicated to the right people in the team or implemented by the team), we can draw at least some conclusions about what we should improve.

BOX 3.2   WHEN THERE IS NO ONE TO TALK TO, OR IS THERE?

Some believe that 10,000 hours of practice will make us masters of a chosen craft. I don't know if it's 10,000 or some other magic number, but the quality of that practice, not just the quantity, will certainly make a big difference. We don't always have someone at hand to tell us if we're doing things right, but one obvious way to check it is to monitor our actions. In the context of working in small- and medium-sized studios, it is worth considering monitoring to be possible during our daily activities, the data to be easily accessible, and the measures themselves to have clear informational value. After all, it is not about multiplying measures to make it look serious, but about methodically improving our practices. On a very basic level we can consider measures like:

- Stakeholder satisfaction – A large part of research is building and maintaining relationships with the team. After all, positive relationships are one of the factors that increase the chances that the research will be perceived as relevant and will

influence design decisions. It is worth asking for a measurable rating of the last study we conducted (e.g. on a scale of one to five stars), but it is crucial to also capture the reasoning behind the rating. For example, I often use the rose-bud-thorn technique, in which I ask the stakeholders in a given study three short questions:
- What was a positive highlight about our collaboration on this study? (Rose)
- Where do you see opportunities for improvement or change to improve our collaboration in the future? (Bud)
- What did not go as you expected or what made our collaboration difficult? (Thorn)

- Research impact ratio – Certainly, it's good to have satisfied stakeholders, but it's worth checking whether they actually use what we provide them with. To check how effectively the results we provide are transformed into actual design changes in the game, it's worth counting how many of the insights we provide have been recommended for implementation in the game, e.g. by counting the ratio of insights used to all those provided from a given study. It is worth taking a look at the unimplemented insights and trying to determine the reason for this, e.g. is it the result of priorities set in the team, or maybe the fact that we failed to effectively communicate the results?

- Research turnaround time – It is good to know how long different types of research take us from the first meeting on a given topic with the team to the delivery of the final report. On the one hand, stakeholders ask how long it takes to conduct a study, and on the other, reducing the study duration suggests that we are achieving some efficiency in our activities. Of course, this measure cannot be optimized indefinitely, and it is worth monitoring whether the quality of the results we deliver is not suffering in the process.

- Research coverage – Tracking the percentage of components and features that were evaluated in research lets us see how well our research approach is addressing different aspects of the player experience. This metric also provides information about which areas of the game carry unspecified or unknown risks, which can be valuable in discussions with stakeholders about future areas for research. At the same time, it's worth noting that this metric doesn't provide information about how the team prioritizes different components of the game (and we'll rarely have the opportunity to look at all of them in detail).

Certainly, it's not about getting perfect results in every metric (although I wish that for everyone), but about checking if we are making progress, reflecting on what led to a particular result and what we can do about it, so that we don't go around in circles. Just by the way, monitoring the effects of our work comes in handy when we have to communicate with our stakeholders, especially while applying for more budget or trying to get support for research initiatives.

3.2.2 ORGANIZATIONAL SETTING

The effectiveness of user research depends not only on budgets, skills, or relationships with the team, but also on where we are in the organizational structure. Just to paraphrase the well-known catchphrase, "structure is the limit". The place of user research in the organizational structure varies from studio to studio, and depending on our place within it, we will have certain benefits, but also face some inherent challenges (see Table 3.1).

It is worth noting that researchers can also work outside the structures of the studio, creating the game. We can work as an external partner (e.g. a freelancer, research agency) or as a

TABLE 3.1

The Place of User Research in the Studio's Organizational Structure and Its Consequences

Structure Type	Description	Pros	Cons
Centralized	We work as a separate team from production, which provides user research services for projects in the studio. In smaller studios, this may be an independent role reporting directly to the board, while in larger studios, it's typically a dedicated user research team with an assigned manager.	Ensures consistency in methods across projects Allows for the development of specialized expertise, especially in larger studios Provides clear ownership of research initiatives Enables the delivery of more strategic insights beyond project-level concerns	Risk of bottlenecks and delays Lack of project-specific context, especially in larger studios Requires more effort to build relationships with the production team, as there are fewer natural opportunities to integrate
Decentralized	We work as part of the team producing a given game. In this structure, we report directly to the people managing the project to which we have been assigned. If there are more people in our studio in user research roles, each of them reports to the people managing the project to which they have been assigned.	Naturally fosters closer collaboration with the team Supports faster turnaround times Makes research activities more easily tailored to the team's needs Shifts research ownership to the team	Can lead to inconsistent methods across projects Risks fragmented expertise, especially in larger studios May result in duplicated research efforts Faces challenges when scaling the team
Hybrid	We are simultaneously assigned to a centralized team providing research services, while at the same time being part of the team producing a given game. Therefore, we report both to the line manager and to the people managing the specific project. This structure is rarely present in small studios.	Consistency in methods while tailoring them to project needs Simplifies research planning and improves resource allocation across projects Fosters knowledge and expertise sharing among user researchers	Requires complex management due to dual reporting structures May face coordination challenges within the UR team, especially in larger studios Risk of research resource conflicts between projects

Annotation. (Own elaboration).

user researcher on the publisher's side. The main disadvantage of both places is that, as an entity external to the project, we have less knowledge about it. Working as an external partner, we are also less likely to collect detailed feedback on our work, and observing our impact on the game may require more work or be postponed (e.g. which recommendations and how they were implemented will be checked only after the release, when the game sees the light of day). In this context, working on the publisher's side allows us to more easily observe our impact on the game, but it's worth to be mindful that how many recommendations and how they were implemented may not be result of substantive premises, but rather effect of power asymmetry in developer-publisher relationship (i.e. the team creating the game will implement a suggested changes in the game not because they were convinced by our results, but because the acceptance of a milestone, and therefore the cash payment for further production, may depend on the implementation of these changes). In many cases, developers have to rely on publishers in the relationship, and nurturing open communication and a trusting relationship between the two can be a challenge in itself, as it requires not only our effort but a certain level of organizational maturity on both ends.

3.3   COMMON MISCONCEPTIONS

In many cases, in smaller studios, we may be the only (and often the first) person to do user research in a deliberate and structured way. Certainly, in those circumstances, various misconceptions we will meet could stem from a lack of understanding of our role, methods, intentions, and the value we provide to the team. On the other hand, I would like us to look at the matter in a less clichéd way than focusing only on what the team doesn't understand. Many times, those misconceptions and attitudes towards user research didn't get out of thin air. People on the team have their own perspectives based on their discipline and experience, and may have developed a particular attitude towards research. Some may have done the research-like activities themselves, others may have hired someone else to do it, and honestly, not everyone may have had a positive experience. If they got a slack-baked cake the first time, let's not judge them for being suspicious about trying another sweet our discipline has to offer. With that in mind, let's dive into some of the misconceptions that may still be alive and kicking in some teams, and the steps we can take to work those misconceptions out (or at least to not reinforce them).

3.3.1   YOU WANT TO MAKE OUR GAME EASY!

In some teams, there is a fear that we will pressure them to simplify the game in order to make it as easy as possible for everyone to play. From our perspective, such fears are unfounded. After all, we are here to help them realize their creative vision, and if the game is intended to be "difficult" (however that is defined), then our job is to support them in achieving that. We could stop there, but this misconception is often based on some common-sense assumptions:

- When the team plays what it creates (which, unfortunately, is not always the case), they inevitably gain familiarity and practice. This may lead them to perceive the challenges in the game as easier than they would be for someone encountering a game for the first time (like a typical research participant). In such situations, when we provide information that a challenge is more difficult than expected, it can be hard for the team to grasp.
- It happens that we can support this misconception, particularly when we forget to distinguish between "action" and "challenge" while offering recommendations on how to solve issues. It can also happen when we don't have a clear understanding of the creative vision. While reading documentation and gathering information about what the team wants to achieve may not be the most ambitious task, it comes in handy if we want to avoid such mistakes.

3.3.2   YOU WANT TO ADD ANOTHER TUTORIAL!

When we notice that players are confused or don't understand something, the immediate thought might be, "We need to explain it to them!". However, our role isn't necessarily to add another tutorial to the game. It's important to first understand what the team intended to achieve (perhaps they wanted the player to feel confused at a certain point) and then dig deeper into why the players didn't understand something. For instance, if the player doesn't understand the purpose of a feature in the game, the solution might not be a detailed explanation, but rather a change in its visual design. At the same time, it is worth being cautious when we report that players don't understand something and the team resorts to saying "we will explain it in the tutorial", as it may be just a way to avoid tackling an uncomfortable design challenge.

3.3.3   You Want to Constrain Our Creative Vision!

Despite the best intentions, it often turns out that the game fails to communicate the creative vision in a way that is understandable or engaging for players. If there is a dissonance between the creative vision and the actual player experience observed during research, it's better for the team to decide how to resolve it, rather than insisting on our recommendations, no matter how effectively they might solve the problem. For instance, in one of the studies discussed in Part 3, players mentioned feeling lost and having difficulty navigating the world, which they found highly frustrating. The game was designed to encourage exploration of an unfamiliar environment while maintaining a sense of being lost. In this case, the creative vision was being realized (players felt lost as intended), but in a way that diminished the experience (players were frustrated by it). Based on the creative vision, the team was hesitant to follow the recommendation to add a marker for the objective on the map (even though it would easily solve the problem), and they chose to explore more subtle ways to guide players.

3.3.4   You Just Told Us Things We Already Know!

Many of the insights we provide may seem obvious once the team hears them (so-called hindsight bias). Another thing is that we don't have a monopoly on knowledge. While creating a game, the team may already be aware of the elements that require improvement. To avoid giving the impression that we are merely stating "the obvious" from the very beginning, it's helpful to ask the team:

- While planning a study: What issues do they expect?
- Before presenting the results: What results do they anticipate in response to selected research questions?

This approach often helps to engage the team more effectively in the research process and also highlights that, although the insights we provide may seem obvious, they weren't immediately apparent from the beginning.

3.3.5   We Do Not Need You – We Are the Players!

Most, if not all, team members are players themselves, which can lead them to assume they can accurately predict the actual players' experience. While it's true that team members may have a wealth of gaming experience, we have to recognize that their preferences, skill levels, and game familiarity may differ significantly from those of the actual target audience. Our role is to provide a perspective on how the game resonates with the actual players, who often interact with the game in ways that may not be immediately obvious to the team.

That said, this doesn't mean we have a monopoly on understanding players. The team's own experiences are a vital part of the creation process. In the relationship between researcher and team, the team knows the game they want to make (at least in principle), and ultimately, the team decides what will be in the game and how it will be shaped. While the team's knowledge may be based on some intuitions and be less structured than insights derived from research, it's something we shouldn't ignore, but support and validate.

3.3.6   We Do Not Need You – We Have Analytics!

When discussing the disciplines involved in game development, we highlighted how analytics can provide valuable data on player interactions, such as where they drop off, which levels they struggle with, or how they navigate the interface. However, analytics alone can't provide context for these behaviours. They can tell us what is happening, but not why. User research, on the other hand, offers insights into player wants, needs, and pains. By combining insights from user research with analytics, we gain a more complete picture of the player experience. This enables the team to make more informed decisions that enhance the player experience and positively influence players' consumer behaviours.

Production-wise, user research plays a key role during the concept and pre-production phase, becoming increasingly supported by analytics as the production phase progresses, and continues to complement analytics in post-production. However, in some studios, analytics and user research methods are often viewed in opposition, with analytics data assumed to have more value, regardless of the question at hand. In my experience, this happens more often with studios that rely heavily on analytics, such as those focusing on free-to-play mobile games. I'm unsure whether this preference stems from the perception that numbers feel more objective, offering a false sense of security (although numbers themselves are objective, they still require interpretation), or from the way research methodologies are often presented in textbooks, where qualitative (user research) and quantitative (analytics) methods are depicted as simply having opposing features. In reality, they can be treated as two sides of the same coin.

3.3.7   We Do Not Need You – We Can Ask Ourselves!

Certainly, it's tempting for the team to think they can handle asking player experience questions on their own. After all, it's just watching people play games. However, people deeply involved in the game's creation may have assumptions or expectations that influence their perspective, often leading to biased results. The team might overestimate the intuitiveness of a feature or misinterpret player behaviour. Additionally, they may lack the expertise to construct effective questions or conduct proper study sessions. That's where we come in! User researchers aim to provide honest, structured, and objective insights into the player experience. However, it's important for us to remember that we're not living in an ivory tower, and game development is a team effort. Rather than herding all research-like activities under our wing like a seagull, it's better to support the team in learning about players on their own and analyzing their creations where our expertise isn't critical. Is the team engaged in a heated discussion about a feature? We can offer moderation to help resolve design arguments using existing knowledge or discover a research topic that we can investigate. Are they playing through the game and providing casual feedback to each other? Let's help them structure their thoughts and draw conclusions. By taking this approach, we build trust and a better understanding of our role in the team.

These are probably not the only misconceptions we may deal with, and the above descriptions are not the only way to look at them [see Hodent 2017]. In any case, it is worth remembering that some of the beliefs may not always stem from a lack of understanding, and we ourselves may unintentionally contribute to reinforcing them. Stay vigilant and listen to your team!

3.4   CHAPTER SUMMARY

In this chapter, we stated that the role of games user researchers is to support game development teams in delivering the best player experience possible according to the intended vision, within given business objectives and technical constraints. We noted that clear communication, empathy, and proactivity, while having ethical considerations in mind, are key to building trust with the team. However, organizational maturity and structure also impact our effectiveness, as our success depends not only on our own effort or expertise. Challenges like limited resources, team buy-in, and inconsistent methods can hinder progress, but tracking key metrics (e.g. stakeholder satisfaction, research impact ratio, and research turnaround time) can help us assess what is happening and plan for improvements. Lastly, we addressed some of the misconceptions about games user research. Although they often arise from misunderstandings of our role, methods, or value we provide, we can unintentionally play a part in reinforcing them. Common misconceptions include the belief that researchers want to make the game easy, add tutorials, constrain creativity, or provide obvious insights. Some developers may feel they don't need user research at all due to their own gaming experience or reliance on analytics. We have to be aware of those misconceptions, address them (or at least not support them) by fostering trusting collaboration with the team, and offering structured and unbiased insights.

3.5   FURTHER READING

Below you will find three books that complement the material we've covered in Chapters 1–3.

***The Gamer's Brain: How Neuroscience and UX Can Impact Video Game Design* (2017) by Celia Hodent**

- In a nutshell: A basic course in psychology and UX for video games.
- Description: Here you will find a description and principle of operation of mechanisms such as perception, memory, attention, motivation, emotions, and learning. All of course, set in the context of providing players with the proper experience. You will also learn a bit about popular game research techniques and their place in the production cycle. It is worth noting that if you are interested in or work in mainstream UX, then much of the information contained in this book may be more or less familiar to you (especially in the part about perception, memory, and attention).

***Game Feel: A Game Designer's Guide to Virtual Sensation* (2008) by Steve Swink**

- In a nutshell: How to design and analyze interactions in video games.
- Description: If you have to deal with how players perceive interactions available in the game world, this book will provide you with a solid conceptual framework and basic tools for analysis. This is especially important reading for designing and researching games that emphasize the speed of reaction and precision of movements (e.g. FPS, platformers, or fighting games) or the representation of a certain physical reality (e.g. racing games, simulators). The book can be divided into three main sections: Introduction, in which the author defines what the titular game feel is. Then you will find chapters exploring the various components of this feeling and its measurable parameters (e.g. input data, control, reaction time). The last part consists of sample analyses of selected games.

***The Art of Game Design: A Book of Lenses, 3rd Edition* (2019) by Jesse Schell**

- In a nutshell: About game design, not just for designers.
- Description: The titular "lenses" (of which the author lists over 100) are perspectives through which you can look at game design. The book also includes a great chapter on conducting playtests. Of course, the question arises: why a book about game design in the list? As we mentioned, our role is to support the team in their efforts to create a game that players will experience in accordance with the creative vision (while also taking into account technological and business limitations). In our daily work, we often communicate with the producer and game designer, and depending on the project, we will also meet a level designer, combat designer, narrative designer… a concept artist, 2D or 3D graphics, UI designer… people with various technical specializations… each of these professions faces specific challenges, so you may encounter very diverse research problems. You're unlikely to be expected to be an expert in every single area mentioned, but it's worth having a better understanding of the common challenges and terms that come up in game development.

REFERENCES

Hodent, C. (2017). *The Gamer's Brain: How Neuroscience and UX Can Impact Video Game Design*. CRC Press.

McAllister, G. (2018). User experience maturity levels: Evaluating and improving games user research practices. In A. Drachen, P. Mirza-Babaei & L. E. Nacke (Eds.), *Games User Research* (pp. 61–79). Oxford University Press.

Part 2

A Ten-Step Recipe for a Single Study

In this part, we will go through the end-to-end research process divided into ten specific steps within a cooking metaphor. The aim is to provide us with a structured approach to research that can be adapted to the varying needs of the development teams in small- and medium-sized studios. To stay pragmatic in our endeavours, we will consider our possibilities and constraints in such organizational settings and illustrate steps of the process with real-world examples. We will start by looking at the selected methods that fit small-studio constraints to understand what we can choose from. We'll then explore how to define the study purpose and select the appropriate method for it. We will also cover how to gather the relevant assets necessary for the study. Next, we'll look at how to prepare methods and tools that best support our study purpose. After that, we'll focus on organizing an effective study setting and fine-tuning our approach and logistics. We'll then move on to recruiting participants and moderating sessions to collect data that supports our study purpose. With the data collected, we'll dive into analysis methods and generate insights to bridge the gap between the "as-is" and "to-be" player experience. Finally, we'll wrap up the whole study with report writing and debriefing the team.

Topics covered in this Part:

- Step 1 - Understanding what's on the menu (Chapter 4) – Capturing the overview of ten selected research methods tailored to a small studio context, and covering each phase of the production cycle.
- Step 2 - Getting to know your guests (Chapter 5) – Discovering the needs of the team through conversations and stakeholder mapping.
- Step 3 - Taking order (Chapter 6) – Collecting requirements for the study and conducting a kick-off meeting to define the study purpose.
- Step 4 - Checking the pots at your disposal (Chapter 7) – Gathering and checking playable and non-playable assets for the study.
- Step 5 - Selecting and preparing utensils (Chapter 8) – Walking through a process of designing methods and tools for the study with a specific focus on study structure, instructions, tasks, interviews, and surveys.
- Step 6 - Organizing kitchen (Chapter 9) – Exploring key elements of the study setting, such as place, equipment, and materials, together with pilot studies.

DOI: 10.1201/9781003501909-5

- Step 7 - Gathering essentials (Chapter 10) – Recruiting participants with focus on who, how, where, when, and how many to recruit, taking into account remuneration and scheduling.
- Step 8 - Slicing and dicing (Chapter 11) – Exploring common considerations and challenges in effective session moderation.
- Step 9 - Cooking time! (Chapter 12) – Analyzing results with focus on understanding what the insight is, organizing data, and exploring selected analysis methods (thematic, differential, temporal, and explanatory) together with insights prioritization.
- Step 10 - Composing and serving the dish (Chapter 13) – Going through the process of structuring and writing the report and conducting debrief sessions for efficient and effective insights distribution.

4 Understanding What's on the Menu
Selected Methods Overview

While running our small user research restaurant, we are subject to certain limitations, so writing about what we could find in larger and recognizable venues could be inspiring, but may not fit our reality and the daily hustles we face. We will look for solutions requiring smaller budgets and logistics (e.g. we may not be able to afford or arrange a multi-seat lab setting), and not requiring us to look for additional competencies (e.g. it may often turn out that we do not have a person in the team who could or would devote time to implement more extensive analytics). However, I do not think that this should stop us from cooking our team some nutritious food for thought. We will go through a list of dishes selected to be both affordable and doable in smaller organizational settings. Let's look at what we have on the menu (Table 4.1).

We will discuss the suggested recipe for each item we have on the menu in Part 3. For now, we'll just cover them enough to be ready to take orders from the team.

4.1 COMPETITOR ANALYSIS

Breaking down and analyzing 3–5 competitive or reference titles, the goal of which is to capture strengths and common pain points in the player experience, as well as to identify opportunities and threats to the game the team is working on. Especially, in the early phases of the production cycle, this can help the team understand the potential scope and quality levels of various game elements that may be required to match, or perhaps even to stand out from the competition. We will discuss the recipe for competitor analysis in Chapter 14.

4.2 CONCEPT TEST

Capturing players' reactions and opinions on specific topics, which can revolve around art (e.g. overall style, character or environment concept arts), narrative (e.g. character background and development, key plot points), marketing materials (e.g. trailers), or even overall game idea (e.g. based on a high concept). The general goal is to understand if the presented concepts are appealing and resonate with the target audience, and whether they are effective in conveying the information, tone, and feel intended by the team. We will discuss the recipe for the concept test in Chapter 15.

4.3 EXPERT ANALYSIS

We act as experts evaluating the game or its selected elements to identify both potential issues and good practices related to gameplay experience (especially in terms of usability and accessibility). Expert analysis can provide valuable insight to the team early in the production cycle and avoid many well-defined pitfalls and mistakes. Expert analysis is generally cost- and time-effective, and as such can be treated as complementary compared to methods requiring participants. We will discuss the recipe for expert analysis in Chapter 16.

DOI: 10.1201/9781003501909-6

TABLE 4.1

Selected Types of Studies within the Game's Production Cycle

Dish	Nutritional Value (to What Extent It Answers Selected Question Type)				Typical Serving Time	Where to Find the Recipe
	Do Players Like What They See or Hear?	Do Players Understand It and Know How to Use It?	Do Players Engage in It?	Do Players Want to Continue?		
Competitor analysis	+	++	++	+	Conception phase	Chapter 14
Concept test	+++	−	−	−	Conception phase	Chapter 15
Expert analysis	−	+++	+	−	Pre-production	Chapter 16
(Co)Design workshop	++	++	+	−	Pre-production	Chapter 17
Team play session (or review)	+	+	+	−	Pre-production and production	Chapter 18
Usability (play)test	−	+++	+	−	Pre-production and production	Chapter 19
Component playtest	+	++	++	−	Pre-production and production	Chapter 20
Experience playtest	++	+	+++	+	Production	Chapter 21
Diary study	+	+	+++	+++	Production and post-production	Chapter 22
Review analysis	++	+	+	+	Post-production	Chapter 23

Annotation. (Own elaboration).

4.4   (CO)DESIGN WORKSHOP

A meeting where we work together with the team (design workshop) and/or players (co-design workshop) to create or improve selected game features. The goal is to engage people who have different perspectives on the feature or will ultimately use it, so that both the needs of the players and the capabilities and intentions of the team are taken into account at the earliest stages of the design. We will discuss the recipe for (co)design workshop in Chapter 17.

4.5   TEAM PLAY SESSION (OR REVIEW)

In this case, we engage the team in sharing more structured feedback on a daily basis to iterate on the assets they create more efficiently and effectively. To make the most of the team's knowledge and experience, we support the team with best practices on sharing feedback, templates for quick reviews, or even facilitating play sessions (i.e. the time when the team plays themselves what they created) to gather more focused and actionable insights. Play sessions and reviews can be treated more of a preparatory step for studies involving players. We will discuss the recipe for team play session (or review) in Chapter 18.

4.6   USABILITY (PLAY)TEST

Observing player behaviours during interaction with various prototypes of the game focused on finding usability issues. This method involves asking participants to perform a series of predefined tasks and gathering insights into the issues that prevent participants from completing those tasks effectively and efficiently. We will discuss the recipe for the usability (play)test in Chapter 19.

4.7 COMPONENT PLAYTEST

Observing player behaviours and capturing their reactions to core game systems. Component playtest is focused on assessing whether and how players interact with selected systems and mechanics that are vital for realizing the creative vision, as well as understanding how various accompanying elements (e.g. art, audio) fit together from a player perspective and build the experience. Typical study uses a collage of different methods and tools (e.g. usability playtest and selected concept test elements) chosen to capture the experience with various layers of the selected component as broadly as possible. We will discuss the recipe for component playtest in Chapter 20.

4.8 EXPERIENCE PLAYTEST

Basically, "experience playtest" can be seen as an umbrella term in which we can find a group of playtests with a similar structure focused on assessing player engagement, which are distinguished by the selected criterion. For example, based on the time of a single research session, we can think about:

- First impressions playtest – lasting about 2 hours, which focus on how much the game encourages the player to invest their time in further gameplay, but also allows to probe potential reasons for returns, which the team will most likely want to address before the launch (it is worth remembering that many distribution platforms allow the game to be returned, as long as the player have not spent more than 2 hours in it).
- Extended playtest – lasting from a few to a dozen or so hours (e.g. we ask players for two 6–8 hour visits to the studio during the weekend), which allows us to assess players' experiences during longer gameplay, as well as to capture how they perceive the game's progression, pace, or difficulty. A variant, in shorter games, is the so-called playthrough playtest, which lasts as long as it takes to complete the game.

We will discuss the recipe for experience playtest in Chapter 21.

BOX 4.1   CAN WE SERVE ENGLISH BREAKFAST FOR DINNER?

If we were to compare the three types of playtests we have on the menu, usability playtests emphasize capturing how well players understand various elements and use them effectively, while experience playtests emphasize capturing player engagement. Component playtests, on the other hand, are a middle ground between the two. All three types have their place in the production cycle, i.e. usability playtests will be a common method in pre-production to ensure that players understand and know what to do, component playtests allow us to refine selected systems between pre-production and production, and in production, when the game will constitute an integrated whole, we will mainly deal with experience playtests. This arrangement also corresponds to how the gameplay experience is built, which we talked about in Chapter 2 (recall that we need to remove potential barriers to entry for players so that they can efficiently learn the rules of the game and use them to finally get engaged in it). However, we shouldn't cling to this pattern, as it may turn out that after conducting an experience playtest in the middle of the production phase, we will find out that players do not understand some mechanics or elements, which may prompt us to conduct a usability playtest as a next step.

4.9 DIARY STUDY

In this method, participants are asked to record their experiences, emotions, thoughts, and behaviours within the game over an extended period (usually days or weeks) in the form of a diary. The goal is to gather insights on how gameplay experience changes over time with all its ups and downs along the way, and understand how players interact with the game in their everyday lives. That way, diary studies help to gather insights that are most often impossible to capture in the short sessions typical of most other methods. Method provides a unique perspective on what builds and what subtracts from the player experience (e.g. which mechanics turn out to be boring after an extended time interacting with them) and what are the expectations for the further development of the game (e.g. what elements or mechanics players lack after a longer experience with the game). We will discuss the recipe for diary study in Chapter 22.

4.10 REVIEW ANALYSIS

Once a game is out in the wild and starts to generate interest from players and experts, at some point, they will start to share their opinions in the form of reviews, let's plays, requests for support, or posts in community spaces. The main goal of review analysis is to collect this scattered information about player experiences, analyze it, and draw conclusions that can be used by the team to spot issues to address, features to add, and prioritize efforts. We may also stumble on so-called silent reviews conducted with journalists or experts before the release. While these are typically overseen by marketing and/or PR specialists, it's worth seeking opportunities to examine them from our own

BOX 4.2   LOOKING FOR A WELL-BALANCED DIET

Worth noting is that our role is not only to provide one specific meal, but to ensure a well-balanced diet that will provide the energy and nutrients needed by the team, while reducing the risk of serious diseases throughout the game's production cycle. This is easier said than done, especially when our resources are limited or uncertain. However, we can refer to specific rules that will help us plan meals throughout the production cycle. After all, we already know that the dishes on the menu provide different nutrients, so we should choose them to ensure balance. In user research, this is called triangulation and involves using multiple methods and tools, theories, and data sources to find answers to the same research questions. We can gather the necessary information based on other games, provide it ourselves based on existing knowledge, work it out with the team, or finally gather it from different groups of potential players. When it comes to methods, we will discover what a game element should be like during both the concept test and the component playtest. Within the component playtest itself, we can use a different mix of techniques like observation supported additionally with an interview or survey. The most important thing is not to rely too much on just one method – especially one that does not take into account the participation of players. The other part of the story is that in small studios we will rarely have the budget to evaluate all the game components or evaluate the same elements multiple times (e.g. we will rarely have a chance to run the same playtest again to find out if the changes introduced by the team had the intended effect) or the will of the team to conduct extensive research in the conception phase. We must also take into account that the team may not have the bandwidth to implement all of our observations. However, this is not a reason to despair. When we find out what the specific goals, risks, and decisions are to be made throughout the production cycle (through both conversations with the team, but also the creative vision, player fantasy, or core pillars), we can think in advance about what the team's priorities will be and how we intend to support them within given constraints.

perspective to better understand what might potentially come. We will discuss the recipe for review analysis in Chapter 23.

As with all cookbooks, these aren't the only dishes available. It is very likely that your and your team's tastes will change over time, so it is worth looking for more advanced or simply different dishes to adapt the menu to the evolving needs and possibilities [for example, see Medlock 2018 or McAllister & Long 2018] or order something you can't prepare yourself in other restaurants (if you will have the budget to do so).

4.11 CHAPTER SUMMARY

We began by exploring the dishes we may serve to provide the team with a well-balanced diet. We have ten methods tailored to small organizational settings and different phases of the production cycle. Each method answers the basic questions to varying degrees (i.e. Do players like what they see or hear? do they understand it and know how to use it? Do they engage with it? Do they want to continue?), so throughout the production cycle we have to remember to not rely too much on just one method (especially one that does not take into account the participation of players), but we mix them to provide the most reliable and complete picture of player experience possible. Although each method has a typical production phase in which it's used, this isn't set in stone, so if necessary, we use a method that's typical for a different phase of the production cycle, as nothing should stop us from serving an English breakfast for dinner, if there's a reason to do so.

REFERENCES

McAllister, G. & Long, S. (2018). A framework for player research. In A. Drachen, P. Mirza-Babaei & L. E. Nacke (Eds.), *Games User Research* (pp. 117–139). Oxford University Press.
Medlock, M. C. (2018). An Overview of GUR methods. In A. Drachen, P. Mirza-Babaei & L. E. Nacke (Eds.), *Games User Research* (pp. 99–116). Oxford University Press.

5 Getting to Know Your Guests
Stakeholder Mapping

As user researchers, we meet with a lot of different people with various backgrounds and stories to tell, who come from both inside and outside of the team. The project documentation and the game build (if available) can tell us a lot about what the team might need. Let's give the documentation a thorough read and play the game as it is. While reading and playing, it's worth jotting down questions that pop into our minds, so that we can ask them later. Armed with this knowledge, we can engage in discussion with various people in the team to gain a better understanding of what they're trying to achieve, their goals and needs, but also blockers and perceived risks. Depending on the organizational climate in the studio, these conversations can take a more or less formalized form. Starting from casual chat over coffee in the studio's kitchen, through hopping into the team meetings, to more structured stakeholder interviews in a 1-on-1 format. When we think of stakeholders, it is basically any person vested in the game we are working on, whether it is a junior specialist, creative director, or management board member. Regardless of the format of these conversations, they will save us time at the preparatory stage of the research and will also make a good starting point to build a relationship with the team, especially at the beginning, when we are just getting to know them and the game. Some of the questions that may be worth asking include:

- Could you tell me a little bit about your role in the team and what you are currently working on?
- What are you aiming to achieve while working on this game? Do you have specific goals? What do you perceive as a risk to achieving these goals?
- What does success look like for this game? What would you like to hear from the players? What would you rather not hear from players?
- What challenges are currently top priorities for you and the team? What decisions need to be made?
- If we were collaborating together on a study for this game, what would be your preferred way of communicating?
- If we were collaborating together on a study for this game, how much would you like to be involved in?
- Is there anything else that would help me or that I should know?

By collecting answers to these and other questions, we can start mapping our stakeholders and trying to determine their level of influence and interest in our work. Stakeholder interviews can also be a good starting point to show the team what our venue has to offer. As it happens in restaurants, some people will book a table in advance by submitting a study request, while others may need more explanation and encouragement to visit us.

In small teams, the conversations themselves will give us a pretty clear picture of the environment in which we will be conducting the research. In larger teams, it may be helpful to organize the collected information. We can use Mendelow's matrix [Mendelow 1991], which captures each stakeholder's relative importance and needs visually (Table 5.1).

To fill out the matrix, we can simply start by adding the names and roles of our stakeholders wherever we see they fit best based on the answers provided. Some of the stakeholders can seem perfectly fit with their interest and influence, e.g. we would expect a combat designer to be interested in conducting research on combat in the game, and having influence on implementing results, so we

DOI: 10.1201/9781003501909-7

TABLE 5.1

Stakeholder Mapping Matrix

		Stakeholder Influence	
		Low	**High**
Stakeholder interest	**Low**	Regular contact	Anticipate and meet needs
	High	Keep informed	Manage thoroughly

Annotation. (Own elaboration based on Mendelow (1991)).

BOX 5.1   SPOTTING CRACKS IN THE PAN

Many of the methods we use, especially in pre-production and production phases, are based on the assumption that the team has developed some relatively coherent creative vision for the game being developed, against which we can evaluate our findings. This is an assumption that is both laudable and often at odds with reality. The mere existence of a creative vision, player fantasy, or core pillars (even in codified form) does not guarantee that everyone on the team understands and implements it in the same way. If we let this go, we can ignore some seemingly trivial elements in our research that are important to the team, providing them with more generic results that would generally apply to most other games. It is a bit like frying scrambled eggs in a pan with the Teflon coating peeled off – basically, something will come out of it, but half will stay in the pan and the other half will be barely edible. For this reason, during stakeholder interviews, it is worth identifying discrepancies between team members, as well as between what they say and what results from the documentation. This way, we can come across certain cracks or large holes in the creative vision that can reduce the value of our endeavours and make it difficult to plan research in the long term. All of this can be signalled and clarified with the team before the study, included in the study design or discussed after the study. In the worst case, even if the discrepancies we notice turn out to be just a false alarm, it is just another opportunity to understand more deeply what the team wants to achieve.

have to keep this person informed and cooperate with them throughout the study. On the other hand, this simple exercise can show us some challenges we may face. If we learn that a crucial member of the team doesn't have a buy-in or time for user research, perhaps we can mark this person's name in red, and adapt our communications, e.g. character artist who is swamped with work may not have time for research, but still will have a lot of influence on how the results of research on combat will be handled, simply by being responsible for the final look of the opponents in the game. Certainly, it would be perfect to have everyone's full attention on our study, but if this approach is not available, sharing the most important information and providing necessary explanations on the study can still do the trick to keep us on track to deliver value.

Properly managed stakeholders can help us remove potential blockers to research and get the resources we need. Like a waiter trying to read the mood in the room, stakeholder mapping can help us better understand the communication preferences and engagement of each team member throughout the study, so we don't end up over-communicating to those who simply don't need it or neglecting those who need it the most. It can also reveal the actual (not just written) decision-making structure of the studio, making it easier to navigate the environment and do our job of supporting more informed design and business decisions. One thing to remember, though, is that stakeholder influence and interests evolve over time, so it's worth revisiting this exercise from time to time to adjust our efforts accordingly.

5.1 CHAPTER SUMMARY

Like a waiter reading the mood in a room, we will want to understand what the various stakeholders (people vested in the project) are trying to achieve together with their goals, challenges, and constraints they face. We have to start by familiarizing ourselves with the game's documentation and build (if available). This will allow us to ask stakeholder questions during daily conversations or in more structured stakeholder interviews. While in smaller studios simply gathering information may be sufficient to understand our environment, in mid-sized ones it may be necessary to map stakeholder information into a matrix to better understand them and align with their interests and influence on the research. During stakeholder interviews and mapping, we also try to identify and explain any discrepancies in the creative vision that can reduce the value of our endeavours and make it difficult to plan research in the long term.

REFERENCE

Mendelow, A. (1991). Stakeholder mapping. In *Proceedings of the 2nd International Conference on Information Systems* (pp. 10–24).

6 Taking Order
Requirements Gathering and Kick-Off Meeting

We know the menu and we have some information on our potential guests, so the task that lies ahead of us now is to take the order from them. While taking the order, we can have temptations to propose the most exquisite or finesse item on the menu, but let's stay down to earth. We focus on what will best meet the needs of the team, while being the most nutritious option under the existing limitations (e.g. time or money-wise). Taking orders sounds easy, but to avoid ending up with the "I didn't order that" reaction, let's go through the typical steps in the process.

6.1 REQUIREMENTS GATHERING

When it comes to user research, it is typical for teams to make reservations. Before we book a table for them, we usually agree on a preliminary research topic, dates, and people who have to be involved in the process. At this point, we'll use "GURCB_01_010101- book - research protocol - template" available at the book's website. It's a document in which we'll gather all the key information about the specific study we're planning to conduct. We can already pre-fill some sections based on the request, our knowledge of stakeholders, and the game. At this stage, we will focus on four sections:

6.1.1 STUDY PURPOSE

This section is used to define what we want to discover. Depending on the goals and specific questions that will appear here, we will later choose methods and tools. We try to formulate the goals in a clear and concise way, so that everyone in the team understands where the study is supposed to lead us. We are looking for answers to questions such as:

- What decisions on the player experience do we need to make?
- What information do we need to make those decisions?
- What player experience or production risks are we trying to assess?

6.1.2 STAKEHOLDERS

It is worth listing the people whose needs a given study is supposed to answer, and those who have an impact on the study itself. Although designers may come to mind first, it is worth remembering that other disciplines also play an important role in our endeavours. For instance, a producer will bring a business perspective and knows the team's workload and schedules, programmers provide us with a properly prepared build for research, and QA specialists ensure that the build we receive is functionally suitable.

6.1.3 PARTICIPANT PROFILE

In this section, we include verifiable information about potential players (e.g. what games they play, platforms they use, etc.), which will allow us to recruit people to participate in the study who fit the profile of the target audience. If we have a better explored target audience, we may list specific player

DOI: 10.1201/9781003501909-8

segments or groups, differing in specific attitudes or behaviours that are important from a business or design perspective (e.g. narrative-driven vs. gameplay-driven players). We will tackle participant recruitment in Chapter 10, but for now, let's keep in mind not to over-focus on socio-demographic variables (e.g. age, sex or gender, education level), especially to narrow down future recruitment without a strong rationale behind it. Basically, we include here answers to questions such as:

- What do we know about the target audience? Who is the player?
- What games do they play or have played?
- What platforms do they have or use?

For the studies that do not include participants (e.g. competitor analysis), we can use this section to list the sources we want to analyze (e.g. specific game titles).

6.1.4   GAME INFORMATION

Here, we try to gather all the relevant information about the game, its creative vision, current design documentation, and existing prototypes or builds. Basically, we want to find out and ensure that we have access to the full set of information the team has, and that this knowledge is up to date.

As the purpose of our study and research questions can still be vaguely defined, we can leave the remaining sections blank. What we can do now is to set up a communication channel for the specific study. For example, on the messaging app we use in the studio, we can set up a sub-channel for the study and invite stakeholders to join it. We will use the same study channel for communication with the team throughout the study. Let stakeholders know that we are planning a study on topic "x", and ask if, from their perspective, we should add someone else to the channel who would be interested in the results or could provide key information supporting the organization of the study. As we want to ensure that our stakeholders are on the same page and to keep them engaged it is also worth sharing a pre-filled research protocol and inviting them to voice out their needs, expectations or concerns for the study by leaving comments in sections "Study Purpose", "Participant Profile" and "Game Information", and asking any questions they might have about the study. At the same time, we can arrange a kick-off meeting, during which we will go through the document together and agree on what will be included in the order.

After agreeing on a date for the kick-off meeting and answering questions, all that remains is to wait for our guest to arrive.

BOX 6.1   BITE OF PRACTICE #1: RESEARCH PROTOCOL BEFORE KICK-OFF

What's the fun in cooking if you can't taste what you're trying to cook? So, to not make it all too abstract, we will recreate the research protocol for the component playtest on combat in *Yupitergrad 2: The Lost Station*. Throughout the creation of the game, the core of the production team consisted on average of 10–12 people, so the stakeholder landscape and communications were rather straightforward. After making significant changes to the combat component early in production, the study request was formulated by the team during one of the routine daily meetings. As specifically defined combat was one of the core pillars, the team wanted to check whether the changes they made reflected their intentions properly. At the time of making the study request:

- The study purpose was defined simply as: What are the players' impressions of the redesigned combat?

- Stakeholders were: lead game designer, producer, art director, and lead programmer.
- Based on previous studies, the participant profile was defined as people:
  - Among the games they played recently, it would be optimal to find at least one of the reference titles for PC/Console (*Metroid* series, *Hollow Knight*, *Doom*, […]) or VR (*Red Matter*, *Compound VR*, *Spider-Man: Far From Home Virtual Reality*, […]).
  - Who prefer action games or action-adventure games ("likes" or "strongly likes")
  - Owns VR headset
  - Both narrative-driven and gameplay-driven players
  - Varied based on gender and age
  - The basic game information was included in the GDD sections on combat and recent game build.

The kick-off meeting was scheduled at the time of making the request with the lead game designer, and due to time constraints, other stakeholders were kept informed on the progress via the study channel.

6.2 KICK-OFF MEETING

Now that our guests have had some time to ponder, we can approach them during a kick-off meeting and start agreeing with them on what to serve. The team may have specific tastes, but it is our responsibility to suggest a specific dish that provides nutritious food for thought. During the kick-off meeting, we want to flesh out what problem the team is actually trying to solve or what kind of decisions they need to make, what information is needed in order to do that, and how we want to gather it. After greeting the team, we may simply share our screen with the research protocol on and go through each section, discussing it with the team:

6.2.1 STUDY PURPOSE

We want to explore and clarify the core challenges, perceived risks, expectations and doubts the team may have, together with what we want and need to learn about players, their behaviours, thoughts, or emotions. If the team listed some questions before the kick-off, we have to flesh them out and categorize them. If not, we have to help them out. Whatever we face, in addition to asking questions listed earlier, it may be helpful asking questions on what the team wants to discover about player experience, for instance:

- Do we want to check if players like what they see or hear?
- Do we want to check if players understand it and know how to use it?
- Do we want to check if players engage in it? Do players find experience optimally paced/difficult/long?
- Do we want to check if players want to continue playing?

The effect of our work should be breaking down the research goal (e.g. assessing the risk of players not understanding the new system) into specific questions (e.g. Do players understand the tutorial prompts? Do players know how to effectively use the mechanics that make up the system? Does the interface in its current state support players in using the mechanics?) that will guide us on fleshing out the methods and tools section. Most of the time, we won't be able to answer all the questions at once (e.g. due to time and budget constraints, and various questions requiring multiple or exclusive methods). We should not be afraid of too many questions from the team (it is usually a good sign for us), as we can always save questions left out for later and follow up on them in another study. It is worth grouping questions by type and prioritizing with the team the most critical ones that will directly influence design and business decisions. On the other hand, we have to watch out for questions that we can't reliably address (e.g. Will players buy the game?) or are too broad or vague (e.g. Do players have fun with the game?). Defining questions more precisely and prioritizing them will help narrow the scope of the study and ensure its focus and feasibility.

6.2.2   KEY DATES

It's good to agree with the team on dates to better understand what this study will require (both from us and them) and to assess constraints (e.g. programmer taking a week off, so we will have to wait longer for the game build to be prepared). To start a discussion on dates, we can simply ask "When do you need the results to be delivered?" and back track from there or ask "When do you have the build ready?" and define dates around it. We will have to revisit this section as the study takes shape, to tweak some dates accordingly.

6.2.3   PARTICIPANT PROFILE

While we may have a definition of the target audience, additional criteria may appear for the specific study, like introducing subgroups or limiting the selection of people to a certain segment. It is worth asking stakeholders if they have any specific requirements for the study, or we can suggest something ourselves if necessary (e.g. we have noticed that players from certain countries have been omitted so far, and therefore we propose to conduct a wider recruitment). If no specific requirements for the participant profile are expressed or needed, we can go with the basic target audience profile.

6.2.4   GAME INFORMATION

When it comes to documentation, it's a good habit to double-check with the team if the listed documents are up to date and exhaustive for the study purpose, e.g. Are these materials up to date? Is there any other relevant information I should know for this study?

6.2.5   METHODS AND TOOLS

Now that we have the study purpose better defined, we can discuss specific methods we have on the menu to get the best answer for the research questions. After the initial choice of the method, it is also worth determining how we want to conduct the study to double-check what is actually doable:

- On-site vs. remote – Deciding in what format we will conduct the research sessions gives us an idea of specific challenges and opportunities, e.g. From what pool of participants can we recruit? How will we make the game build and other materials available to players? The choice of format may be dictated by formal reasons (e.g. if the team is concerned about leakage, they may prefer to conduct the study on-site only) or logistical ones (e.g. if the team distributes the build in a way that allows easy granting and withdrawing access, then remote research may be taken into consideration more easily).
- Moderated vs. unmoderated – Moderated studies generally require us to devote more time (we have to be present and active for the entire session), but they provide us with more in-depth conclusions. We can ask participants about various things as they pop up or even ask them to think aloud (i.e. comment out loud what they're doing, thinking, or feeling) as they interact with the game. On the other hand, unmoderated studies will save us time (we don't have to be active through the whole session) and will be more convenient to be run

in a group format, in which several people take part in the study at the same time. So, here we are wondering about two things:

- Is the game in a state where we can put players to play it on their own with minimal instructions?
- Will we get the necessary answers when we don't have the opportunity to observe and ask the participants what they are doing at a given moment?

- Test environment – Here we discuss what will be the subject of the study, in order to prepare techniques later and agree on the necessary assets with the team. **After all, examining combat in the gym** (i.e. separate scenes/builds used to test specific mechanics and gameplay systems) **will tell us a lot about this component in relative isolation, evaluating combat in a specific mission will tell us how it behaves in the context of other game elements, and evaluating combat over several hours in fragment of the game will tell us how the experience with this component changes in time**.

Depending on the method agreed and details on how the study is about to be conducted, we will flesh out the rest of the methods and tools section after the kick-off meeting.

6.2.6   Session Duration

For studies involving participants as a matter of self-check, and as an input for planning research sessions, it is helpful to understand how long the single session will take, and how the time is distributed between various methods we plan to use. For now, we can set an overall cap on time for a single session or leave it blank, as we will flesh out this section only after having a methods and tools section ready.

6.2.7   Session Schedule

For studies involving participants, we can use this section to write down basic information on when participants are scheduled to take part in the study, so the team has one place to check where to observe sessions and/or if there are observer slots available. For now, we leave it blank, as we will start to fill in this section only after the start of the participant recruitment.

BOX 6.2   THINKING ALOUD OR BEING IN THE MOMENT?

Generally, asking our participants to think aloud gives us a window to their thought process, and helps to better understand various issues they encounter when it comes to understanding or using something in the game (e.g. interface element, their idea to approach a puzzle). However, it comes at a cost. Main drawbacks of using thinking aloud are that when a participant is talking about something, they have to analyze it more, and are likely to reflect more on the in-game situation they're in, which may end up spotting issues that wouldn't occur normally. We can deal with it when it comes to studies focused on accessibility and usability (e.g. usability playtest). However, if we add to this that thinking aloud makes the research session situation even less natural than it would be without it, it makes thinking aloud not the best choice for studies focused on experience (e.g. experience playtest). Basically, most players won't comment aloud on what they do or think to themselves while playing, but will rather spend their emotional and cognitive resources to actually play and engage with the game. Certainly, even with its limitations, thinking aloud can provide us with deeper insights, but it is not a technique that will allow us to find reliable answers to all our questions.

6.2.8 Assets

In this section, we discuss what materials will be needed to find answers to the research questions within the selected methods and tools. Especially, in the case of game builds, it is also worth discussing what debug options we have at our disposal to conduct a study in an efficient and trouble-free manner (e.g. Is there a way to skip content such as levels/quests/puzzles? Can we unlock content or features such as spawning specific items or opponents, or adjust the game state on the fly by changing things such as player health level?). Generally, during the kick-off meeting, we want to agree on assets that have to be delivered by the team, e.g. Is the game build enough for us, or do we need the team to provide us with some audiovisual or narrative assets as well? Do we need any assets prepared or adjustments made to the game build specifically for the study, and when can the team deliver them?

6.2.9 Deliverables

Given that we know the scope of the study and time constraints, we can discuss the deliverables (actual dish), so the tangible artefacts of our work for the team to consume:

- Top findings – A short one to two-page document that contains three to five key insights from the study. The document is usually delivered the day after the last research session. It can have a wide audience beyond those directly working on the game (e.g. board members who usually do not need to go into the details presented in the full report). In research conducted under strong time pressure, in order not to block the decisions and actions of the team, we may want to deliver such a document after about half of the planned sessions have been conducted. If this is the case, we are dealing with preliminary findings.
- Full report – A document containing a description of the insights from the entire study. **The full report does not have any limit on the number of insights or pages included, but as a rule, it should be exhaustive in describing the results without exhausting the recipients**. Depending on the study and the techniques used, the report can be created from several days (e.g. in a usability playtest) to even weeks (e.g. in a diary study). We will discuss reporting in more detail in Chapter 13.
- Debrief – A meeting during which we present the results to stakeholders. It is important that the meeting takes place as soon as possible after the completion of work on the full report, when the team's attention hasn't yet been shifted from the study to other tasks. We will discuss debriefing and other forms of results sharing in more detail in Chapter 13.
- Data – Some stakeholders ask for access to data collected during the study, most often full recordings of sessions and the answers given by participants in surveys. Our role is basically to ensure that they don't have to look there (after all, they didn't come to a restaurant to cook for themselves), but if such a request arises, I usually side with making study data available to them after the debrief.

Certainly, filling in the research protocol may require going back and forth to adjust various sections, as they are interdependent (e.g. what kind of deliverables we will be able to prepare depends on the time we have). After the first run through the protocol, it is good to revisit sections like stakeholders (e.g. "Based on what we discussed so far, are there any other people who should be engaged to make this study happen?") and key dates (e.g. "Based on what we discussed so far, are there any potential blockers to the schedule?"). When everything is covered, it's time to agree on the next steps and close the meeting. If we covered all the necessary topics during the kick-off meeting, now we have to wait for the specific assets to be delivered by the team. In the meantime, we can focus on fleshing out the methods and preparing the necessary tools. After the meeting, we can post an update on our study channel to let the team know what we agreed on, and what are next steps in the process.

BOX 6.3   BITE OF PRACTICE #2: RESEARCH PROTOCOL AFTER KICK-OFF

Before the kick-off meeting, the team left some comments in the research protocol on the risks and things they weren't sure about in the redesigned combat system in *Yupitergrad 2*. At the same time, they required further discussion and clarification, because proposed topics touched on different layers of the game – from single customization options, through the appearance of opponents and the experience of encounters, to the reception of the environments in which the combat was to take place. The effects of the discussion with the team were reflected in the research protocol with the following sections updated:

- **Study purpose** was divided into main and optional goals with wording reflecting the agreed risks and trade-offs:
  - Main:
    - Checking the basic usability and feel of combat, including:
      - Checking whether participants recognize opponents' characteristics from their form.
      - Checking the ease of use of the boltgun (basic weapon) and minigun (additional weapon), together with switching between them and recognizing their state (e.g. minigun overheat).
      - Checking whether participants can find effective ways to win encounters with opponents of various types (speedy, regular, heavy).
    - Checking whether participants discover that they can avoid encounters in corridors.
    - Probing perceived opponent diversity.
    - Probing how the reception of combat depends on the environments (shape of the corridor or arena type).
    - Probing the reception of the environments in which combat takes place.
    - Probing the reception of the audio layer for combat (weapon sounds, opponent sounds).
  - Optional:
    - Checking potential issues with HUD readability.
    - Probing the reception of the combat customization options (aim assist; opponents' accuracy).
- **Participant profile** – The information gathered earlier was confirmed, and information on the number of participants (i.e. five to six) was added after agreeing on methods and tools.
- **Methods and tools** – When agreeing on the study purpose, we discussed with the team that we could encompass proposed topics within one study, but there is a risk that some of the results may not be fully reliable. While for the topics revolving around the usability layer, we could say that we would "check" and provide reliable results, for the experience layer, we could only "probe" to get some idea of the potential problems and strengths of the game. In a perfect situation, we would schedule at least two studies with a smaller scope, like the usability (play)test, followed by an experience playtest, to reliably check the proposed topics. However, based on the budget and the time available, this wasn't an option for the team at the time. As the limitations and risks were discussed, and trade-offs for proposed methods accepted, we decided to proceed with the component playtest. To meet the study purpose, we decided that for the test environment, the team would prepare a game build containing a combat gym (allowing for spawning opponents) and selected levels and

arenas combined in the order they would appear in the game. The build was also to have a debug menu enabled to change selected options (menu screens were not yet implemented) and to modify the player's equipment as needed. Additionally, we needed visuals of the opponents to probe whether participants could recognize their characteristics from their form, as well as selected sounds for combat. Since the team was sharing the builds in a way that allowed easy granting and revoking access, we decided to conduct the study in a remote format to have access to a wider pool of participants. Additionally, due to the adopted study purpose, the test environment, and the remote format, the study adopted a moderated format.

- **Assets** needed for the study were further specified as:
  - Game build with gym for combat and selected levels and arena types.
  - Opponent black and white 2D silhouettes based on 3D models.
  - Opponent screenshots based on models on a neutral background.
  - Audio for combat (opponent sounds, player weapon sounds, environmental sounds, music samples).
- **Deliverables**
  - Full report
  - Debrief

During the meeting, it also turned out that one of the key stakeholders would be the programmer responsible for co-designing and implementing the changes to combat so far, so immediately after the meeting, he was invited to collaborate and share his perspective on the planned study. The game information section didn't change any further, and was only confirmed by the team. At the very end, we defined key dates, aligning the team's needs with the user research bandwidth.

In the next five chapters (7–11), we will focus on studies involving participants, as most of the time they require us to prepare much more elaborate input than studies focused solely on analysis (expert analysis, competitor analysis, or review analysis). For presentation purposes, we will discuss them in order. However, we have to keep in mind that in real life, we will prepare pots and utensils, gather ingredients, and organize our kitchen much in parallel.

6.3 CHAPTER SUMMARY

Knowing what we can offer and what our guests may need, we can begin taking orders. We're prepared for both those who wish to book a table themselves and those who will need more encouragement to visit us. We gather the basic information needed for the study and fill it into a research protocol, which we then share with the team so they can add their questions, risks to be considered, and design and business decisions they need to make (study purpose). We also ask stakeholders to provide us with specific information needed for the study (i.e. stakeholders, participant profile, game information). Then we arrange a kick-off meeting to get more details on the aforementioned information together with fleshing out other sections of the research protocol (key dates, methods and tools, assets, and deliverables). We remember that while the team may have their own preferences, it remains our responsibility to propose a method that provides adequate food for thought.

7 Checking the Pots at Your Disposal
Gathering Assets

During the kick-off meeting, we discussed with the team what exactly will be needed to fulfil the study purpose, and we also agreed on when we can expect it to be delivered. On the other hand, this does not exempt us from monitoring and checking for cracks in the pots once we receive them. So let's go over some of the typical assets we may request from the team. We can put them in two basic categories – non-playable and playable ones.

7.1   NON-PLAYABLE ASSETS

Especially in the earlier phases of the production cycle, we will be dealing with assets, such as concept arts, narrative beats, interface wireframes, or control layout screenshots. Generally, these materials do not have to be final, but they have to be developed enough to convey the team's ideas behind them. In the later phases of the production cycle, we may use actual screenshots made in-game or in-engine, or marketing materials like key visuals or trailers. In general, when agreeing with the team on the assets needed for our study, we want to make sure that they will allow us to answer the questions posed in the study purpose (e.g. Is the function of the character clearly signalled by its form?). **We also want to ensure a certain standardization of assets by presenting them to participants in the same form and quality, while paying attention to the context in which we present them** (e.g. if we are assessing the reception of various characters, we will first present them against the same – often neutral – background, so that the situation in which we presented them doesn't affect the results, and only then we will check how they are perceived in the context).

BOX 7.1   BITE OF PRACTICE #3: NON-PLAYABLE ASSETS

In the component playtest for combat in *Yupitergrad 2*, we wanted to find out whether opponents would be easily distinguishable from each other, and whether the form of the different types of opponents clearly signalled their characteristics and behaviour. Additionally, the team designed combat with the intention for the player to constantly move during encounters to avoid being killed, and the game often presented opponents from great distances. So players were put in situations where they couldn't always see all the details of the characters, because they were either too far away or the player's attention was paid to other activities. Based on those assumptions, we decided to check how participants perceived the silhouettes of opponents, to see if they were distinguishable on the most basic dimensions, such as size or shape (Figure 7.1), and only then check if more complex elements (e.g. weapons) were recognized by the players as intended (Figure 7.2).

While preparing visual assets with the people responsible for the art in the game, I reached out to the team member responsible for the audio, to learn that due to other obligations they had at the time, we had to postpone testing on audio assets to another occasion. As other

---

DOI: 10.1201/9781003501909-9

FIGURE 7.1 Art assets with opponent silhouettes used in *Yupitergrad 2* component playtest on combat. (Courtesy of Gamedust.)

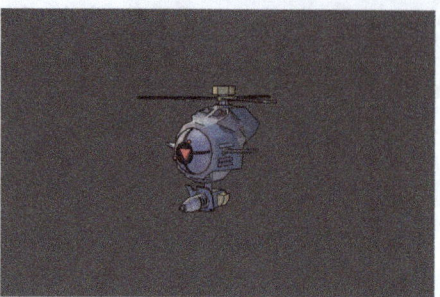 

FIGURE 7.2 Art asset with screenshots of in-engine enemy models used in *Yupitergrad 2* component playtest on combat. (Courtesy of Gamedust.)

assets were confirmed to be prepared on schedule, stakeholders agreed to proceed with the study with more general questions on the audio layer, without probing information on specific sounds.

7.2 PLAYABLE ASSETS

Certainly, most of the time, we will be focused on checking gameplay experience, and to do this, we need to confront participants with actual gameplay. As we already said when describing the production cycle in Chapter 2, we will initially have prototypes at our disposal, which will eventually give way to fragments of gameplay, ending with the entire game. Let's not forget that along the way, there may also be gyms that the team creates for their own needs, in order to be able to test selected mechanics and systems in relative isolation from the rest of the game. Sometimes, we may even have a build specially prepared for the purpose of the planned study. **Regardless of the form of the game build we will have at our disposal, our primary goal is to check whether it will allow us to achieve the study purpose**. Simply, we will have to play it before sitting our participants in front of it. Therefore, it is worth double-checking the stability and functional quality of the build, and how the debug options work.

7.2.1 THE STABILITY AND FUNCTIONAL QUALITY OF THE BUILD

Generally, our role is to assess whether the gameplay experience is accessible, usable, and engaging, and we assume that various game elements have to be functional in order to do that. In mid-sized teams, we will typically have allies in QA people who strive to ensure that the functional issues are known and taken care of, and that there are workarounds available (i.e. instructions on what we should do when something goes wrong). However, it's not always the case for the small teams where QA support may be available only at specific points in the production cycle, and having responsibility to test the game split among the team members most of the time. Regardless of the situation we are in, it is our role to ask the team about known issues and potential workarounds. Certainly, the game build doesn't have to be perfect. However, when it's full of bugs and crashes during planned activities and interactions, it may be a prompt for us to discuss with the team, if they are able to solve critical issues before the study or, at worst, postponing the study till the game is in better shape. For a vivid example, encountering screen freezes and frame rate drops below 60 frames/s in a VR game will most likely expose our participants to very unpleasant symptoms, preventing us from drawing meaningful conclusions, so it might be better to spare everyone the trouble. Regardless of the hardware platform we will be evaluating the game build on, during our own playthrough, we should ask ourselves (and the team) questions such as: Does the game crash or freeze during typical player activities and interactions? Are all the features we plan to evaluate during the study working and responsive? Are there bugs that disrupt activities or tasks we plan to evaluate during the study? Are there any platform-specific issues present (e.g. frame rate drop below a specific level)?

7.2.2   How the Debug Options Work

During the production cycle, the team creates various tools that help them see what's happening with the game to quickly identify and fix technical issues, and to test and iterate on their work. And the good news is that some of those tools can be actively used for our purposes. For example, if a participant can't finish a task or overcome a challenge, the debug feature to skip a selected part of the game allows us to move on to the next part of the study without having to instruct the participant what to do and hope that this time they will succeed, or worse, overcome the challenge for them. Some of the debug features may be game-specific, and it is worth checking with the team what options we have at our disposal in a situation where we encounter bugs that make it impossible to continue the game or the player is unable to cope with a task or activity we have planned.

Whether we use playable, non-playable, or a mix of both types of assets in our study, it may take some time for the team to deliver them, so we will typically not wait till we have all of them to start preparing our utensils. Especially, since we have already collected much of the key information needed to do it.

7.3   CHAPTER SUMMARY

Knowing what dish we want to cook, we first have to check the pots. We gather the assets available or prepared by the team for the study. Whether it's a non-playable (e.g. character art, narrative beat) or playable assets (various game builds), we want to make sure that they will allow us to answer the questions posed in the study purpose. With playable assets, we also ensure that builds are stable and at the functional quality level, giving us the possibility to conduct the study. We also want to learn known workarounds and check how the debug options work. Having the assets ready, we can move on to designing the study structure and preparing methods and tools.

8 Selecting and Preparing Utensils
Methods and Tools

We know what we want to cook, and we know the pots at our disposal, so we can now select and prepare the necessary utensils that will allow us to prepare what the team has ordered. We now have to flesh out the methods and tools section of our research protocol template.

8.1 STUDY STRUCTURE

Although the structure of the study will vary depending on the tools and methods chosen, we can generally list the following steps:

8.1.1 INTRODUCTION

Each study begins with some form of introduction and prepares participants for what is about to happen during the session. After all, right after they arrive, we do not immediately throw them into the game or work with materials. A typical introduction includes information about who we are, a description of the research session, what information we are collecting and what we will do with it, obtaining informed consent from the participant, signing an NDA, and a description of what we expect during the session (e.g. that they will try to play as if they were at home; that we are not testing them or their skills, but the game).

8.1.2 WARM-UP

Here, we ask general questions that are easy for participants to find answers to, to break the ice (hence, we call them icebreakers), make them feel at home, and encourage them to talk. Usually, we use this occasion to learn some additional information, like facts about them, their preferences and habits, e.g. Before we begin, I was wondering, what games have you played recently?

8.1.3 PRE-TEST

After the warm-up, we may want to collect or provide additional information that may affect the results of the study. For example, as part of the pre-test for a VR study, we may ask participants to complete a survey about how they are feeling and whether they are experiencing any symptoms that may affect their experience with the game, such as headaches, stomach aches, or eye strain. On the other hand, if the game trailers are already publicly available at the time of the study, we may show them to participants and ask them about their expectations for the game. If such materials are not yet available or we are concerned that they could distort the results of the study too much, we may forgo the pre-test.

8.1.4 TEST

This is where the "actual study" comes in. In studies where we want participants to experience specific activities or game elements (e.g. usability playtest), this section is where we list specific tasks and arrange their order, e.g. to reflect their actual flow in the game. If our study is less structured

DOI: 10.1201/9781003501909-10

(e.g. freeplay during an experience playtest), the test section is much shorter and is where we consider what instructions we need and want to provide. Of course, we can have a whole range of semi-structured variants (e.g. a component playtest where there are both specific tasks and more general instructions).

8.1.5 POST-TEST

After conducting the actual part of the study, we can collect information about the remembered experiences of our participants or test additional hypotheses (e.g. show a gameplay trailer and ask participants to what extent their experience during the game was consistent with what they see in the video). **While we attach great importance to how someone actually experienced the game (e.g. based on observation and analytics), information about how someone remembered that experience (e.g. collected through a survey or interview) helps us create a more complete picture of the issues and strengths of the game.** pre-test is also a place to repeat selected measurements we did in the pre-test. For example, we can repeat our survey, so we can compare whether the participants' well-being changed after the experience with the game.

8.1.6 WRAP-UP

When we finish what we have planned for the session, we owe our participants some kind of closing. At this point, we thank them for taking part in the study and sharing their opinions, we also remunerate them for participation (or inform them when we will do it) and if we conduct participant recruitment ourselves, we encourage them to send their friends the recruitment form for the studies we conduct.

With the basic study structure outlined in the research protocol, we can begin elaborating on it in the moderator's guide, which we will rely on during the research sessions. In the "GURCB_01_010101- book - moderator guide - template" available on the book's website, you will find generic instructions covering each step of the study structure that can be adapted for the needs of different studies. Although the research protocol and moderator's guide are closely related, they serve different purposes. **We use the research protocol to keep a bird's-eye view of the entire study and to easily communicate with the team, so we have to keep it concise. In contrast, we will use the moderator's guide to communicate with participants during specific research sessions, so we will flesh out the details there.** For our purposes, in the coming sections, we will indicate which of the two documents each of the elements we produce will go into.

BOX 8.1   BITE OF PRACTICE #4: STUDY STRUCTURE

We want to organize the study structure in such a way as to limit the influence of individual parts on each other (e.g. checking whether participants recognize opponents' characteristics from their form should be done before participants have the opportunity to encounter them in combat). It can be tricky, especially in studies involving multiple goals, but giving it attention will save us trouble during analysis and limit the possibility of getting confounded results.

For our component playtest, we decided to go with introduction, warm-up, and wrap-up, similar to the ones you can find in the "GURCB_01_010101- book - moderator guide - template". However, when it comes to the rest of the study structure, few methods were combined to realize the agreed study purpose:

- **The pre-test** focused on testing non-playable assets (e.g. graphics depicting silhouettes and models of opponents) to capture what information participants can extract from their form before experiencing them. Since we were conducting a playtest for a VR game, a permanent element of the pre-test was also checking the well-being of participants.

- **The test** was all about exposing participants to various combat situations. At this stage, we knew that participants would have to face encounters with single opponents and groups of them, as well as a variety of contexts in which combat takes place. With the help of the lead designer, we selected typical encounters, both in terms of types of opponents, their number, and the structure of the places in which they take place.
- **The post-test** was planned to capture both general impressions of the combat and to probe topics related to various elements that make up the combat system, which might not have arisen spontaneously during the session (e.g. perception of the environments in which combat took place or sounds of combat in the game). As part of the post-test, it was again necessary to ask participants about their well-being to check whether the game didn't cause any unpleasant symptoms.

8.2 INSTRUCTIONS AND TASKS

In studies involving participants, we usually provide some instructions so that the participants know what to expect and what we expect from them. If we additionally want to observe specific activities or gameplay elements, we usually have to supplement them with tasks. Depending on the research goals and adopted methods, instructions and tasks can take a more or less elaborate form. During the later stages of the production cycle, when the key systems are implemented in the game, but also when the tutorials take shape, our instructions will take a more general form. For example, during the experience playtest, we can simply ask participants, "Now you can start the game and play it freely as you would at home". On the other hand, in the earlier phases of the production cycle, when various game elements and systems are still being worked on, there is often a need to provide more detailed instructions or additional information. For instance, we will more often instruct our participants to familiarize themselves with the control layout before starting to play independently or perform tasks. We may ask our participants, "Please explore for a moment how to use various game controls" before moving on to the actual tasks or gameplay fragments. Familiarizing with controls can even be treated as a task in itself. In *Yupitergrad 2*, our pre-production usability playtests typically started with asking participants to describe their intentions and expectations before using a specific input while self-learning the controls. We simply wanted to understand what control layout would be comfortable and intuitive (meaning quickly and easily discoverable, and consistent with expectations) for players. This allowed us to better adapt the basic control scheme, but also indicated the need to implement control presets (as providing full remapping wasn't an option due to the business and technical constraints).

When it comes to preparing the tasks our participants will face during the session, we start by looking at the goals the game will set for the players. However, these goals don't have to be always explicitly communicated by the game. For example, the basic goal that many games set for the players is to defeat opponents or to solve puzzles. In order to achieve these goals, players undertake a series of activities in the game. If the players' goal is to defeat opponents in ranged combat, in order for them to succeed, we should ensure that they know how to recognize opponents, select the appropriate weapon from the menu, aim, shoot, and adapt their tactics to their health level and the context in which the combat takes place. We have to note that for each activity we should identify a verifiable end condition, i.e. something after which we will clearly state that the activity has been completed or not. For example, we know that the participants know how to choose a weapon if they actually select a weapon from the inventory and equip it.

After defining the activities, we have to consider in what context we want to observe them. For example, we can observe combat during a single encounter within a specially prepared gym, where we will spawn various opponents and weapons in controlled conditions. This should allow us to take a closer look at individual mechanics and elements of the combat. We can think of prototypic

BOX 8.2   EXERCISE: PEANUT BUTTER AND JELLY SANDWICH

Our task during a study is often to observe and analyze complex activities performed by the players (e.g. reloading a gun). Breaking those complex activities down into simple ones occurring over time allows us to better locate, understand, and describe the problems players encounter (e.g. noticing the clip is empty → reloading → noticing the gun has reloaded → going back to action). Certainly, we should look for a granularity level for our breakdown to remain useful in the context of the game we're working on (e.g. if reloading in a wide open is not an intended option for the players, and they should find cover first, we have to include this in our activity breakdown).

This kind of approach also proves helpful in generating instructions and formulating questions. To practice this, I encourage you to do a simple exercise. You may know how to make a peanut butter and jelly (PB&J) sandwich. It's quite simple, so you can probably describe how to make one to someone who doesn't even know how to begin. The instructions for the exercise are also very simple: gather the ingredients for a PB&J sandwich, write a list of instructions for making it, and ask someone to follow them exactly. Then, iterate until you get the intended result. If you don't feel like eating a sandwich, you can try another activity, like brushing teeth. GLHF!

BOX 8.3   BITE OF PRACTICE #5: DEFINING TASKS

With the planned study, we wanted to capture the potential issues and strengths of basic combat elements (e.g. weapons and opponent types), but also understand how they work together in more complex situations (e.g. fighting multiple different opponents) and different contexts (e.g. encounters in corridors and encounters in arenas) that players would encounter in the final game. At the time, we also knew that the redesigned combat required us to check if the planned control scheme was easily discoverable and learnable for the players, even if there was no tutorial available. It ended up with formulating four tasks in the research protocol, which were arranged in a way that reflects what players will experience during the game:

- T1: Control layout exploration
  //Gym with opponent spawning on demand
- T2: Encounters with a single opponent
  //Gym with opponent spawning on demand; encounters with various opponent types; aim assist and opponent's accuracy option on/off; testing primary weapon (boltgun).
- T3: Encounters with multiple opponents
  //Gym with opponent spawning on demand; encounters with various mixes of opponent types; testing additional weapon (minigun).
- T4: Encounters in various environments
  //Selected game levels with encounters in corridors and arenas.

situations during gameplay, e.g. we can expect that the combat will proceed differently in narrow and limited spaces to the combat taking place in an open space. We can also think about observing the combat on various maps or levels of the game, which will provide us with a better chance to observe issues dependent on context. Knowing what goals and activities the players will face, as well as the context in which we want to observe them, we can define the tasks for our study (e.g. encounter with a single opponent on a gym level). Once we have written down the tasks, we can compile them into an ordered list. **As a rule, we will start the list with the easier tasks and, if possible, order them to reflect what players will actually experience in the game**.

Having an organized task list, we can add them to the research protocol and move on to writing specific instructions in the moderator's guide. First, for each task, we want to provide the players with the appropriate information. If the players have to use specific elements of the game or reach a specific location to start the task, we have to provide them with this information, just not to leave them guessing. **To make it easily readable for our participants, we keep instructions simple, short, and with the use of action verbs (instead of passive statements)**.

However, there are things we want to avoid. Using words populating our interface or specific to our game (e.g. opponent names) can make tasks easier and lead participants to correct answers (e.g. when we ask participants to "spawn a heavy enemy" in a gym level, we provide them with a hint to what to expect from this opponent). Instead, we could use synonyms or neutral code names (e.g. instead of "spawn a heavy enemy", we can ask participants to "spawn an enemy A"). It's also good to avoid adding surplus adjectives (e.g. Now you'll fight an unusual opponent A) or phrases (e.g. This task will be more difficult than the previous ones), as again they can influence participants' expectations or even put them in an awkward situation (e.g. imagine that the participant lost with an opponent we labelled as "easy").

BOX 8.4   BITE OF PRACTICE #6: WRITING DOWN
INSTRUCTIONS IN THE MODERATOR GUIDE

Players in *Yupitergrad 2* move their character in a spiderman-like fashion by shooting ropes with suction cups at the ends. As the tutorial wasn't ready at the time, we had to explain this basic movement mechanic to the participants. At the same time, we wanted to explore whether the basic rules for movement (suction cups sticking only to blue surfaces) and supportive mechanics (adjusting rope length) were discoverable and understandable for the participants. All of it was reflected in the instructions for the first task.

[T1: Start] "Now that we are in the game, I would like to share with you the basic controls. We will start with movement. The buttons under your index fingers, the triggers, are used to shoot the suction cups. When the suction cup sticks to a surface, you can try to pull yourself towards it by moving your hand. Now, explore the room you are in, and comment on the actions you take".

[Additional instructions]

If the participant has not discovered that the suction cups only stick to blue surfaces: "The suction cups only stick to blue surfaces".

If the participant has not discovered that the length of the rope can be adjusted with thumbsticks: "You can move the controller sticks forward or backward to lengthen or shorten the rope".

[T1: End] Finish the task when the participant shot suction cups only at blue surfaces to move around, and adjusted the length of the ropes. "OK, now please move to the room behind the glass".

Whenever possible, it's a good idea to make the end of one task the introduction to the next one, in order to maintain a smooth flow of the study.

[T2: Start] When the participant reaches the room behind the glass: "Now let's check out the other possibilities. In this game you can use weapons. Press and hold the Y button to enter the menu. Select settings, then debug options. Turn on the boltgun and close the menu. The buttons under your middle fingers are for shooting - please check how this works".

[T2: Opponent A] "Even though you're behind glass, when you're in this space, enemies can't see you until you leave it. The buttons you see on the wall summon enemies to the level we're in. To start with, I'd like you to click the button under the "A" label once. Remember to describe everything you do, think or feel during the fight. OK, now leave this space and try to defeat this enemy".

[Additional Instructions] After two failed attempts, ask the participant to customize their experience: "OK, before we proceed we could explore some of the customization options available. Press and hold the Y button to enter the menu. Select settings, then debug options. Click the "enemies accuracy" option and close the menu".

[T2: Opponent A - End] Proceed to the next section when the participant defeats the opponent for the first time or after four attempts. Ask the participant: "What do you think of this enemy?"

[T2: Opponent B] "Now go back to the room behind the glass and click the button labelled "B" 4 times. Leave this space and defeat the enemies whenever you are ready".

[...]

After going through the available enemy types in "T2: Encounters with single opponent", the participant was asked to turn on an additional weapon (minigun) through debug options, and received similar instructions for the task "T3: Encounters with multiple opponents", except that instead of one type, the participant spawned different mixes of them. So let's fast forward to instructions for "T4: Encounters in various environments".

[T3: End] Finish the task after the participant answers "Okay, now leave this room through the yellow door".

[T4: Start] When the participant passes through the yellow door, "You'll now see different levels planned for the actual game. Feel free to go through them at your own discretion, and describe what you're doing, thinking or feeling as you play".

[Additional instruction]

After each level, ask: "What was your experience with this level?"

After two failed attempts at any level, ask the participant if they want to customize their experience. If the customization options are already on, skip to the next level after the third attempt.

[T4: End] "OK, that's all the gameplay we've got for today. You can now close the game. Take off your VR headset and press "Alt+F4" on your keyboard".

Although the moderator guide is a script for us to standardize the research sessions course, it is worth remembering that the instructions contained in it may not (and usually won't) cover all the issues that participants will encounter. Certainly, we can write down additional instructions or questions for the participant "just in case", which may prove helpful. However, this doesn't exempt us from ongoing monitoring and reacting to what is happening during the session, which we will discuss in more detail in Chapter 11.

With the instructions and tasks prepared, we can move on to the specific questions we would like to ask our participants.

8.3 QUESTIONS

When we look at our work from the outside, it basically comes down to us asking questions to the team to get questions about the game, which will allow us to generate questions for the participants, which will lead us to some answers (and most probably generate more questions). We could even say that the answers, however important, are merely a byproduct of our kitchen antics. To approach the topic smoothly, we can start with the observation that for various studies, we can rely on six basic questions [Schell Games 2015]:

- What was the most frustrating moment or aspect of what you just played?
- What was your favourite moment or aspect of what you just played?
- Was there anything you wanted to do that you couldn't?
- If you had a magic wand to wave, and you could change, add, or remove anything from the experience, what would it be?
- What were you doing in the experience?
- How would you describe this game to your friends and family?

Asking these questions will certainly give us a pretty good idea of what issues and strengths were associated with the gameplay experience. However, many times there are other things we might be interested in. After all, we will want to ask about behaviours and attitudes, thoughts and feelings, but also facts and opinions that make up players' experiences.

8.3.1   QUESTION TYPES

We will ponder a bit about generating questions, because asking the right ones in the right format is half the battle. Let's start by looking at basic question types.

8.3.1.1   Closed or Open-Ended

Closed-ended questions require participants to provide a short response and often include a suggested response format – from a simple "yes/no" (e.g. Did you enjoy the experience with the game?) to a predefined list of responses (e.g. Which statement best describes your experience with the game?) – making it easier to summarize and compare the results of multiple participants. Closed-ended questions help with fast gathering of specific information, but at the cost of it being relatively superficial. In contrast, open-ended questions give participants much more freedom and encourage more elaborate responses (e.g. What was your experience with the game?), which provides more in-depth information. At the same time, gathering the information and its analysis are relatively more time-consuming.

8.3.1.2   General or Specific

When we want to explore a topic broadly, we ask general questions (e.g. How was your experience with combat in the game?). When we want to narrow down the participants' answers to a chosen aspect, we ask more specific questions (e.g. How was your experience with the boltgun?). It is worth noting that the **most basic way of structuring lists of questions is to arrange them into a funnel, from general to more specific ones** (e.g. after participants play the game, we will start with questions about their overall experience, then about combat experience, and finally about experience with specific weapons).

8.3.1.3   Direct or Indirect

When we refer directly to the information we want to obtain from participants – like simple facts (e.g. What games do you like?), descriptions of real situations (e.g. Describe a situation in which you wanted to do something, but the game didn't allow it) or hypothetical ones (e.g. Imagine you could play for a few more hours, what elements and situations would you expect to see?) – we are dealing with direct questions. However, there are situations when the information we are interested in may be more difficult to obtain, because answering a question may be difficult for participants or there is a risk of biased answers. On such occasions, the indirect questions will come to our aid. For example, some participants may find it difficult to share what frustrated them most (to not hurt our feelings), but it may be easier for them to answer questions like "How many stars on a scale of 1–5 do you give the game?" followed by "What would have to change for you to give it one more star?".

To gain a better understanding of how to frame our questions effectively, let's have a look at the question types we should avoid. The typical suspects include:

8.3.1.4 Leading Questions

Questions that lead participants to an answer or suggest to them what answer is considered to be "correct" (e.g. Tell me how much you liked this game?). It is worth for us to note that whether a question is leading may depend not only on the question itself, but also on the context in which it is asked (e.g. In one studio recruitment survey I found the question "How well would you rate your skills at first-person shooter games?", which is not a bad question per se, but the lack of questions about other genres may invite potential participants to do the more intense guesswork about recruiter intentions).

8.3.1.5 Threatening Questions

Obviously, we don't want to intimidate our participants by asking them confrontational questions, because in addition to being rude, it can result in defensive and biased answers (e.g. Why did you fail so badly at that challenge?).

8.3.1.6 Assumed Expertise Questions

These are questions that assume participants know the answer (e.g. asking "What were your experiences using a jetpack during gameplay?" when we don't know if the participant has had the opportunity to use it). While during moderated studies participants will most likely let us know if they are unable to answer this type of question, such questions negatively affect their engagement during the session. The remedy is simple: if we are not sure that participants know or have experienced something, we could use filter questions before asking the actual question (e.g. Have you had the opportunity to use a jet-pack during gameplay?). Similarly, questions that use unclear or unfamiliar terms can be confusing for participants (e.g. Would you prefer this information to be conveyed in a more diegetic form?). This can result in difficulties in providing answers, and sometimes biased answers (participants can wrongly assume that they understand various terms or understand them differently than we do). If we have to use specific terms or jargon, it is worth asking participants about them first (e.g. Have you come across the term diegetic? How do you understand it?) or provide a simple definition.

8.3.1.7 Double-Barrelled Questions

Questions that cover two or more different topics and allow participants to answer one of them (e.g. Do you think this item is easy to use, and do you find it overpowered?). As a result, we may not be able to decipher which question the answer is about or only get an answer to one of them. Simply, we ask only one question at a time to avoid that.

8.3.1.8 Behaviour in Time Questions

Asking about past behaviour (e.g. How many hours per week did you spend playing on average in the last year?) or future intentions (e.g. How likely is it that you would buy this game?) can give us inaccurate or unrealistic results. **Generally, we avoid questions about future intentions, as they can lead us to misleading results**, if only because the relationship between attitude and behaviour weakens over time, as we discussed in Chapter 2. When it comes to past behaviours, we generally want to learn them, but memory is not a perfect record of past events, and it becomes blurred over time. If we need to obtain information about some past behaviour, we can ask participants to refer to some objective source to get more reliable answers (e.g. based on the information in your Steam library, write down what games you have played most in the last three months).

8.3.1.9 Out of the Context Questions

We will often want to ask our participants about many things. However, we have to remember that participants' attention is a limited resource. For this reason, we do not jump abruptly from topic to topic, and we abstain from asking questions that are not relevant to the player's experience at the moment (e.g. asking a participant "Do you enjoy puzzles in games?" when they are trying to solve a timed puzzle might not be the best idea in this regard).

8.3.2 FORMULATING QUESTIONS

That's enough for us in the context of question types. The thing we may now wonder about is how to come up with specific questions. Well, it certainly depends on the study purpose. Based on it, we simply need to map the topics we want to learn about. We start by writing down the things that might be worth looking at more closely within a given topic. This process can be aided by both the information we've gathered from the team and by referring to general knowledge about the player experience (such as the one we discussed in Chapter 2). For example, when studying combat, we might want to look at such topics as how players react to different types of weapons, how players handle weapons, how they perceive different types of opponents, what their experience is like during combat, how that experience changes depending on the environment in which combat takes place, and what expectations players express before, during, and after the combat experience. If we want to map a single topic, such as opponents, we might be interested in understanding subtopics of how they are perceived by participants in terms of appearance, behaviour, diversity, difficulty, and the expectations they generate. After mapping out the topic, we can move on to formulating specific questions in a form that will facilitate obtaining the information we want (i.e. open-ended vs. closed and direct vs. indirect). Once we generate questions for one topic and its subtopics, we repeat our process for the others. The process for a single topic is illustrated in Figure 8.1.

This approach focuses on formulating a lot of questions, but as a rule, **we want the study to exhaust the topic within a given timeframe, not the participants**. Therefore, it is worth marking the questions that we consider the most impactful (i.e. they can act as a basis for design or business decision), and necessary for the study purpose to be realized, while saving the rest of them for the future.

Once we have prepared and selected questions, we need to consider what kind of answer we expect or can expect to a given question in order to choose the right format and time during the session in which to ask it. As two basic formats, we can consider an interview or a survey.

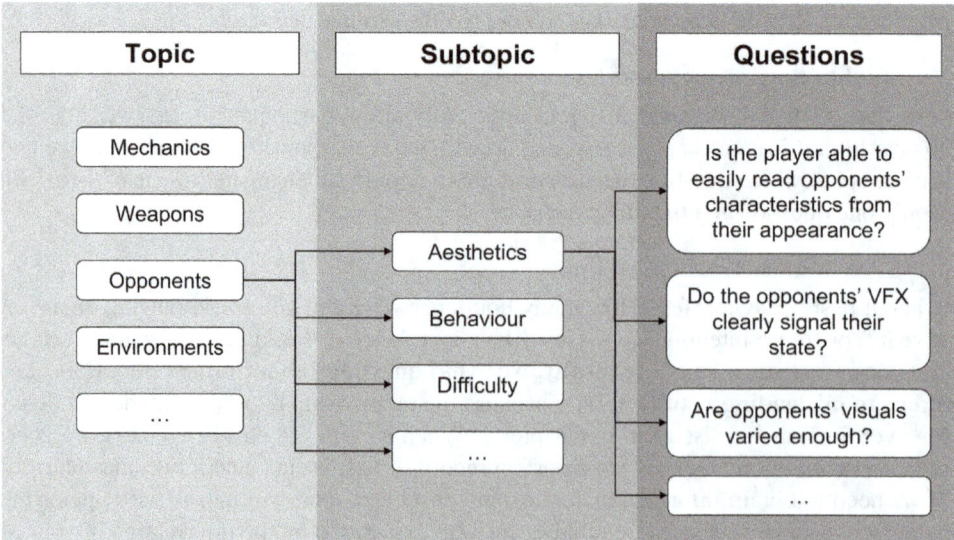

FIGURE 8.1   Process of mapping topics into questions.

8.3.3 INTERVIEW

We ask a lot of questions orally throughout the session. This ranges from the aforementioned icebreakers during warm-ups, to questions asked during the session (especially in moderated studies), to the post-test interviews at the end of the research session. In some studies, such as concept test, individual or group interviews can often be the primary research method.

When asking questions **in the interview format, we focus primarily on understanding the "why" behind player experiences** (reasons for various behaviours, as well as the motivations and emotions behind them). We look for answers to questions such as: What's the issue? Why is this an issue? How do players feel about it? Asking questions in the interview format also comes in handy when dealing with complex or sensitive topics that require us to explore the various contexts and nuances present in player experiences in more depth.

Interviews can take many forms, from structured (asking questions in a predetermined order) to unstructured (asking general questions to start a more loose conversation with the participant, which we continue based on the answers we get). As a rule of thumb, the less we know about a topic (e.g. we're exploring mood and art style for the game in the concept phase), the more unstructured the interview format will be (and an interview in general is more appropriate than a survey). This generally corresponds to the production cycle, where in the conception phase we explore what kind of game we want to make, and in the later stages we specify how we want to make it, and then we monitor whether we are successful in this process. But even in pre-production and production phases where we are conducting research on something interactive (e.g. interface prototypes or gameplay fragments), we will rarely anticipate all the topics that will emerge during the session, so we may often end up with semi-structured interviews. Here, we will focus on semi-structured interviews, which we will conduct at the end of the research session as part of various (play)tests.

When structuring our interview, we organize topics in a logical way so as not to jump between them during the interview (e.g. we start with questions about general impressions of combat, moving through selected elements of that component such as weapons, opponents, and others, and ending with expectations for combat in later stages of the game). At the same time, we use the funnel structure mentioned earlier – moving from general questions to more specific ones within the topic.

While the questions we selected and ordered will be the core of our interview, it is worth ensuring that both the introduction and the end of the interview are conducted in a smooth and natural manner. I tend to start the post-test interview with a very general question like "How was it?", to capture the participant's impression and what first comes to their mind before we go through the other topics. At the end, I ask, "Is there anything important from your perspective that I didn't ask about that you would like to add?", to capture threads that may not have come up during the interview. Sometimes we can spot an important topic this way, but it's often an opportunity for the participant to sum up their thoughts before we close the session.

BOX 8.5 BITE OF PRACTICE #7: POST-TEST INTERVIEW

In the component playtest on combat in *Yupitergad 2*, we prepared a post-test interview, which, in addition to summarizing impressions from the entire study, was planned to allow us to explore more specific topics that might not have popped out spontaneously during the gameplay. Since the interview was supplementary to other techniques used in the study, depending on the time left until the end of the session, not all questions had to be asked (questions that were needed to keep the structure of the interview or key for the team were marked with "(*)").

1. (*) How was it?
2. (*) Was there anything that happened during the game that you remember most?

3. (*) What was the most satisfying aspect or event in the game for you?
4. (*) What was the most frustrating aspect or event in the game for you?
   4.1 Were there any actions in the game that were difficult to perform?
5. (*) What were your tactics to win the fight?
6. What do you think about…
   6.1 … the way weapon switching works?
   6.2 …the way the weapons are presented?
   6.3 …aiming?
7. (*) Did any of the weapons you tested have recoil?
8. How do you feel about…
   8.1 …the sounds and music during combat?
   8.2 …the appearance of the enemies?
   8.3 …the appearance of the arenas?
9. (*) Was there a moment during combat when you wanted to do something but the game wouldn't let you?
10. (*) If you could change, add, or remove one thing from your experience with the game, what would it be?
11. What are your expectations for further gameplay?
    11.1 What game elements would you expect to be introduced?
    11.2 What would you expect from the next levels of the game?
12. (*) Imagine this game being released tomorrow, in the same state it is today. On a scale of 1–5 stars, how would you rate the combat right now?
    12.1 (*) What would need to change for you to give it one more star?
13. (*) Is there anything significant from your perspective that I didn't ask about that you'd like to add?

8.3.4 SURVEY

When our questions are more focused on the "what" and "how much" (e.g. How many players are struggling with this issue? To what extent? How often?) and the responses we want to collect are numerical (or otherwise measurable) in nature, a survey will generally be the format we strive for. Also, when the topic of interest is better explored or we want to quickly collect information from a large number of participants, it may be more convenient for us to ask questions with a predefined response format afforded by surveys. While we're on the subject of survey response formats, let's take a closer look at what we typically have at our disposal.

8.3.4.1 Ranking Questions

When we want to understand the relative preferences or how participants prioritize specific items (e.g. which features are most important to them), we can ask them to rank them in order based on the criteria provided (e.g. Rank the character designs in order from the one that best fits the provided description to the one that least fits it).

8.3.4.2 Single and Multiple Choice Questions

When we have a predefined list of items and ask participants to select one of them (single choice) or one or more of them (multiple choice). We use the single choice format when there is only one answer applicable or we want to get the single answer (e.g. Please select the option that best describes how you felt while playing the game). On the other hand, we use multiple choice when there can be more than one valid answer (e.g. From the list below, please select up to three features you would expect to see in the game). As a rule of thumb, if we do not have confidence that the list we prepared is finite, it is worth including the option "other, please specify" to capture the things we might have missed.

8.3.4.3 Scale

When we want to gather participants' responses to specific statements on a defined scale (which makes it easier for us to compare their answers), we can use:

- Rating – If we want participants to provide us with a quick and general evaluation (e.g. How would you rate your experience with the game?) on a numerical scale (e.g. one to five stars; one to ten).
- Likert-type scale – When we want to capture participants' opinions and attitudes to specific statements, we can ask them to rate their level of agreement (typically selecting from five options "Strongly disagree" - "Disagree" - "Neither Agree or Disagree" - "Agree" - "Strongly Agree"). It is worth noting that we can ask not only about the level of agreement with the statement, but also about the frequency (e.g. "Never" - "Always"), importance (e.g. "Very Unimportant" - "Very Important"), or other aspects of interest to us. Likert-type scales are used in many varieties (e.g. version with seven options; the forced-choice version, where there is no "Neither..." option), which, to a better or worse extent, address potential problems (e.g. participants giving answers "Neither..." due to fatigue).
- Semantic differential – when we want to capture participants' emotions or their perceptions of the experience, we can ask them to rate it on a scale between two opposing adjectives (e.g. Based on the image above, this character is: "friendly - _ _ _ _ _ - hostile").

8.3.4.4 Matrix

When we ask participants to respond to a variety of statements that are thematically related, using the same response format each time, we can organize them into a matrix format, where the rows are statements and the columns are response options. In general, we use this format to increase the clarity of the survey and to make it easier for participants to respond efficiently (e.g. Instead of asking separate questions in the survey such as "How do you rate the aesthetics in the game?" or "How do you rate the music in the game?", we can ask a single question "How do you rate the following elements of the game?" with subsequent rows covering items like aesthetics, music, and so on).

Certainly, if we want to get a very specific answer (e.g. the participant's age in years or the three games the participant has played the most in recent months), we can use the open-ended response format and ask participants to write in answers rather than providing them with a list of possible answers. We can also ask more general questions if we want to obtain additional information on a specific topic. Within the methods we have on the menu, using a mix of closed- and open-ended questions can be an effective approach to getting a more complete picture of the player experience, as it gives us both a measurable answer along with a rationale for it. At the same time, we have to be mindful that this requires more effort from participants to answer, which, especially in longer surveys, can lead to discouragement and lower response quality. However, asking open-ended questions in surveys focusing on "whys", may sometimes be the only feasible option (e.g. asking several open-ended questions in a survey as part of an experience playtest, which typically adopts a group format, is much more feasible than interviewing each participant individually).

The format in which we formulate the question may seem obvious (e.g. for things such as gender or level of education we will usually adopt a single-choice format), but it's essentially the result of our more or less informed decision about the level of detail and precision of the answer we want to obtain (e.g. we can ask about age by asking the participant for their date of birth, asking them to enter it in years or to choose from a list of predefined age groups). **When choosing the format, it is worth remembering that the way we ask the questions will affect the answers we get** (e.g. we can get completely different answers by asking participants to write down three features they missed during the game compared to asking them to choose three from a predefined list of that they would like to see in the game). Simply, what we ask is what we (might) get.

We can organize the questions in a similar fashion to our post-test interview (i.e. organizing it by topics and funnels). However, it is worth providing instructions within the survey, together with the time estimated to complete it. When it comes to survey building tools, before we choose paid solutions that allow for custom response formats and provide for complex logic, it is worth relying on tools that may not be as extensive, but will be easily accessible to us (e.g. Google Forms or Microsoft Forms).

BOX 8.6   BITE OF PRACTICE #8: PRE-TEST AND POST-TEST SURVEY

For the component playtest on combat in the *Yupitergrad 2*, two separate surveys were administered – one in the pre-test and one in the post-test part of the study.

Each survey opened with instructions (Figure 8.2), and participants were asked to rate their well-being on a separate scale.

In the pre-test survey, we devoted one section to participants' expectations about the gameplay trailer (e.g. What are your expectations about the gameplay based on what you saw in the trailer?). The next sections concerned participants' perceptions of NPCs (non-playable characters – any character that the player does not control) and their characteristics based on the provided graphics (Figure 8.3). The last section consisted of sections containing questions about the form and characteristics of weapons that players will be able to use during the game.

In the post-test survey (i.e. after players had a chance to play a prepared gameplay fragment), our questions focused on various elements that make up the combat system. The survey opened with a section with questions about general gameplay impressions (Figure 8.4), and the subsequent sections focused on:
- General combat experience including pacing, difficulty, and length of encounters (Figure 8.5).

Read the instruction
We'd like to hear your impressions of the game.

Completing the survey should take approximately 30 minutes.

When completing the survey, please remember:
- We're not testing you, we're testing the game.
- Please rate the game based on the content in the version you've played, not what you think will be in the final version.
- Answer questions based on your experience, not how you think other players would feel.
- Answer honestly - we value your honest opinion (and your answers will remain anonymous).
- Please be thorough in your answers. Even the smallest details are important to us.
- If any question is unclear, ask a moderator for clarification.

FIGURE 8.2   Post-test survey instructions. (Courtesy of Gamedust.)

- Player character including controls and ease of use of various combat mechanics (Figure 8.6).
- Opponents (including their behaviour, diversity).
- Environments in which combat took place (including their size, diversity).

NPC #1

NPC (*non-playable character*) - a term for any character (friendly/neutral/hostile) that is not controlled by a player.

Briefly describe what you see in the image above: *

Your answer

This character is... *

	(-3) Hostile	(-2)	(-1)	(0)	(1)	(2)	(3) Firendly
.	○	○	○	○	○	○	○

FIGURE 8.3 Survey fragment with an open-ended question and a semantic differential. (Courtesy of Gamedust.)

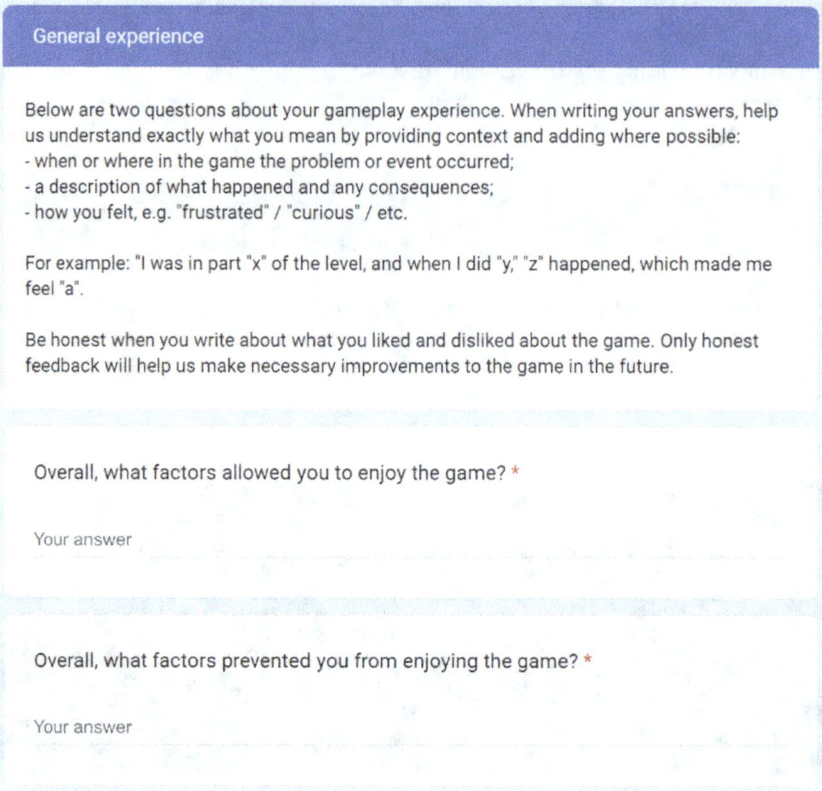

General experience

Below are two questions about your gameplay experience. When writing your answers, help us understand exactly what you mean by providing context and adding where possible:
- when or where in the game the problem or event occurred;
- a description of what happened and any consequences;
- how you felt, e.g. "frustrated" / "curious" / etc.

For example: "I was in part "x" of the level, and when I did "y," "z" happened, which made me feel "a".

Be honest when you write about what you liked and disliked about the game. Only honest feedback will help us make necessary improvements to the game in the future.

Overall, what factors allowed you to enjoy the game? *

Your answer

Overall, what factors prevented you from enjoying the game? *

Your answer

FIGURE 8.4 Survey fragment with additional instructions and two open-ended questions on general experience. (Courtesy of Gamedust.)

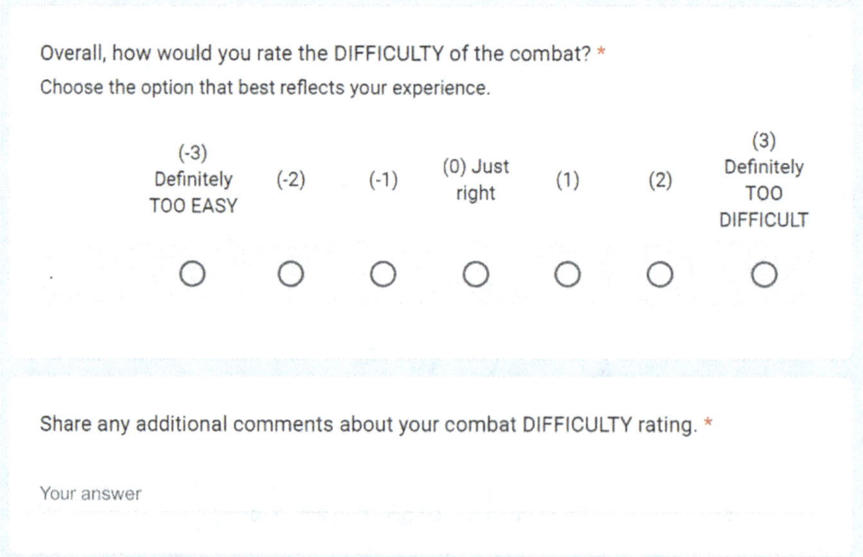

Overall, how would you rate the DIFFICULTY of the combat? *
Choose the option that best reflects your experience.

(-3) Definitely TOO EASY	(-2)	(-1)	(0) Just right	(1)	(2)	(3) Definitely TOO DIFFICULT
O	O	O	O	O	O	O

Share any additional comments about your combat DIFFICULTY rating. *

Your answer

FIGURE 8.5 Survey fragment with a closed question (scale) and an open question regarding perceived difficulty. (Courtesy of Gamedust.)

Game elements - Player charcter & enemies

During gameplay, how clear was it to you: *
Choose the option that best reflects your experience.

	(1) Completely unclear	(2)	(3)	(4)	(5) Completely clear
How to select or change weapon	○	○	○	○	○
How to use a weapon	○	○	○	○	○
That the enemy is attacking you	○	○	○	○	○
That you deal damage to your opponent	○	○	○	○	○
That the opponent is dealing damage to you	○	○	○	○	○
That your health level is decreasing	○	○	○	○	○
How to retreat or skip a fight	○	○	○	○	○

FIGURE 8.6 Survey fragment with questions organized in a matrix format. (Courtesy of Gamedust.)

8.4 SESSION DURATION

We usually plan a specific session length to avoid participants getting tired or discouraged. The length of the session itself is also information that we provide to potential participants during recruitment. It allows us to plan the session schedule (after all, we will plan differently if we fit three research sessions into one day instead of two), and it can guide us when determining the remuneration for participation in the study (we will naturally reward someone more generously for longer sessions).

Certainly, there is no magic session length, but for our purposes, we can assume that one usability (play)test session will usually last 60–90 minutes, and one component playtest session can last up to 150–180 minutes. However, there is nothing to stop us from planning a usability (play)test for as short as 45 or even up to 120 minutes. With longer sessions, it is worth remembering that we don't wait for participants to ask for a break, but plan them in advance during natural pauses in the study (e.g. after completing a part of the study, between tasks, or after closing a topic in a long interview). At the same time, everything has its limits, and if our usability (play)test is about 4 hours long, it's worth considering conducting two separate studies. Therefore, when preparing the study structure with all its methods and tools, it's worth checking whether we haven't overdone it. We can make a rough estimate of the time it will take to complete each method (e.g. trying to complete tasks or a survey on our own) and put it in the session duration section to check whether a single session is not too long or whether there is still time for some extras. Although our estimates may initially seem like guesswork, it's worth practicing estimating to have a basic check that any of the methods aren't being used against our intentions (e.g. if we planned to focus on observing tasks and interviewing, then a survey that will take half the session time is probably not what we were aiming for). After we iterate the study structure section of our research protocol, we can post an update on our study channel and invite the stakeholders to give it a look and leave comments or questions.

With the study structure prepared, we can copy specific parts (tasks, interview, survey) to our moderator guide and move on to arranging our kitchen workspace so that we can easily get to work as soon as we have the ingredients needed for our dish.

8.5   CHAPTER SUMMARY

Knowing what we want to cook and what pots we have at our disposal, we begin selecting the appropriate utensils. Our task is to outline the study structure in the research protocol (introduction, warm-up, pre-test, test, post-test, wrap-up), and then develop general instructions, methods and tools, such as:

- Tasks – we start by defining and selecting the activities for tasks, breaking down those which are complex into simple ones, all with defined end conditions. Then, we consider the context in which we want to observe specific activities (isolated, in the context of other game elements, or over several or more hours). Next, we write instructions, remembering to keep them simple, short, and to use action verbs.
- Questions – we begin by outlining the themes arising from the study purpose to define the questions we seek answers to. Keeping in mind that questions can be closed or open-ended, general or specific, direct or indirect, we select the appropriate method of asking them:
  - Interview – when we focus more on: What's the issue? Why is this an issue? How do players feel about it?
  - Survey – when we focus more on: How many players are struggling with this issue? To what extent? How often?

When developing questions for interviews or surveys, we remember to organize them (e.g. by topics and funnels). After developing methods and tools, we estimate the length of a single research session and make any necessary adjustments to achieve the desired effect. We then supplement our moderator guide with appropriate instructions based on the prepared methods (i.e. tasks, interviews, surveys).

REFERENCE

Schell Games (2015). *The Definitive Guide to Playtest Questions.* https://schellgames.com/blog/the-definitive-guide-to-playtest-questions-for-video-game-playtesters

9 Organizing Kitchen
Setting and Pilot Study

One of the important things that will save us problems when cooking is the proper preparation of the workspace in our kitchen. We don't want to trip over unnecessary things, desperately search for utensils, or make any other unnecessary mess, because after all, we will be the ones responsible for cleaning up. Let's now look at how to prepare our research setting so that it doesn't bother us during sessions, while saving us from typical problems.

9.1 SETTING

To remind myself of what needs to be done when preparing a research setting, I came up with the acronym PEM, which can be deciphered as: **Each study requires a suitable Place, appropriate Equipment, and readily available Materials**. We will take a closer look at each PEM element.

9.1.1 PLACE

As a rule, the place where the research takes place should be neutral, so as not to affect the participants in any way. Looking at the conditions in small and medium-sized studios, we will rarely, if ever, have a dedicated room for conducting research. Most often, we will have to use a conference room or conduct sessions remotely. On the one hand, we don't try to intimidate our participants by placing statuettes, gadgets, or other evidence emphasizing the coolness of our studio, and on the other hand, we don't try to imitate the gamer room, pretending that the research situation is completely natural. Let's be moderate – the presence of a large table, chairs, office equipment, or plants in the conference room or conducting the session against the bright wall background as part of a remote session will be completely natural (and most of the time neutral). Another thing that interests us is ensuring sufficient privacy and minimizing potential external disruptions during the session. Conducting a session at a trade show or while the team is actively discussing some functionality in the next room may not be the best idea. In the case of remote sessions, we also ask participants to ensure privacy and a quiet environment for themselves for the session duration. Certainly, we can think of other possible environmental influences, such as temperature or lighting conditions, which can affect the comfort of participants (and ourselves) and therefore the results obtained during the session. It's not about running around with a thermometer, but ensuring the room is neither too hot nor too cold, and it's worth remembering to let in some fresh air between the sessions. Finally, for on-site studies, it's worth considering where participants will be able to safely leave their belongings, telling them where the toilets are, as well as considering where and how we will take care of participants during breaks in the session (both planned and unplanned).

9.1.2 EQUIPMENT

Depending on whether our study has adopted a group or individual format, we will face different logistical challenges. In individual studies conducted on-site, we will need a computer on which we will display non-playable assets and/or run the game build, record what is happening on the screen, as well as allow participants to fill out surveys. Additionally, we will need a webcam and microphone (unless we are using a laptop with built-in ones) to record the participant.

DOI: 10.1201/9781003501909-11

In this arrangement, it's worth having an additional monitor – on one, we will display materials, the game, and surveys to the participant (we have to secure an additional keyboard and mouse for providing input), and on the other, we will have a view of the software recording the session. The most basic choice for PC and console games in the context of recording software is Open Broadcaster Software (OBS), in which we can capture several sources in a single recording (e.g. what is happening on the screen and the recording from the webcam), there are also readily available plug-ins that allow us to display input used by participant on controllers, and we can even stream the session to the observers. In the case of mobile games, it is worth getting a document camera to record what is happening on the screen during the session (some of them come with black pads that make it easier to obtain the right contrast on the recording). In group studies, we will necessarily need more computers, which may involve conducting it during the weekend (in smaller organizational settings, we will most probably have to borrow additional computers from other team members). In case we don't have a photographic memory, we will certainly need an additional laptop or tablet on which we will display the moderator guide for ourselves and will take notes from the session (the other option is to go the traditional way - print the moderator's guide and take notes with pen and paper). In the case of remote research, we pass on the responsibility for having the right equipment to run the game, an appropriate internet connection, webcam, and microphone to the participants, but this requires us to make sure during the recruitment process that they have such equipment and prepare it for the study (e.g. make sure that they have full batteries in their controllers). The advantage is that on our side we will only need a computer with recording software, webcam, and microphone, and for our own convenience we can try to arrange a second monitor – one with the moderator guide and notes open, and the other one with the video conference app (e.g. Google Meets, MS Teams, or other).

9.1.3 MATERIALS

In addition to the materials that we directly use to conduct the study, such as the moderator guide, which contains the content of tasks, questions, and necessary links (e.g. to surveys), we have at least three key things that we should prepare, namely NDA (Non-Disclosure Agreement), informed consent, and remuneration for participants. With NDA, we want to protect ourselves against potential leaks of information about the game in the making and sensitize participants to this. Depending on the legal standards in our country and the policy of our studio, an NDA can take a more or less extensive form. At the same time, we aren't legal specialists, so it's worth obtaining an NDA form for research purposes from the person providing the studio with legal services. Most often, we ask participants to read the NDA and sign the document immediately before the session or we do it at the recruitment stage in electronic form (e.g. using an electronic signature service provider). Another thing we mentioned is informed consent. Regardless of the format (paper or oral), the most important thing is to provide participants with the necessary information and explanations about what awaits them during the study (e.g. that we want to record the session, that people from the team may watch it, that the session will include playing, filling out surveys and going through interviews), so that they're aware of what will happen and only then agree (or not) to participate. The moderator guide template prepared for this book is a variant in which informed consent is in oral form. Last, but not least, we would like to thank our participants for taking part in the study. Regardless of whether our "thank you" takes the form of money, vouchers, games, or merch, let's have it ready at hand so that we don't have to look for it at the end of the session. We will talk a little more about selecting remuneration type and amount in Chapter 10.

With the setting prepared, we can update our moderator guide with any necessary instructions (e.g. sharing screen and information on running game build for remote session) and organize a pilot study.

BOX 9.1 SMELLY CA... PLAYTEST

When planning our research, it is worth taking care of both our own hydration and that of our participants. After all, we will want them to tell us a lot about their experiences, and it wouldn't be nice for a dry throat to discourage them from doing so. During the on-site session, it is worth offering something to drink – water, tea, or coffee – and as part of remote sessions, it's worth reminding the participants to prepare something to drink.

If we are planning for longer sessions (e.g. as part of extended playtests) and are considering some meals or snacks for our participants, it's worth ensuring that they are simple and nutritious, as well as adapted to the requirements or dietary restrictions of our participants. Over-reliance on pizza, spicy foods, chips, sodas, and sweets can ultimately provide a temporary energy boost, only to end up with an energy crash for our participants later. Not to mention all the smells or sticky hands, which aren't the best aid for focus during the session.

9.2 PILOT STUDY

It's time to check everything. How we do it depends on whether we already have the necessary assets to conduct the study (e.g. game build) or we still have to wait for them to arrive. After all, when we don't have the assets yet, it can be difficult to verify all the elements of the study (for example, whether the instructions for the tasks are understandable and do not contain "obvious errors"). To get around this, especially with our first studies, it is worth conducting a pilot study in two steps.

9.2.1 PILOT STUDY – STEP 1

When we have closed the study structure, moderator guide, and prepared the setting, we can try to trace the path that the participant has to follow from the moment they arrive at our studio (or another place where we conduct the study) to the moment they leave the building. It's worth doing this literally, i.e. walking around the building and trying to look at the instructions that we have in the moderator guide through the eyes of the participant. We look if there is anything missing or if the information is provided in the right order (e.g. Did we point out to them where the toilets are, and where the food would be served so they could become a little more familiar with the unfamiliar space? Did we anticipate that someone might arrive earlier and have to wait?). It is also worth sitting in the place reserved for the participant and trying to act out the activities that we have prepared for them (e.g. from reading and signing the NDA and informed consent, through reviewing materials and playing the build, to the interview, filling out surveys, and receiving the remuneration), while noting the gaps and checking whether all elements of the setting work according to plan. During this dry run, it's worth measuring the time it took us to complete individual parts of the study to have a better approximation of the session duration in the research protocol.

9.2.2 PILOT STUDY – STEP 2

This is a kind of general rehearsal that allows us to make final corrections to what the actual participants will experience. We can start the second step when we have all the assets ready. To conduct this part, it's worth asking someone from the team or friends and family to take on the role of the participant and comment on anything unclear for them. We go together through the entire study with them, and again check for any gaps or elements to update. We can measure the time again to verify whether the structure of the session and how long it lasts do not deviate too much from our assumptions.

BOX 9.2   KEEP YOUR CUPBOARDS TIDY

Some of us may have noticed that the templates in this book have rather specific names. This is the naming convention for files assigned to a given project. If we don't have a large repository (and in a small- or medium-sized studio, this will likely be the case), keeping the file and folder structure organized will help us avoid some of the problems of keeping track of what's where. Especially since we'll be creating at least several files for a single study.

Let's recreate the file naming convention with the example:

"GURCB_01_010101- Component Playtest - research protocol - template".

The file name consists of several elements:

- "GURCB" – project code name
- "_01" – ordinal number of the study
- "_010101" – creation date or file status date change in "yymmdd" format
- "Component Playtest" – type of study
- "research protocol" – file type
- "template" – file status, which can be "template", "draft", "ready", "submitted"

Knowing the above, we can also reconstruct the name of the folder containing the files, which is the project code name and type of the study (i.e. "GURCB_01- Component Playtest"). Certainly, the point here isn't to use this specific file naming convention, but to ensure that we have one that is useful for us, and stick to it consistently to avoid potential chaos in the files we create or receive for research purposes.

Preparing for the session requires paying attention to many elements. At the same time, with subsequent studies conducted in a specific setting, "Pilot Study – Step 1" will bring us less and less information and will prove to be skippable at some point. Thus, it is worth using various less time-consuming aids instead, such as a checklist with the necessary steps and elements to check. At the same time, we don't give up "Pilot Study – Step 2" completely, especially if time allows us to do so.

9.3   CHAPTER SUMMARY

We need to organize our kitchen in a way so that slicing and dicing together with cooking the dish runs smoothly. After finalizing the methods, we move on to organizing our study setting, paying attention to preparing a suitable study place (whether remotely or on-site), organizing the necessary equipment (e.g. a second monitor or webcam, software for recording sessions), and materials (e.g. NDA forms, participant remuneration). Finally, we conduct a pilot study to ensure that the prepared methods and setting will allow us to conduct the study in an efficient and problem-free manner. Throughout the entire process, we remember to keep the files we create for the study organized not to get lost in them later.

10 Gathering Essentials
Participants Recruitment

As we may remember from the first part of this book, the player experience is the experience that the player has with the game. Although the game (more precisely, assets such as game builds, concept art, narrative beats) can be seen as the pot, the main ingredients of our dish will be the players' behaviours, thoughts, and feelings. Having everything prepared, we can now do some search for the essentials.

Recruitment itself can be quite a challenge at first. We may want to resort to common-sense solutions, such as conducting research at events and fairs or inviting friends and family. In special cases, this will make sense, but as a rule, such shortcuts when recruiting can bite us later. After all, the quality of the dish depends on the quality of the ingredients. On the other hand, using the services of a professional recruitment agency will require us to secure an additional budget, which can be a challenge in itself. That's why we will go over the steps we can take ourselves to recruit the right participants for our studies. Doing this groundwork will save us time and money in the long run.

10.1 WHO TO RECRUIT?

One of the biggest disappointments in conducting research is when we realize that the participant who is taking part in the session is not representative of our target audience. Certainly, we can try to explain to ourselves that we will find out how our game is perceived by a wider audience, but the matter comes down to the fact that there is a small probability that this person will buy or download our game and leave a review. In one of the studies for a racing game, I had a participant who was incredibly dissatisfied with how the car was driven in the game and that the driving model was in every possible way different from his expectations. After asking a few questions, it turned out that he actually liked racing games, but simulator-like ones (i.e. aimed to faithfully reflect the behaviour of the car while driving) and characterized by graphic realism. Well... we playtested a game that had an arcade driving model and cartoon-like graphics. So, instead of harvesting carrots, I ended up gathering parsnips – similar in shape but suspicious in colour and taste for the dish I was preparing. So, let's take a look at how we can protect ourselves from potential disappointments of this type.

To put it simply, we have to check whether potential participants represent our target audience before inviting them to participate in the study. First, we have to select the criteria based on which we will conduct this check. In Chapters 1 and 2, we devoted attention to game typologies and a number of factors that influence players' decisions and behaviours. In this regard, we listed economic, socio-demographic, and psychological factors. However, some of them may be difficult to obtain (e.g. people are rather reluctant to share their income in order to participate in a game study), and we will rarely have the opportunity to check all of these variables at once (otherwise we would exhaust or alienate our participants before we even have a chance to invite them). Fortunately, in most cases, we can limit our attention to familiarity with reference and competitor games, game genre preferences, hardware platforms owned and/or used, and consider basic socio-demographic information.

10.1.1 FAMILIARITY WITH REFERENCE AND COMPETITOR GAMES

The general assumption we make is: "if you bought or played game 'x', you will probably like game 'y', which is similar to 'x' in terms of 'z'". Knowing whether someone has played specific reference games (i.e. those that inspired the solutions in our game) also helps us determine the probability that a potential participant will understand the conventions adopted in our game. In the case of competitor games (i.e. those that will be considered as a purchase option together with our title), we also want to capture the participants' opinions on whether our solutions are better or worse compared to existing titles, to better understand our competitive edge and differentiators. If our team doesn't yet have precisely defined reference and competitor titles, it's worth establishing such a list together to be able to select research participants more accurately.

10.1.2 GAME GENRE PREFERENCES

This is a less precise indicator than specific titles, but it can still give us some insight into whether a title has a chance of appealing to someone. After all, we won't always find people who have played specific reference or competitor games. The problem here, however, is that boundaries between genres are often blurred, and participants may understand them differently than we do, e.g. someone who indicated that they like racing games may just as well mean their experience with *Forza Horizon* as with *Mario Kart* (and they may sincerely dislike one of these options). If we decide to recruit based on genre preferences, it's worth having a list of genres that is specific enough to encompass our game while also including example titles to not leave potential participants guessing.

10.1.3 HARDWARE PLATFORMS OWNED AND/OR USED

We already know that the hardware platform is crucial because it largely determines whether our game will be considered as a purchase option. Additionally, knowing whether the player uses a hardware platform allows us to gather initial information, whether they know the typical conventions (e.g. control schemes) used in games on a given system. We know the hardware platform (or platforms) for which our game will be created early in the production cycle, so it is worth collecting this information from potential participants to avoid a situation in which we invite someone who, although may be interested in our game, is not our target audience member. Certainly, an exception to this approach will be new platforms that are niche or are just introduced on the market, e.g. Around 2015, for research on VR games we recruited people who had no contact with this platform, as well as those who had only the opportunity to interact with it occasionally (e.g. at various events), because the group of owners was relatively small.

10.1.4 BASIC SOCIO-DEMOGRAPHIC INFORMATION

After discussing socio-demographic factors (e.g. age, sex or gender, education level) in Chapter 2, we know that they don't necessarily translate into the actual experiences of individual participants. Although at first glance asking about socio-demographic variables may seem less important for this reason, it can still provide us some hints, allowing us to recruit a potentially diverse group of participants, e.g. by recruiting people of different sexes (or genders), ages, and education levels, we have a better chance of capturing a greater number of perspectives resulting from different needs and experiences, both in gaming and in life. At the same time, only in specific cases, we will decide to narrow down recruitment based on specific socio-demographic characteristics (e.g. when conducting a study on a game designed for children).

Depending on the creative vision and the study purpose at hand, we may also be tempted to ask about playstyles or ways of spending free time or books and films participants are familiar with (e.g. when conducting concept test for a game based on a book, we can expect that reception of concept arts or narrative beats will depend on whether someone is familiar with the literary original). For free-to-play games, we may want to learn about participants spending on in-app purchases (e.g. if and what they buy). If we are conducting research on a specific hardware platform, such as VR, it's good to ask about how comfortable someone feels while using the platform, as well as about experiences related to simulator sickness. On a more basic level, if we are conducting remote sessions, it is worth asking about internet connection speed, camera, and microphone to avoid technical issues during the session.

BOX 10.1   JUDGING A PLAYER BY THEIR PLAYTIME

It is worth considering the selection and mix of recruitment criteria, as some of them that come to mind, when taken alone, can be misleading at best. One of such criteria is the time someone spends in general on playing games (typically during a week). We already know that 5 hours is something different for a teenager and something else for a person in their forties. However, it turns out that the time someone spends on games can also be related to the genre or the type of game. And so, among the population of players, 5 hours spent on strategy games can be a lot in reality, compared to spending 5 hours on MOBA games [see Sobczyk et al. 2015]. So, if information about time spent playing is crucial for us for some reason, then in addition to taking into account information about the participant's age, we collect information about what genres (or specific games) it applies to. Certainly, we can decide not to collect this information at all and consider this issue closed, but I think it is more important for us to have some reflection on the way we check and set recruitment criteria, not to accidentally exclude participants who may nevertheless belong to our target audience.

10.2   HOW TO RECRUIT PARTICIPANTS?

Having selected the recruitment criteria, we have a choice of how we want to collect this information in order to gather a pool of participants from which we will invite selected people to our study. Looking at solutions that will not generate additional monetary costs for us, we can consider sign-ups through email, community, mailing list, and recruitment forms.

10.2.1   EMAIL OR COMMUNITY SIGN-UPS

We create an announcement in which we encourage participants to express their willingness to participate in game research by sending a message to the provided email address, or signing up as part of the community to a specific person from our team (e.g. on the Discord server). We will usually only collect critical information (e.g. If you want to take part in the study organized by <studio name>, write us an email with the title "playtests". In the email, write the titles of games you have recently played and the dates when you can visit our studio). The advantage of this solution is the ability to quickly select potential participants and recruit them for a specific study. However, in the long run, it can become cumbersome and difficult to maintain.

10.2.2   MAILING LIST SIGN-UP

This solution requires us to use a mailing list maintenance tool. Similar to the previous solution, we create an announcement in which we encourage participants to take part in game research, but this time we ask them to sign up for the mailing list. The main advantage is the low entry threshold for potential participants (all they need to do is provide an email address) and the ability to quickly gather a pool of potential participants. The disadvantage, however, is that we don't know anything about these people, so we have to verify to what extent they meet our criteria (e.g. by sending them an additional message with questions verifying it).

10.2.3   RECRUITMENT FORM SIGN-UP

We can try to create our own pool of participants by using easily accessible tools (e.g. Google Forms, Microsoft Forms). While this solution requires our effort to create a survey and for participants to complete it, in the long run, it's a solution that will allow us to build a pool of potential participants that we can easily use for various studies and games. You can find sample recruitment form questions in the file "GURCB_01_010101- book - recruitment form - template".

10.3   WHERE TO LOOK FOR PARTICIPANTS?

Regardless of whether we choose to select a community, mailing list, or a form, the quality of our participant pool will largely depend on where we source them. There are at least several ways of finding people for our study (see Table 10.1).

TABLE 10.1

Advantages and Disadvantages of Various Sources for Recruiting Participants

Source	Pros	Cons	When We May Want to Rely on It
Friends and family	Quick access to participants. Participants know us (or are familiar with us) and are most likely eager to help, so it's easy to contact them and schedule a session.	Participants from our circle may be more likely to give us the answers we want to hear, so as not to hurt our feelings or jeopardize the friendship, instead of honest and constructive feedback. Participants may have some knowledge about the project and some attitude towards it, which may affect their perception of the game. The group itself may be specific due to some characteristics (e.g. socio-demographic or economic), so we have a greater risk that it will not reflect the target audience well.	When we are just starting our research endeavours, it is worth not adding stress to ourselves and conducting a few trial sessions with friends. It may not always provide us with insights about the game, but we can certainly ask them for honest feedback on what did not work for them during the session. Simply put, when we do not have the budget. However, it is worth having them meet the basic recruitment criteria so that the study with their participation makes sense. If we have the budget, it is worth reserving those that meet the criteria for conducting pilot studies so we don't have to use participants recruited elsewhere. On rare occasions, it may turn out that people from our circle are the right and convenient group to conduct our study.
Events (e.g. trade shows, conferences, webinars)	We have direct contact with potential participants to share information about the study and invite them to participate. Events usually attract people interested in a given topic, so there is a greater chance of finding the right participants (e.g. among people who came to our stand at the fair).	Events are usually limited by time, location and number of attendants, so we have limited reach. They may require from us additional preparations or costs (e.g. we may want to print leaflets with a QR code for registration for the study and hand them out to attendees).	Whenever our studio exhibits at a consumer trade show, it is worth coordinating with the people from our team responsible for the event preparation to include information about playtests with a link to sign up (e.g. QR code) in selected marketing materials. It can be an effective form of recruiting Delphi groups (i.e. consisting of experts in a given field), e.g. the creative vision assumes a faithful representation of the historical realities of a given period, so in the concept phase, we decide to interview historians.

(Continued)

TABLE 10.1 (*Continued*)

Advantages and Disadvantages of Various Sources for Recruiting Participants

Source	Pros	Cons	When We May Want to Rely on It
Studio-owned communication channels (e.g. studio's Facebook page, X profile, but also channels like studio's Discord server)	We have broad access to potentially large and diverse groups of people. People who follow our channels may be more willing to engage with our research announcements. By using paid posts or ads we can reach a specific group of potential participants (e.g. in terms of demographics, interests). In cooperation with people from the team responsible for social media, we can easily rely on communication channels that are already operating in our studio.	To put it simply, our posts can easily get lost in the stream of information that people see on their social media walls. Although it depends on the number of followers of our channels and their engagement, if we want to ensure a wide reach for our recruitment, in most cases it will be worth supporting it with paid activities (e.g. ads). We have to stay vigilant while recruiting through our communication channels (e.g. studio's Discord server), as we generally don't want to invite most ardent fans of our games or studio to flatter us during research sessions.	Especially when we want to quickly recruit people who are in some way interested in our studio or games. If we have a budget to support recruitment with paid activities, this source can be helpful in building a participant base pre-filtered by specific criteria.
Community forums or servers (e.g. Discord, Facebook groups, online forums)	Based on competitive and reference games, we can easily identify and find communities where we will find people who are most likely to meet the basic recruitment criteria. Different online communities bring together people who share a common interest in a topic, but often differ in terms of economic and socio-demographic variables.	Some communities may be passive or uninterested in activities not directly related to their topic, so it is worth being prepared for a potentially low response rate.	When we want to recruit participants who share common interests, such as hobbyists, fans, or people interested in specific genres or titles of games, films, or books. When we look for people who may have specialist knowledge on a topic that can be vital for creating the intended player experience (e.g. if we want to faithfully replicate forklift driving in a game, we may want to recruit from places like groups with job offers for forklift operators)
Recruitment agencies	The basic assumption is that agencies specialize in providing the participants matching our criteria to save us time and effort. Providing a diversified, but also reliable group of participants, ensuring that they will show up for the session.	Basically, it's money. Agency fees may be a significant factor excluding it as a source of participants for us. We have less control over recruitment, and sometimes may stumble upon so-called pro-participants (i.e. people who make participation in research as an additional income source or a way of spending time).	When we have very specific criteria for recruitment or we're looking for participants who are hard to reach through other sources. Relying on recruitment agencies can come in handy when we are looking for participants who are players of competitor games or are unsatisfied with other games of our studio (e.g. previous entry in the series)

Annotation. [own elaboration].

With all their pros and cons, we will most often use those sources in combination to obtain a possibly large and diversified participant pool for a study at hand and future ones. If we have decided to build and maintain our own participant database, we must bear in mind that over time it may become outdated for various reasons (e.g. people lose interest in participating in our research, their contact details change). To keep our participant pool in good shape and readiness, we have to repeat sourcing from time to time.

10.4 WHAT TO OFFER PARTICIPANTS IN RETURN?

Once we have determined what we want from potential participants and how and where we want to recruit them, we have to consider what we can offer them in return. After all, we don't want only the most ardent fans and supporters of our studio to take part in the study. Such research would provide us with results that are, at best, incomplete, and at worst, completely unrealistic. We also have to note that some of the stakeholders may not perceive participation in our studies as work, which does not change the fact that we intend to ask random people to devote time that they could spend the other way (e.g. on work or with family), which is a cost for them (maybe not always monetary, but certainly economic). To balance this cost, we can choose different forms of remuneration for taking part in the study, which come down to two basic types of incentives.

10.4.1 MONETARY INCENTIVES

Incentives such as money, vouchers, and gift cards can be used by participants to meet their various needs, which can encourage a wide group of people to participate in our study. They can help encourage people who would not otherwise take part in the study (e.g. because they are working at the time). Of course, the basic blocker to using monetary incentives may be the budget, but also administrative and legal challenges (e.g. in some countries it may be necessary to sign additional contracts and later settle them with the tax office). Another important issue is that incentives of this type can potentially skew the results and lead to obtaining lower quality insights (e.g. too high incentives compared to the time spent may encourage potential participants to cheat in application surveys or put pressure on them during the study).

10.4.2 NON-MONETARY INCENTIVES

In most cases, incentives such as merch, copies of games, thank-yous in game credits, or even a studio transfer of money to a charity, most of the time will pose a smaller budgetary, administrative, or legal challenge for us. Properly selected incentives can encourage participants more thoughtfully, and in some cases, to analyze the game more carefully (e.g. expansions, DLCs, or battle passes for the playtested game), providing us with better quality results. However, they are naturally attractive to a narrower group of potential participants, because they don't provide flexibility in meeting needs. The perceived value of non-monetary incentives can significantly differ between participants, which also affects their motivation to participate in the study.

Both monetary and non-monetary incentives can be effective in motivating potential participants, but we have to consider who we want to recruit. If we are looking for participants who actually use a specific platform (e.g. Steam), it's easier to discourage those who don't by offering a voucher to be redeemed on that platform. On the other hand, if we are looking for experts or people who may have a mixed attitude towards our game (e.g. players who bought the first part of the game, but are unhappy about what they hear about the sequel), then hard cash may be the thing that will encourage them to participate in our study. Finally, let's remember to give participants the option to withdraw from the study at any time, even after it has started. We can encounter various approaches to answering the question "What about remuneration if a participant shows up, but doesn't complete the study?". The answers range from no remuneration (treating it the same as if they did not come), through partial to full remuneration, regardless of the degree of completeness. Regardless of what we adopt, we transparently communicate this to participants before they start the study. In my practice, for most of the time, I fully remunerated participants for shorter studies (e.g. concept test, usability playtest) regardless of the level of completeness (it was enough for the participant to show up). For longer studies (e.g. extended playtests, diary studies), I used tiered remuneration. For example, in a diary study, participants received a small part of the remuneration for completing subsequent weeks of the study, and a separate remuneration for the post-test interview, which was conducted at the very end of the study or at the moment when the participant reported that they didn't want to continue playing (to capture the reasons for abandoning the game).

Now that we have determined who, how, and where we want to recruit, and what we will offer in return, all that is left for us is to publish an announcement about our study (or general recruitment form for studies conducted in our studio) and monitor the response.

10.5   HOW MANY PARTICIPANTS ARE NEEDED FOR A STUDY?

In the context of small organizational settings, we are more sensible to ensuring that our research is cost-effective and feasible within given constraints. Generally, we aim for a short research turnaround time to keep up with the pace of the team and deliver insights when they're most needed to inform decision-making and mitigate risks, while having a keen eye on the budget. Therefore, in this book, we focus on methods typically conducted on small samples (i.e. number of participants) to dive deep into the "what" and "why" of their experience. For most methods we have on the menu, we will often need 5–15 participants to reach results saturation [Nielsen and Landauer 1993] (i.e. to get to the point where an additional participant doesn't provide us with new information). To keep things simple, each recipe listed in Part 3 includes a suggested number of participants to balance the cost required with the value gained. **Essentially, we're more focused on finding holes in player experience and less on seeing how many players fall into them**.

We need to remember, though, that our target audience most of the time will not be a homogeneous monolith, but rather a diverse set of players. We have to keep our eyes open for the existence of potential subgroups or segments (e.g. narrative-focused players vs. gameplay-focused players) that have specific needs and requirements that may affect their perception of the game and their purchase decision. In identifying these groups, in addition to our own efforts (e.g. competitor analysis, concept testing), conversations and joint analyses with people involved in marketing in our studio can be very helpful. However, the more such groups we find, the larger the number of participants we should invite to the study (e.g. if we have identified two player segments, it will be good to about double the sample size to cover them in one study).

We also have to decide how we select people for a specific study from our participant pool. Most of the time, we will want to invite a group of participants who meet our basic criteria (e.g. reference and competitor games played), but are diverse on other relevant dimensions (e.g. genre preferences, sex, age, interests, education) to include a variety of perspectives. After all, if it turns out that people with diverse backgrounds and experiences have similar ups and downs with our game, then there must be something to it. However, sometimes, based on the study purpose, we may want to explore only selected segments or subgroups to pinpoint their specific pains and needs. On such occasions, we will narrow our group to participants similar on selected dimensions (e.g. for instance, we will recruit only participants experiencing specific barriers while playing).

Finally, we need to acknowledge that in a single study, we have little information on "how much" something we will find is an issue, and most of the time, we can't generalize our results to the broader player population. Later in the production cycle, we can turn to analytics to fill in this gap. But earlier in the production cycle, we can address this in part by evaluating player experience across multiple methods and occasions (remember that we want to provide our team with a well-balanced diet). Typically, when we see the same issue appearing across multiple studies, we can safely assume that it's the issue that needs to be fixed. **As a rule of thumb, it's better to conduct ten studies with eight participants each throughout the production cycle than to conduct one study with 80 participants at a single point**.

10.6   WHEN AND HOW TO INVITE PARTICIPANTS?

While our participant pool is filling up, we can start sending invites to our study to people selected from it (or even randomly selected, if there are enough potential participants in our pool who meet the criteria). In reality, we will rarely start sending invites after all the pots, utensils, and kitchen space are ready. After all, recruitment, like any process, will take time, and we want to lose as little time as possible between completing the preparations for the study and conducting the sessions. As we mentioned, many elements of the preparations will happen in parallel, so our task is to monitor with the team, if the dates we agreed on for delivering assets are at risk of delay, and adapt our approach accordingly.

When it comes to timing, we don't want to send invites out too early nor too late. If we send them too early (e.g. a month before the session), people may lose interest or their plans may change in the meantime, and if we send out the invites too late (e.g. a day before a study) more of the potential participants may already have plans set and will be more reluctant to rearrange them. As a rule of thumb, if we're giving short notice, it's better to do it over the phone (or via chats, e.g. if we recruited participants via the studio's Discord server) to complete the whole process and schedule participants in one conversation. The obvious downside is that we have to gather some additional information beforehand (e.g. participant's phone number), then invite them one at a time, and do it at times of day when someone is likely to answer the phone. So if we have more time, we can email many participants at once, but we have to guide them step by step. We will focus now on inviting participants via email, to have a better feel of the various steps in the process.

10.6.1   SCREENING POTENTIAL PARTICIPANTS

Depending on the recruitment method and criteria we have chosen, we may want to send the invitation immediately (e.g. if we have already verified that the potential participant meets the criteria based on their answers in the recruitment form) or conduct a so-called screener (a brief set of questions that we ask to check if the person meets our criteria) before actually inviting someone to the study (e.g. if we have chosen to recruit participants via mailing list sign-up, then collecting additional information may be necessary). The screener can be shared as a short survey via email or conducted verbally by phone.

10.6.2   SENDING INVITE TO SELECTED PARTICIPANTS

If a participant doesn't meet our criteria, we thank them for their interest and inform them that we may contact them for future studies. If they do meet our criteria, we can send them the study invite in which includes information such as:

- What is the study about in simple language?
- What commitment is required to participate in the research session (e.g. estimated duration, remote vs. on-site)?
- What are we offering in return (i.e. incentive amount and form)?
- How can a person confirm participation?

When we agree on specific dates, and depending on our studio policy, we may need to send the potential participant an NDA, which should be signed before the session begins. While this is common practice in remote studies, in on-site studies, some researchers prefer to sign the NDA immediately before the session, when the participant arrives at the studio. Once we decide on how the NDA will be processed, we can send the participant a confirmation email that includes:

- Agreed date and time (with time zones for international studies).
- Information about the location, i.e. a link to the video call or the studio address with information on how to get there (e.g. a map).
- How to prepare for the study (e.g. devices needed, internet connection).
- Information to contact us (with contact details) in case the participant is late for the session or if they experience any technical issues.

10.6.3 SENDING REMINDERS AND OVER-RECRUITING PARTICIPANTS

We can say that now all we have to do is wait for the participant to arrive, but it's good practice to send reminders before the research session (we can even ask for the confirmation or cancellation of the session on agreed date) to reduce the likelihood that someone will forget about the session and not show up, thus creating a gap in our calendar. Reminders can be sent about 24 hours before the session with a recap of the key information (e.g. date and time, place, and request to contact us if the participant is about to be late or needs to cancel the session). Moreover, we should not just count that all participants we selected will show up and that all sessions will run smoothly. **To save ourselves potential stress, we usually invite 10%–20% more participants than we plan to have, to be more certain that at the end we will collect the desired number of observations**.

10.6.4 INVITING OBSERVERS

When inviting participants, we shouldn't forget about communicating with our stakeholders. Especially since we have a session schedule section in the research protocol, where we let them know when the sessions will be held. We want to encourage the team to see for themselves what the reactions and experiences of potential players are. When it comes to the presence of observers during the session, on the one hand, we don't want to overwhelm the participants with too many people watching their actions, and on the other hand, we want as many people from the team as possible to be able to observe the research session. We also mentioned that observers may want to ask additional questions, and they can be an irreplaceable help when something in the game doesn't work as it should. One solution is to stream the session so everyone in the studio can access it, and then encourage team members to share their observations and questions in a chat we created for the session. The loose format (observers drop in and out of the stream as it suits them) may not be the best choice in times of high workloads and can end up with team members losing context by only observing certain parts of the session. Certainly, our role will be to fill in that context and clarify nuances of what happened after the session, but we may find that an alternative approach works better for some teams. In some of the studios I have worked with, stakeholders or people on their teams were encouraged to reserve observer slots (which were usually limited) for specific research sessions, and the time spent on observing was taken into account when dividing workload among the team. While fewer people had the opportunity to observe the live sessions, more had a more complete experience of the sessions and a deeper understanding of the context in which certain issues or strengths of the game were revealed. To sum up, the approach we take depends largely on the organizational setting in which we operate, as well as the willingness (or possibilities) of the team to engage in observing sessions.

As the date of our first research session is fast approaching, all that remains is to check everything one last time and wait.

10.7   CHAPTER SUMMARY

As the main ingredients of our dish will be the players' behaviours, thoughts, and feelings, we have to do some search for the essentials. When preparing to recruit participants, we need to define:

- Who to recruit? (based on criteria such as familiarity with reference and competitor games, genre preferences, hardware platforms owned and/or used).
- How to recruit participants? (through email or community sign-up, mailing list sign-up, or recruitment form).
- Where to look for participants? (friends and family, events, studio-owned communication channels, community forums or servers, and/or relying on recruitment agencies).
- What do we offer participants in return? (monetary or non-monetary remuneration).
- How many participants are needed for a study?
- When and how to invite participants to the research sessions?

In the whole process, we don't forget about inviting team members to observe the sessions.

REFERENCES

Nielsen, J., & Landauer, T. K. (1993). A mathematical model of the finding of usability problems. In *Proceedings of the INTERACT'93 and CHI'93 Conference on Human Factors in Computing Systems* (pp. 206–213).

Sobczyk, B., Dobrowolski, P., Skorko, M., et al. (2015). Issues and advances in research methods on video games and cognitive abilities. *Frontiers in Psychology, 6:1451*.

11 Slicing and Dicing
Moderating Research Sessions

The big day has finally arrived. When participants arrive (whether on-site or remote), it is worth remembering that participating in a research session is not an everyday and natural event in their lives, so there is no need to add to their potential stress. It is worth welcoming them and talking to them for a while before the session begins. If we are conducting research on-site, we take care of the basics, such as something to drink and indicating where the participant can leave their belongings, as well as where the toilet is. Although we have prepared a moderator guide that organizes the course of the research session, it is like a script for an actor – it still needs to be acted out. So, let's look at what is worth paying attention to when taking on the role of the person conducting the session.

In terms of tone and manner of running the research session, we strive to maintain a certain standardization (i.e. that every participant receives the same information in the same way – this is supported by the moderator guide) and neutrality so we don't bias the results ourselves. When we think of "being neutral", it doesn't mean being unapproachable, withdrawn, and cold in contact. We simply shouldn't impose our views and opinions on the participants, whether about the game or in general. **Although we want to obtain specific information, the tone of our meeting should resemble a conversation, not an interrogation**. As in any conversation, we may make a mistake or touch on a sensitive topic. There is no reason to feel guilty about that, but to make participants feel comfortable and give them the option not to answer some of the questions (e.g. "I'll ask some questions during the session. If you don't feel comfortable answering a specific question, just let me know by saying, 'I don't want to answer that question,' and I won't bother you about it, and we'll move on"). At the same time, however, let's maintain our own boundaries. If participants ask us about sensitive information or something that could affect the course of the session, we don't have to be evasive, but let them know clearly that we won't answer that question (e.g. participant: "When will this game be available?"; researcher: "Sorry, but I can't answer this question"). At the same time, the language we use should be adapted to the participants, as after all, they have to understand the meaning of the instructions and the questions asked. However, it's not the best idea to resemble the participants in terms of intonation, slang, or elements of dialect – let's remain ourselves in this matter. We may start to wonder how active we should be during the research session. In general, apart from giving instructions and asking questions, the participants do most of the talking. Our role is to steer the session to obtain important information, observe and listen to the participants, keep them motivated, and help them verbalize any issues they encounter.

11.1 OBSERVING WITHOUT INTERPRETATION

During the research session, we will have the opportunity to observe the actions of our participants. However, we have to be patient and not immediately make assumptions or draw conclusions about what we see. First, we want to see behaviours without interpreting them through the prism of our own knowledge, experience, or prejudices. Therefore, we **focus on what is happening at the moment and note the actions, words, and behaviours of the participants without jumping to conclusions and explanations**. The idea is to avoid potential biases such as confirmation bias (i.e. preferring an interpretation of events that confirms our previous expectations, regardless of whether it is true) or projecting our own experiences onto the participants. By refraining from quick interpretations, we give ourselves more time to analyze what we see during the session, which helps

DOI: 10.1201/9781003501909-13

BOX 11.1   EXERCISE: DO PIGEONS LIKE TO DANCE?

Observing players' behaviour without interpretation is a skill that helps us achieve unbiased results. And like any other skill, it requires training, which is quite specific, because we have to learn to spot specific things in our own thinking. And there can be a lot to spot, e.g. the basic attribution error (i.e. the natural tendency to attribute a person's behaviour to their characteristics, not environmental factors), confirmation bias (e.g. when we focus mainly on events that confirm our assumptions) or availability biases (e.g. focusing mainly on explanations of players' behaviour that we already know from experience) among many others. These types of biases can have serious consequences for us, from missing important observations to leading and maintaining false beliefs in the team that can cost us not only the confidence in our work, but also reduce the chances of the game's success. The mere awareness that there are different biases we are prone to is helpful, but to develop the skill of "thinking about our own thinking", we will need a little practice, so I invite you to do an exercise.

In your immediate environment, find an animal (e.g. pigeon at a bus stop, a bird sitting in a meadow, or a cat in the yard) and observe it for a few minutes. When observing, your goal is to simply note what the animal does (e.g. how they move or how they interact with the environment). It can be tempting to automatically attribute different thoughts, emotions, and intentions behind those observed actions, and this is what we want to capture and unlearn, so try to refrain from putting labels or guessing (e.g. animal wanted to…; it was smart/stupid/intentional/…). In this exercise, avoid observing loved ones or your own pets, because you can have many more assumptions or preconceived narratives at play, which may be hard to spot.

to make the conclusions drawn more accurate. To share an example that illustrates this approach, I will refer to the study that forms the background for this Part of this book. In *Yupitergrad 2*, the player character has a weapon in each hand. Players control each of these weapons separately (left – with the left controller; right – with the right controller). During the sessions for component playtest focused on combat, we observed that "some participants behaved chaotically during encounters with several opponents and had difficulty winning with them". The first interpretation that came to our mind was "the fight becomes too difficult as soon as several opponents appear", which could lead to the conclusion that the behaviour and statistics of opponents need to be further explored and worked on. However, after a closer look at the actions performed by the participants, it turned out that the problem occurred for those of them who held the same weapon in both hands, which resulted in two identical crosshairs being displayed on the screen. Players simply couldn't clearly tell which crosshair was assigned to which hand, and the difficulty became apparent when more elements (i.e. opponents) were competing for their attention, resulting in behaviour that looked "chaotic" from the outside. To sum up, during the session, it's important for us to first focus on the observation, allowing patterns to emerge, and only then interpret and look for causes of the observed behaviour.

11.2   ASKING QUESTIONS AND LISTENING TO ANSWERS

We stated that a session should resemble a conversation, not an interrogation. Therefore, when conducting a moderated session or an interview, we don't bombard the participants with a barrage of questions. Our goal is to understand what the participants wanted to tell us. In order to do this, we give them time and space that will allow them to collect their thoughts and feelings, and then give the fullest possible answer. **We ask one question at a time, and only move on to the next one when we are sure that we have actually understood the participants**. In this context, we have to note that a participant being silent for a few seconds after a question is not necessarily a bad thing.

In some situations, participants may just need a bit more time to express themselves. We don't disrupt these brief moments of silence, and only repeat the question if we notice that the participant didn't hear us or if we feel they haven't fully understood what we meant. Another part of the story is that we don't ask questions merely to stick to a predetermined order or plan – like a koala clinging to a tree (for a charming and instructive story, see Bright & Field 2017). We remain open and adapt to what is happening during the session. For instance, if we notice unusual behaviour or if we believe that participants are struggling with something (e.g. not following the intended order or method for overcoming a challenge for an extended period), we might ask, "What are you trying to do?" to help uncover the source of the issue.

Naturally, our role is not only to ask, but also to listen to our participants' answers and comments, and not just to listen in any way, but to listen actively. Actively means that we observe and listen attentively to what participants have to say, while letting them know that they are not only heard but also understood. This helps us build rapport (i.e. a good relationship with the participant), which gives us a better chance that participants will share their actual thoughts on the experience, whether they are positive or negative. We can express that we are actively listening in many ways, such as by simply nodding our heads or saying "Uh-huh...", "Okay...", or using verbal affirmations such as "I see" or "That's interesting". But there is more to it than just nodding. Ultimately, we want to gather information from our participants that will help us realize the study purpose. Let's look at some other active listening techniques that we can use to help our participants verbalize their thoughts and feelings.

11.2.1 PARAPHRASING

We repeat what the participant said, but in our own words. Paraphrasing is particularly useful when we're unsure whether we've fully understood what the participant wanted to convey. Even if our paraphrase isn't fully correct, it reassures participants that we are listening and opens the chance for them to clarify or elaborate on their thoughts (e.g. Participant: "I'm not sure if this is the right approach to solve it", Researcher: "So, you're uncertain about whether this is the correct approach?", Participant: "Yeah, I just don't know what these signs mean").

11.2.2 CLARIFYING

When we want to ensure that we gathered clear and complete picture of the participants thoughts or feelings, we can ask follow-up questions or ask them to elaborate more, especially when the participant's statements are vague or judgmental (e.g. Participant: "Something is wrong here", Researcher: "Can you explain what exactly feels wrong to you?" or Participant: "That was good", Researcher: "When you say it was good, could you explain what specifically stood out?").

11.2.3 SUMMARIZING

When we want to bring some structure to our conversation or confirm our own understanding of what was said, we can provide participants with a concise summary of the key points of their statements or what happened in the session. Apart from checking our own understanding and bringing some structure to the session, summarizing gives participants the opportunity to further explore themes or ideas important to them (e.g. Researcher: "So, what you're saying is that the navigation was easy to follow, but you felt the colour scheme was distracting. Is that right?").

11.2.4 REFLECTING

When we want to provide participants with some space to express their thoughts in a more elaborated way, we can try to reflect some of their statements back. We can do so-called "echoing" (i.e. repeating exactly what the participant just said), ask questions using parts of the participant's statement we want to understand better (e.g. Participant: "I felt confused about the options", Researcher: "You felt confused?", Participant: "Uh… I just don't know if the aim assist is on or off"). We also use reflection when participants ask us questions while interacting with the game, instead of giving them instantaneous answers (e.g. Participant: "I don't know what to do", Researcher: "What do you think you should do?").

BOX 11.2   TYPICAL NUTS TO CRACK DURING THE SESSION

In research, as in life, things don't always go as planned. While the people we invite usually take on the role of participants, and we support them in that role by giving instructions, they won't always behave according to the instructions given or fully concentrate on answering questions. Such behaviours can understandably make us feel tense. After all, as researchers, in our role, we may expect to be in control of the session, and it's natural to feel a little bit anxious when we perceive that this control is slipping away. Even if we feel a bit of a twinge when our participants aren't behaving as we expect them to, it's good to remember that they are only humans in an unusual situation. Although there are no wrong emotions, instead of focusing on our internal state or scolding participants, we can treat our emotions as a signal to take corrective action. And we have some means of action in this regard:

- When participants talk too much… – Sometimes participants may get off topic or provide more detail than necessary. Of course, most of us do this from time to time and there's nothing wrong with that, but if it happens too often, it's worth taking action, because the session has a limited time and defined goals. It's worth catching the moment of pause in the participant's speech and bringing them back on track by summarizing their statements and asking a follow-up question to narrow the scope (e.g. "That's interesting, but let's talk about <specific topic> for now. Could you tell me…"). We can also ask more closed questions or use less verbal affirmations to invite more brief answers.
- When participants talk too little… – At the other end of the spectrum, participants' answers and comments during think-aloud or an interview may be too scant to be useful for our purposes. Certainly, in such situations, we want to encourage them to say more. To do this, we can rely on using clarification or reflection, or ask open-ended questions such as "Can you tell me more about this?" more frequently to encourage them to elaborate. Another reason why participants will not talk much may be simply that the question is too difficult or broad. If we suspect this is the case, it is worth using an inverted funnel in asking questions (i.e. starting with more specific questions and working towards more general ones based on the answers). Certainly, there may be even more prosaic reasons for not talking too much, such as the participant having a dry throat or the fact that a participant's current activity is cognitively or emotionally demanding.
- When participants talk for others… – Sometimes it may happen that participants start telling us about how something will be received by other people (e.g. "I think other players may have difficulty with this"), this is the so-called projection (i.e. a mechanism in which someone attributes their thoughts or feelings to other people). It may sound interesting, but we are interested in the individual experience of the participants we have in front of us, so we redirect the conversation back to their own experiences (e.g. "I would like to know, how was it for you?").

- When participants want to do something else... – If participants want to engage in something else than what we asked them to (e.g. instead of focusing on the task, they want to freely explore the game), we can acknowledge that and refocus them on the question or task at hand. For example, "I can see you're interested in what's out there. For now, let's focus on our task, and if we have time later, you can explore that". Controlling the flow of the session while giving participants a sense of flexibility can help them stay engaged.
- When participants get distracted... – Although we planned session length to not exhaust our participants, some of them can get tired anyway or get distracted (e.g. by a door bell with unexpected delivery during remote session), so it may be good to offer them a short break to not torment them, "How about we take a short break before continuing?". After a break, we could provide a summary of what we discussed or have done so far and continue the session from there.

However, if we see that most of our participants don't follow some of the instructions or struggle with specific questions, this may suggest that something went wrong on our end. It's worth taking a closer look at these issues and considering what might be the cause (e.g. complicated instruction or confusing question), and then making the necessary corrections. All in all, we don't want to punish our participants for not following the plan, but to make them at ease, while gathering the information necessary to realize the study purpose.

11.3 TAKING NOTES

Running a session can be quite an energy-consuming task. After all, we observe what our participants are doing, listen to them, and engage in conversation, while also paying attention to what is happening in the game and whether everything is working as it should. Some say that conducting sessions requires three sets of eyes – one to focus on the participant and their actions, another to follow what is happening with and in the game, and a third to document the whole thing. When it comes to documenting the session, we could come to a conclusion that if we record it, why bother more? Essentially, while recording objectively captures the session, it doesn't replace the value of note-taking, which helps us to:

- Capture the Moment - Being in the moment can be different from how we remember it. When we take notes during a session, it encourages us to actively filter information and focus on the most important observations, patterns, or emotions. On the other hand, our memories are not perfect, so notes can be helpful not only to go back to certain moments during the session, but also when we forgot to hit the record button or experienced technical issues during the session.
- Reflect While Doing - Taking notes forces us to actively analyze what's happening. Writing down various thoughts or questions that pop up in our minds can be useful both during the rest of the session or when analyzing the results later. After all, a recording doesn't capture things that happen in our heads.
- Analyze More Efficiently - While taking notes, we want to capture moments that are somehow meaningful (e.g. when a participant is struggling, shows emotion, or says something important to the study purpose). After the session, it will be easier to find those moments in the recording without having to watch the whole thing again. In this sense, notes supplement the recording by informing our actions during the analysis.

Although note-taking during the session helps us stay focused, reflect, and aid our analytical efforts later, we have to remember that our own attention is also a limited resource. Certainly, we want to take detailed notes, but we have to strike a balance between jotting things down and staying engaged with the participants. So, let's look at some hints to make effective notes during the session:

- Timestamps – marking at what point in the session we note observations, e.g. in the hh:mm format. This makes it easier to later find the moment of interest on the recording.
- Key observations – in principle, we do not want to note everything to duplicate what we will have on the session recordings. We only want to capture key events during the session (e.g. when the participant experiences difficulties or emotions), which will make it easier to review the recordings during later analysis.
- Direct quotes – we can very accurately capture the experience of participants during observation, but nothing speaks to the imagination of the team like seeing the experience through the eyes of the participants. It is worth noting the statements of participants that directly refer to or sum up their difficulties, pains, but also positive experiences.
- Abbreviations – to note more efficiently, we can use acronyms or tags for typical things that we can expect during the session. We can of course develop a certain extended language for our purposes, e.g. we can use the first letters of various words to note types of observed issues E, U, and A (standing for Experience, Usability, Accessibility) or emotions Su, Ha, An, Sa, Fe, and Dg (standing for Surprise, Happiness, Anger, Sadness, Fear, Disgust). Regardless of what acronyms we come up with, the most important thing is that we use them consistently at least within one study, so as not to make later analysis more complicated than it would be without them.
- Comments – it is also worth noting what comes to our own minds during the session (e.g. questions, ideas). Noting our own thoughts can give us inspiration to ask the participant additional questions during the session or support later analysis, but it's also a way to capture potential biases of our own.

To take notes, we can use a simple notepad (paper or digital one), a spreadsheet, or we can use our moderator guide. I usually use a spreadsheet or create a separate copy of the moderator guide for each participant, where I write down my observations under the appropriate section (i.e. I write down what the participant does or says under a specific task or interview question). However, this is not the only way to take effective notes. Especially in more structured studies (e.g. usability (play)test), mind maps can be a very good alternative (for a guide on how to take notes using this technique, see Bromley 2020).

11.4   MANAGING TIME

In addition to observing, asking questions, listening to answers, and taking notes, it's worth checking our watch. After all, the session has a specific time that we have agreed with the participants, so it would be nice not to overdo their courtesy. If we notice that some part of the session deviates too much from the time we have assumed in the research protocol, we can do a few things apart from asking participants to spend 10 minutes more with us or allocating more time for subsequent sessions. We can modify the format of the questions we ask, e.g. using closed questions more often and focusing on exploring only the most important topics for the study. In studies that include some interaction with the game or its elements, if we have already obtained answers to our research questions during observation (especially supported by the participants' comments spoken aloud), we can shorten, or in the worst case, skip less important parts of the session, such as the post-test interview. Here, we stick to the assumption that the observed behaviour has greater value for us than the declaration. Of course, it may happen that the participant will perform the prepared tasks much longer than we expected and we won't stand a chance to guide them through all the tasks that we have planned for a given session. In such situations, it is worth not interrupting the participant abruptly, but letting them finish at least the current task and then moving on to the next parts of the study.

11.5   MANAGING OBSERVERS

Yes, of course, we invited some observers to participate in the session. Team participation in the session is invaluable because it gives them the opportunity to see how someone from the outside reacts and engages in the thing they are creating. Additionally, in situations where some elements don't work as they should (e.g. a participant has encountered a bug that prevents them from performing an action in the game), observers will often be the first to notice it and let us know about it. During the session, we can ask them directly for help in such situations, while letting the participants know that there has been a technical issue that is not their fault (e.g. "I see that we stepped on a bug. <name of the observer> could you tell us how we should proceed now?"). Another thing is that observers are an extra set of eyes watching the participants' actions, and we've encouraged them to share their questions. So, during the session, it's worth checking the study channel we've set up for them to catch any questions that come up there – after all, it's the team's questions that we're supposed to answer. At the same time, let's remember that we control the flow of the session, so the time and form in which we ask these questions depend on us. Finally, right after the session, when we've said goodbye to our participants, it's worth staying for a few minutes to discuss with the observers their impressions and observations about what happened during the session, so as to capture what we may have missed.

Between sessions, it's important to keep our stakeholders updated on progress via our communication channel. We also remember to send reminders to observers about upcoming sessions. Transparent communication will also be crucial, in situations where a session has had to be postponed or even cancelled (e.g. due to a participant not showing up), as it may impact agreed key dates. We also want to inform the team when everything is going according to the plan (e.g. "Today we conducted 5th of the 7 sessions scheduled for this week"). After all sessions have concluded, we mention when and how we plan to share the first results with stakeholders (e.g. "Today we completed the last session scheduled for this study. You can expect the Top Findings by the end of the day tomorrow at the latest").

We may get a headache from the number of things that we need to pay attention to during a research session. That is why it's worth taking care of ourselves, planning enough long breaks between sessions, taking care of meals, and proper hydration. It may seem obvious, but it's easy to forget about it when preparing for research. Another thing is that, especially at the beginning of our research endeavours, we primarily focus on the key aspects of conducting the session, giving ourselves room for mistakes and gradually expanding competencies. As Alan Watts once said about learning to play the piano, "Don't be afraid to play a wrong note, just keep the right rhythm". In this context, the most important thing is to build rapport with the participants and obtain the required information from them, and practicing asking questions and active listening will help us in this. We can fill in most of the gaps in the notes and observations by reviewing the recordings. We will simply have to spend a little more time analyzing the results.

11.6   CHAPTER SUMMARY

With everything prepared, we move on to slicing and dicing. While moderating the research sessions, we remember that this is not an interrogation, but a conversation with another person. We support participants in verbalizing their thoughts by actively listening (we rely on techniques from simple nodding, through verbal affirmations, to paraphrasing, clarification, summarizing, and reflecting). We also remember that a research session is a rather unusual situation in the participant's life, so we don't get anxious when something doesn't go according to plan (i.e. when participants talk too much/talk too little/get distracted/want to do something else). Instead, we support our participants in providing us with the information needed to fulfil the study purpose. During the session, we take structured notes that can be used in later analysis, and remember to manage the session time and the observers we invited.

REFERENCES

Bright, R., & Field, J. (2017). *The Koala Who Could*. Hachette Children's Group.

Bromley, S. (2020). *MindMaps: Get In front of game design decisions* [YouTube video]. Games User Research SIG Virtual Summer Camp 2020. https://www.youtube.com/watch?v=sR-09PA_jZM

12 Cooking Time!
Analyzing Results

Every cook has their own preferences, habits, and "secret sauces". Ultimately, depending on what we do with the ingredients we have collected, we will obtain different flavours and aromas. However, it's not just about showing off finesse; after all, we have a specific order and a designated time to prepare it.

12.1 FINDING AN(D) INSIGHT

Analyzing results, from the perspective of our goal, is the process of actively processing data about the players' experience, "as is" needed to make decisions that bring us closer to the players' experience "to be". A properly conducted analysis is based both on the player experience we observed and the information we have on the game (e.g. its creative vision), tailored to the specific context (e.g. business or technical constraints). The effect of our analysis is conclusions derived from the data in the form of insights. Insights are like single bites of the dish we are about to prepare. **In order for something to be called an insight, during the analysis, we aim to capture answers to specific questions:**

- **What is happening? (descriptive function)** – While observing sessions and analyzing the collected data, we aim to describe what we're seeing and identify emerging patterns.
- **Is this good or bad? (evaluative function)** – We want to assess the consequences of what we have observed and described. In other words, we want to know whether it supports or hinders the player experience.
- **Why is this happening? (explanatory function)** – We want to figure out the reasons behind the pattern we observed, relying on what we captured during the session (e.g. participants' behaviours and comments) and general knowledge (e.g. theories, models, or guidelines).
- **What could we do about it? (corrective function)** – Based on what we described, we then move on to identifying possible improvements or other ways to address the issue and improve player experience.
- **What will happen if we do nothing? (predictive function)** – Lastly, we want to figure out if the issue stays as it is, how this might affect the player experience in the long run (e.g. will it lead to frustration, confusion, or issues with other game elements).

The features of an insight described above can be treated rather as a model, which is worth striving for. In reality, in which we are subject to limitations resulting from the methods used or the time and resources we have, we will not always provide a corrective and predictive function (e.g. writing a recommendation that will be useful for the team may require additional time and effort, and the report usually must be delivered on a specific date). Let us have a look at the sample insights below (Figures 12.1 and 12.2).

Certainly, not all things that we cook up during the analysis will take the form of a full-blown insight. **We may have some observations that may be of interest to the team, but if we can only describe what is happening – it's called finding.** In this book, we use the clear distinction between findings and insights, and after describing them, we can assume that every insight is also a finding, but not every finding is an insight. Findings can be a good supplement to the report (e.g. showing

DOI: 10.1201/9781003501909-14

SELECTING EQUIPMENT

CRITICAL

(2.3) When adjusting the rope length, participants mistakenly changed equipment as both features rely on interaction with thumb stick: Participants accidentally changed equipment while trying to adjust rope length during movement, which left them confused, as both functions were mapped on thumb stick (i.e. adjusting rope length mapped on moving thumb stick up-down; changing equipment mapped on thumb stick press). The issue was persistent, even though some participants were fully aware that their problem stems from control mapping.

Fragments of session recordings:
- „I kind off switched away my gun by accident" P01, 1:09:20-1:10:05
- „Ahhhh... my weapon wasn't ready" P02, 38:45-39:15

P04 about selection wheel: *So that it does not involve pressing the stick, but rather one of the keys on the controller.*

P03: *I personally don't like this solution, because I personally think that whether on a console or on Quest games, pressing and then holding down to select something isn't very reliable. [...] Just like on a console, where you have to press something under this button and then select or do something else in between, I'm not a fan of that. [...] It seems to me that in dynamic games it's not very reliable, as if pressing this button when you're excited could be accidentally pressed [...]*

14/60

FIGURE 12.1 Sample insight in the form of an issue. (Courtesy of Gamedust.)

EQUIPMENT PRESENTATION

STRENGTH

(2.6) The way the equipment was presented in the game was very positively received by participants: Participants emphasized that the equipment complements the rest of the game's visuals and (in the case of the Minigun and Nozzles) clearly presents its function. The equipment swap animation was also perceived as highly satisfying. It's also worth noting that the way equipment is presented in the game environment (before being acquired by the player) was similarly perceived as highly satisfying.

P01: *That's pretty nice with the stuff coming out, so you can totally... you totally understand what you are doing. If the nozzles were on the backpack you wouldn't know, you can control it sideways. That's a pretty neat feature.*

P01: *It looks red, it looks pretty cool. And it have a nice crosshair now. Yeah, that's cool.*

P02: *I like the way it looks like it's cartoonish, it's slightly goofy, but it matches the design of the thing, so you have this plunger with the machingun attached – so yeah, I like it, it looks great.*

P04: *It looks pretty impressive, that gatling gun.*

17/60

FIGURE 12.2 Sample insight in the form of a strength. (Courtesy of Gamedust.)

some potential questions for studies in the future). However, they act more like a garnish, not the dish itself, so we do not rely on them alone.

In order for the dish we are creating not to be bland or, even worse, not to harm our guests, while combining insights, we should aim to be precise, accurate, objective, and adequate.

12.1.1 BEING PRECISE

We want to be specific to help the team take the necessary action, avoiding generalizations or leaving room for vague interpretations (e.g. Instead of writing "Participants struggled with the settings menu", we try to point out exactly what they struggled with and how "Participants couldn't see the 'Save and Exit' button due to its low contrast"). When it comes to being precise, we also want our insight to be:

- Exhaustive, but not exhausting – This may sound paradoxical at first, but we aim for clear and simple explanations which at the same time contain the necessary details and nuances so that the team can fully understand what is happening and what options they have for action without the need to do an academic degree. At the same time, we are mindful of avoiding jargon resulting from our specific knowledge and experience, which may be unfamiliar to the team (e.g. "Lack of feedback frustrates participant's need for competence").
- Not limited to classification – The mere fact that we observed an obvious violation of the rules we know (e.g. lack of information about the number of coins violates Nielsen's heuristic on visibility of system status) doesn't guarantee that the team will be able or willing to take action on this basis. We aim to provide information that is meaningful to the team in the context of the game being created.

12.1.2 BEING ACCURATE

We want to best reflect what is happening, based on the gathered data (e.g. writing "Participants didn't use weapon 'x' which was available in the inventory" when they didn't have the opportunity to use it, it's not the most accurate statement in this regard).

12.1.3 BEING OBJECTIVE

We want to best reflect the player's perspective, not our own assumptions or preferences (e.g. instead of serving our interpretation "Map was too big and there was nothing meaningful to do", we focus on what actually happened "Participants described finding their way through corridors as 'confusing' and 'frustrating' because the game didn't inform or prompt where to go").

12.1.4 BEING ADEQUATE

When we're writing an insight, we have to take into account the specifics of a given game (including its creative vision) and production context to not provide recommendations on a hit or miss basis (e.g. if players complain about the lack of a quick save in a game that is intended to allow saving only at checkpoints, it requires from us deeper analysis of the root-cause than a suggestion to add quick saves).

Now that we know what the bites of our dish might look like, let's take a look at how we could obtain them.

12.2 ORGANIZING DATA AND SETTING THE MINDSET

Armed with our notes, recordings, and survey data, we can get down to the dirty work. First, we need to review and organize what we have. Just like in cooking shows, we divide everything into appropriate bowls. If our study included tasks, we can put observations from individual participants together with their answers to survey or interview questions for specific tasks in one place. We can also use any other logical division that makes it easier for us to find answers to the questions asked by the team (e.g. Combining data on combat in corridors into one group, while keeping combat in the arenas observations in a separate one). Most often, for this purpose, we will use a spreadsheet, a board with post-its (digital or physical), or simply a piece of paper and a pencil. We write down our observations and participant statements as subsequent lines in the spreadsheet or as subsequent post-its on our board. If we have time, we can prepare data for various analyses by marking the participant ID (e.g. P1), time of occurrence (e.g. using timestamps or steps like "Pre-test, Test: T1, Test: …, Post-test), and the method from which the observation comes (e.g. make a note on a post-it "P1, survey, Post-test" or add separate columns for participant ID, time of occurrence, and method used in a spreadsheet). We put reviewing and organizing data in short sentences, but our data will rarely be perfect, so the work itself may turn out to be tedious and require us, for example, to return to the recordings to clarify what we meant when we wrote "participant didn't manage and fell".

Another thing worth doing before starting the analysis is to answer the question "How will we come up with specific interpretations of the data?". Sounds philosophical at first, but it boils down to the fact of how we will use our existing knowledge and experiences in the analysis. There are two basic approaches in this regard. When we start with existing theories, frameworks, or research questions and use them to guide what we look for in the data, it's called deductive or "top-down" analysis. It's great when we're validating assumptions or measuring specific criteria, or we are just short on time. It ensures we stay focused and align insights with business or design goals. The obvious drawback is that we may easily omit things that don't fit the picture painted by the theory. On the other end, we have inductive or "bottom-up" analysis, where we let patterns emerge from the data itself. We approach the data with minimal assumptions, trying to carefully understand what happened during the sessions. As we go through the data (notes, recordings, etc.), we identify recurring themes, behaviours, or issues. It helps us explore the data more openly and prevents us from narrowing down the analysis too early. However, it can be time-consuming, and the derived conclusions may be much less coherent than those guided by "top-down" analysis. We can probably see that inductive analysis is more often a starting point in the research methods we apply in the early phases of the production cycle, leaving room for deductive analysis later on. However, most of the time we will switch between or blend both approaches. For instance, in the component playtest, we may begin deductively (guided by the study purpose), but at the same time, we stay open to inductive findings that challenge or enrich our understanding. We can also start by exploring the scores participants gave in the surveys, which will later guide us through analyzing observations and specific comments made by participants.

Apart from theoretical considerations, the key is to be aware and intentional when we're applying specific theory, and know when we're letting the data speak for itself. This awareness may help us produce insights that are not only grounded in data but also more nuanced and less biased.

After organizing the data and being honest with ourselves about the approach we want to take, we can move on to the actual analysis. Depending on the study purpose and the methods and tools used, we can start our analysis from various angles, e.g. we could analyze the figures in the surveys first, so they will guide us on analyzing what we observed and what participants said or wrote during the sessions, but we might as well use the figures obtained in the surveys only as a summary of the insights we derived from other data sources. For presentation purposes, we will start with a basic approach to analyzing the survey responses we received for the closed-ended questions. Then, we will spend much more time analyzing what the participants did, said, and wrote (in response to the open-ended survey questions) during the session.

12.3   ANALYZING RESULTS – FINDING WHAT'S IN THE NUMBERS

In the studies involving small numbers of participants we discuss in this book, we will not rely solely on figures we obtained (e.g. the game received a median rating of 80 out of 100 among participants), because taken alone they will not tell us much about what the team should do to improve the game, nor will the single study be large enough to draw more general conclusions (e.g. the overall rating of our game is better than that of competitor titles). However, we can still use some of the basic descriptive statistics and statistical tests to our advantage.

12.3.1   DESCRIPTIVE STATISTICS

At the beginning of the analysis, we will want to explore the numbers a bit to find potential places to investigate further and guide our actions. At the end of the analysis, we can use the data to summarize our observations. For this purpose, some of the metrics used to describe the data will come to our aid, namely:

- Mode – This is the most frequently occurring value in the responses to a question, e.g. in a data set consisting of the values 1, 1, 3, 4, 4, 4, 5, the mode is 4.
- Mean – An average value taken from all the responses to a question, which provides us with an overall tendency among participants, e.g. in a data set consisting of the values 1, 1, 3, 4, 4, 4, 5, the mean is 3.14. However, the mean is easily affected by various data imperfections, which can often be found in small samples such as outliers (values that stand out from others in the data set).
- Median – This is the middle value among the responses to a given question. In other words, it is the value that divides the set in half (i.e. 50% of the results in the set are higher and 50% of the results are lower than the median), e.g. in a data set consisting of the values 1, 1, 3, 4, 4, 4, 5, the median is 4. As a rule, the median is preferred over the mean in small samples because it is less susceptible to various imperfections in the data set.
- Quartiles – This is what we get when we divide the results of our participants in response to some question into four equal parts (i.e. each of them will contain 25% of the results). When describing the results, we use three quartiles:
  - the first (Q1), above which there is 75% of the data.
  - the second (Q2), above which there is 50% of the data (this is a value equal to the median).
  - the third (Q3), above which there is 25% of the results.

From this, we can determine the interquartile range (IQR) between Q1 and Q3, which helps us understand how dispersed our results are (e.g. the larger it is, the greater the variability of the participants' responses or results).

The good news is that these and other descriptive statistics come as built-in functions in widely available spreadsheet tools (e.g. Google Sheets, Microsoft Excel), so they do not require any extra effort from us to use them.

BOX 12.1   BITE OF PRACTICE #8: NOTE ON DATA VISUALIZATION

As we pointed out when discussing the deliverables for the study, if the team requests the data set, we usually end up sharing it. At the same time, our role is to translate the data into conclusions for the team (they didn't come to a restaurant to cook for themselves). Certainly, metrics such as mode, median, or average can tell something about the data we've collected. However, on their own, these metrics can be too abstract for the team or draw their attention to single figures taken out of the context (e.g. the average overall rating of the game), and this may lead to misleading or oversimplified conclusions.

We can prevent it by presenting metrics in the right context for the study purpose. First, we have to know the message we want to convey, as this will help us determine the specific form of data visualization. For instance, if we want to show how the perceived difficulty rating changed between the multiple game levels, the line chart may be a good choice to show potential ups and downs (it's good to show error bars for each game level aggregate rating to better present uncertainty in the data). However, if we want to illustrate how participants'

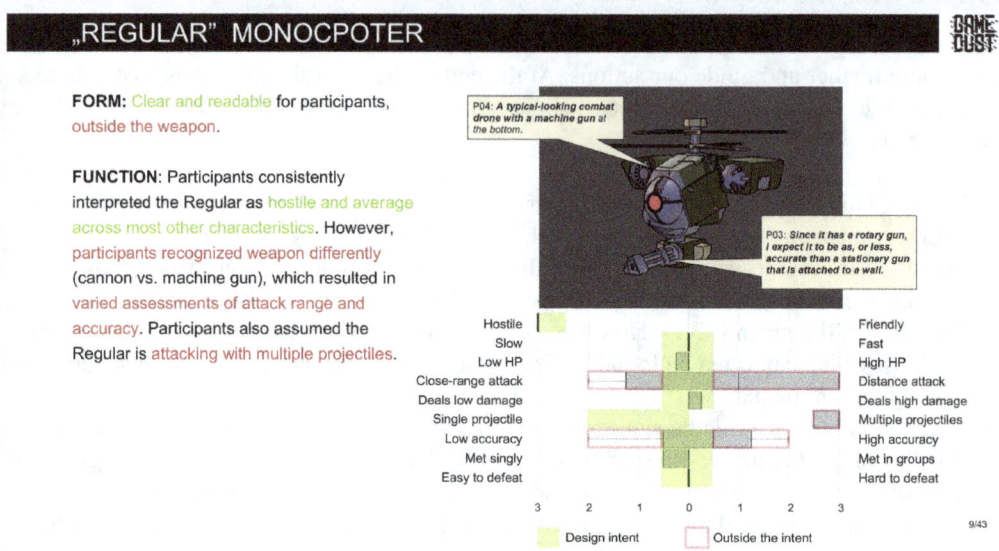

FIGURE 12.3 Report page with insights on recognizing opponent's characteristic from its form, with participants' survey responses visualized in a box plot. (Courtesy of Gamedust.)

difficulty ratings were distributed for a particular game level, a bar chart would be a good choice. And when we want to check whether participants' well-being, measured in the pre-test, affected the difficulty scores in the first level, we can use a scatter plot to explore if there is a potential relationship. Next, we provide context for the data or the "reference value" (i.e. the value against which we are comparing the results) that come from the study at hand, previous ones, or are defined by the team. Generally, we want to paint a picture for the team that shows what's going on to drive a conversation focused on actions and decisions.

As we may remember, in the component playtest on combat in *Yupitergrad 2*, we wanted to assess whether the form of the different types of opponents clearly signalled their characteristics and behaviour. To that end, we prepared survey questions to evaluate them on various dimensions. Given the small sample size, when analyzing results, we relied on values such as median and quartiles, and used box plots to show how the answers among participants varied. To provide context for the participants' answers, we assessed their responses against the ranges provided by the stakeholders (Figure 12.3).

One thing worth noting for us is that giving the data proper context and presenting it in an appropriate form helps shift the team's focus from individual metrics to thinking about the reasons why participants left such and not other ratings, which is crucial for proper reception of the insights we provide.

12.3.2 Statistical Tests

When we need to compare certain outcomes (e.g. which of the proposed character concepts scored better on a particular question) or find patterns, we can use a variety of nonparametric tests. We call them nonparametric because they don't require the data to meet certain parameters (e.g. a bell-shaped distribution), which is often the case with small samples. Although this flexibility comes at a price. Instead of telling us the exact difference in values between the things being compared, these tests tell us which thing was rated higher more often. For example, instead of concluding that "Concept A scored an average of 4.8/5, while Concept B scored 3.9/5, which is a difference of 0.9 points in favour of Concept A", we could simply say that "Concept A scored higher more often than Concept B". Some of the nonparametric tests at our disposal are:

- For independent groups (i.e. when comparing results from groups of different people, as if we were comparing apples to pears):
  - Mann-Whitney U Test – allows us to compare two groups of people (e.g. narrative-driven vs. gameplay-driven players).
  - Kruskal–Wallis H Test – allows us to compare more than two groups of people (e.g. beginners vs. intermediates vs. experts). If at least one of the groups is significantly different (the test reaches a p-value less than 0.05), then we will need to compare the groups pairwise using the Mann-Whitney U Test.
- For dependent groups (i.e. when we compare the scores of the same people at different points in time, as if we were comparing apples before and after peeling them):
  - Wilcoxon Signed-Rank Test – allows us to compare one group of people in two different situations (e.g. scores of the same people on a well-being scale before and after the test).
  - Friedman Test – allows us to compare one group of people in more than two different situations (e.g. scores given to the game by the same people after completing the first, second, third, etc., level in the game).

Although most of these tests will require us to perform additional calculations (even in widely available spreadsheets), the good news is that there are simple calculators to be found on the Internet (just type in the "test name + calculator"). One thing to keep in mind, though, is that when using these (and any other) statistical tests is that we see something called a "p-value" among the test results. In general, the p-value tells us whether the difference that we see between the groups isn't something random. Usually, when the p is less than 0.05, we can look if the difference bears any practical consequences, and when p is greater than 0.05, we can assume there's no difference on a statistical level.

There is certainly much more to statistics than meets the eye, but using the above descriptive statistics and tests can be a good starting point to familiarize ourselves with the topic without risking adverse reactions from the get-go (we may even find a true love for it in the process).

12.4 ANALYZING RESULTS – UNDERSTANDING THE ISSUES AND STRENGTHS OF THE GAME

As we've taken care of the numerical data, and found some hints on what may be worthwhile to investigate further, we can move on to analyzing a whole ton of materials that are of a more immeasurable nature (i.e. our observations and participants' statements, both verbal and written) to prepare the insights. **We want to stay open to the fact that the way we structure and analyze the data affects what we will ultimately obtain**. After all, we will bring out one flavour by frying something and another one by steaming it. We can also think of applying various analysis methods as a kaleidoscope (depending on how we arrange the glasses, the image we observe changes). Given that we reviewed data earlier, we will now focus on a few selected analysis methods adjusted to our purposes, to look at our data from different angles.

12.4.1 THEMATIC ANALYSIS

One of the most common analyses, which can often be treated as a starting point for other ones. Our aim is to identify common themes and patterns among our participants that emerge from their behaviours and statements. In order to do that, we organize the data into meaningful categories (e.g. based on similarity in topic, structure, or time of occurrence) that will allow us to answer the team's questions and identify issues and strengths of the game.

Key questions we ask ourselves:

- What is recurring in the data?
- Are there any patterns emerging?

How to perform it in five steps [Terry et al. 2017]:

I. Coding – We go through our notes, recordings, and open-ended survey responses we reviewed earlier, marking statements or behaviours that stand out or repeat across participants. Some statements may be so complex that we will want to split them into several smaller pieces that are easier to code.

II. Grouping – We then group the statements or behaviours we coded similarly on a board with sticky notes or move them closer in lines within a spreadsheet.

III. Labelling – We give each group a clear, descriptive name (i.e. theme) that best reflects the data in it.

IV. Refining – We go through the data again to ensure that the names represent it in a consistent and reasonable way.

V. Generating insights – For each theme, we aim to write a summary in the form of an insight and use participant quotes, screenshots, or sample recordings to illustrate it.

We can perform thematic analysis in a top-down or bottom-up manner or as a mix of both. The process described above relies on a bottom-up approach (i.e. we are looking for themes emerging from data). We can also start analysis in a top-down approach, with a predefined list of themes (e.g. based on a theory or framework), so we don't have to discover them from scratch. We then group data under themes, skipping the labelling step (because the themes are already there), refine them as needed (e.g. by breaking the theme into smaller ones), and then we move on to generating insights. This approach can be useful when we are short on time. The one thing to note for us is that whether the approach we take, the steps in the process are iterative (i.e. we may go through coding, grouping, and refining a few times as insights emerge).

12.4.2 Differential (or Comparative) Analysis

This type of analysis helps us explore and understand differences in player experience across our participants. Differential analysis is useful when some of the issues aren't experienced by all the participants or when we want to understand the differences in scores given by participants in the survey. The aim is to spot differences and identify the best available explanation based on the data, to better adjust suggestions for the team (e.g. assessing if there is a need to tailor the experience to specific player groups or giving higher priority to issues impacting the vital parts of the target audience).

Key questions we ask ourselves:

- Who is experiencing what?
- What is the difference in player experience between participants who faced the issue and those who did not?
- What is the difference in player experience between participants who rated the game higher and those who rated it lower?

How to perform it in five steps:

I. Identifying groups – We start by selecting a criterion for dividing participants into groups that makes sense in the context of our study purpose and the data we gathered.

Issue	P1	P2	P3	P4	P5	P6
Didn't notice or had difficulty reading where they were receiving damage from	✓	-	✓	✓	✓	✓
Didn't notice changes in their HP levels during fights	✓	-	✓	☐	✓	✓
Mistakenly pressed the grip button instead of trigger to shoot	✓	✓	✓	✓	✓	✓
Didn't notice that wave of enemies or the entire arena was completed	✓	✓	☐	✓	☐	✓
Didn't see glass and tried to pass through it	✓	✓	✓	-	-	✓
Couldn't recognize interactive elements in the environment	☐	✓	☐	☐	✓	☐
Mislead by narrative dialogues about their current objective	☐	✓	☐	✓	☐	☐
Didn't notice prompts on HUD	-	-	✓	✓	✓	✓

FIGURE 12.4   Example participant issue matrix.

II. Comparing the data between groups – We check which of the themes or issues we found during thematic analysis apply to specific participants.

III. Spotting the differences – We look for any major differences between the groups.

IV. Looking for explanation – We try to understand what in the data or context of the study may explain the differences we spotted (e.g. prior experience, specific event during the session).

V. Generating insights – We describe what was different, for whom, and why it matters for the game.

One way to organize the initial insights for differential analysis is to create a participant issue matrix (although I prefer to call it a participant insight matrix, because we can also analyze discovered strengths this way) to see if and what differences there are between individual participants (Figure 12.4).

Again, our analysis can be performed using either a top-down or bottom-up approach. The key difference lies in how we define the groups. In a top-down approach, groups are defined when we prepare the study (e.g. by recruiting novice vs. expert players) with the aim to compare various subgroups or segments of our target audience. Alternatively, we can take a bottom-up approach, where we define the groups based on the gathered data (e.g. dividing participants based on the median survey score for a specific question, or by whether they finished the task or not). While the top-down approach helps us stay aligned with target audience definitions existing in the studio and makes insights easier to communicate, the bottom-up approach may help us uncover new sub-groups or reveal less obvious insights.

12.4.3 TEMPORAL ANALYSIS

Here, we focus on exploring how the player experience of our participants unfolds and evolves over time. Temporal analysis is useful when we want to spot issues or strengths that are interdependent, or when we want to check how various events during the session may have influenced participants' later behaviours and statements (e.g. early difficulties with navigating through the settings menu

BOX 12.2   LOOK INTO THE NEGATIVE SPACE

Many times, finding an insight is not about looking at what participants did or said, but thinking more about what they didn't. Certainly, we may have a feeling that most of our job is pointing out the issues experienced by participants and providing suggestions on how to improve the game. This is a true and incomplete picture at the same time. If we only focus on what we saw and heard during a session, we can narrow our attention too much, leaving out areas of the game that may be important from a design or business perspective. That's the reason it is good to ask our stakeholders about their goals and what they would specifically like to hear from players (apart from that they will love our game), and look for the hints in the documentation (if available). For instance, some level designers state that the most memorable moments during a single level are used to better plan for the intended player experience. If, during a study, we ask participants, "What were the most memorable moments of this experience for you?", and we don't find those stated moments in response, this may be a clue for level design to modify their approach. Certainly, we can't expect to always have such precise information, but even a high level information about creative vision, player fantasy, or core pillars can help us to explore the negative space.

leading to later issues during gameplay, as participants weren't adjusting options, or participants' initial excitement about a feature gradually giving way to boredom after repeated interactions). The aim is to order the issues and strengths as they occurred during the session to spot key moments in the experience, and gain a better view of how things that happened earlier influenced later events, and identify issues that occurred repeatedly during the session. As a result, we gain deeper insights and input to prioritization by understanding which issues players are coping with over time, which ones are persistent, and which are dependent on context.

Key questions we ask ourselves:

- How do earlier events affect what happened next?
- How do the issues experienced by participants change over time?

How to perform it in five steps:

I. Ordering the data on the timeline – We organize issues and strengths we've identified earlier, by the time of occurrence (e.g. by session steps).
II. Noting when issues occur – We look for specific points at which participants had more significant difficulties, experienced something particularly positive, or changed their behaviour or tone.
III. Spotting the patterns – We look for issues occurring at the same session step for multiple participants (e.g. issue "x" seems to be persistent, as it consistently appears in levels 1, 4, and 5), and which issues are consistently related in time (e.g. issue 'x' always precedes issue "y").
IV. Looking for time links – We try to understand how early events may affect what happened later.
V. Generating insights – We describe what happened, when, and how it changed over time, and how it affected the player experience.

While we want to perform temporal analysis, it's worth considering some things before deciding to do it. First, it's good to decide on the time resolution of our analysis (i.e. are we analyzing the session on a minute-by-minute, level-by-level, or day-by-day basis?). Certainly, we want to keep analysis

BOX 12.3   WATCH OUT POOH, THIS ISN'T HONEY!

What participants say and what they do can turn out to be quite different. Participants have imperfect memories; they may also struggle to explain their internal experiences clearly, and they may even alter opinions to reflect social norms or politely agree with us. And these are just some of the reasons why we pay more attention to what participants do than to what they say.

However, we need to have both types of information, as both what people think or feel and how they act are inherent parts of their player experience. The mismatches between player attitudes and behaviours are often a great source of insights. So, instead of concluding that our participants have imperfect memories or "lied to us" (as some might put it), our goal is rather to explain the discrepancy we observed. In this regard, we can use temporal analysis to help us uncover how various events during the game may influence what participants say about the experience.

feasible, and we will find some hints in the methods and tools used (e.g. we could analyze changes from game level to level during component playtest, but it might be better to focus on analyzing whole sessions within diary study). Second, it is worth considering the level of detail we want or can achieve within our constraints (i.e. we may focus solely on the player's interaction with the game, but we could additionally consider game and participants separately, or we could even take other factors like changes in the environment in which the session took place). Certainly, the higher the level of detail, there is higher the possibility of finding something both surprising and vital to the study purpose. However, opting for a higher level of detail has a tremendous impact on the time we will need to perform the temporal analysis.

12.4.4   EXPLANATORY ANALYSIS

With this analysis, we focus on understanding why specific issues or strengths occurred. Although the answer to the "why" question may come to our minds intuitively, as some of the issues experienced by participants may have relatively simple explanations (e.g. text was not visible due to low contrast) or we may know them from experience, there are times when we encounter issues that are much harder nuts to crack. In such cases, explanatory analysis can be particularly helpful in our efforts. The aim is to provide a deeper understanding of the root causes behind the observed issues (or strengths) by exploring how various factors interact to lead participants to experience a particular issue, providing us with the most probable explanation.

Key questions:

- How do different things we observed during the session (e.g. the game, the participant, but also the environment) contribute to or cause the observed issues?

How to perform it in five steps:

I. Scratching below the surface – We focus on asking why something is an issue or a strength. We can rely here on using techniques such as "5 whys" [Ohno 1988] (i.e. asking the why question every time we come up with the answer, which, after the fifth attempt, may lead us to identifying one of the potential root causes).

II. Defining context – As we explore what may be the potential cause of the issue, we can start to note various factors that may be worth considering (e.g. participant mindset and condition, what happened in the game, external distractions).

III. Cross-referencing data – To get a more complete and refined view, we check if we included data available from various sources (e.g. observations, statements, context, we may even look at recruitment survey data), and resolve potential contradictions (e.g. differences between what participants did and said).

IV. Identify contributing factors – As we have potential factors listed, we now clarify which of them contributed to the problem and in what way.

V. Generating insights – We describe what caused something to be the issue or strength.

One example technique that can help us analyze potential root causes of issues is the Ishikawa diagram [see Ishikawa 1976], also known as the fishbone diagram (Figure 12.5). The "fish's head" is the issue we want to understand, and the fishbones on the left are potential causes, with subsequent smaller branches containing additional details or sub-causes.

The thing to have in mind while performing explanatory analysis is scoping what factors we assess. As a starting point, we examine factors related to the game, the player, and the experience resulting from the interaction between the two, many of which we described in Chapters 1 and 2. However, to ensure our explanation is the simplest, most coherent, and comprehensive one, we extend our view to less obvious, but potentially important influences (e.g. factors related to Place, Equipment, and Materials, which we discussed in Chapter 9). While some of the explanations may emerge directly from the data, referring to the existing body of knowledge (e.g. frameworks like MDA or Rational Game Design; theories like GameFlow, Self-Determination Theory; models on player behaviour and decision-making) will give us a basic structure to guide our thinking. Similar to the previous analyses, the process is iterative, as new information emerges, context may shift, and new factors can be spotted during cross-referencing data. Finally, **explanatory analysis, more than the previous ones, gives us a notion of the uncertainty that accompanies us through all research endeavours. And it's something that is worth getting comfortable with, as in research, "we can rarely be sure we're right, and there's always a chance we're wrong"**.

Now that we have gone through the selected analyses, we can summarize them in Table 12.1.

By using a specific analysis, we can stay focused and avoid being overwhelmed by too many questions about the data at once. At the same time, by analyzing data from multiple angles, we can gain a more complete and detailed picture of the player's experiences. However, the question that remains is "Do we need to do all of these in every single study?". Of course not. While thematic

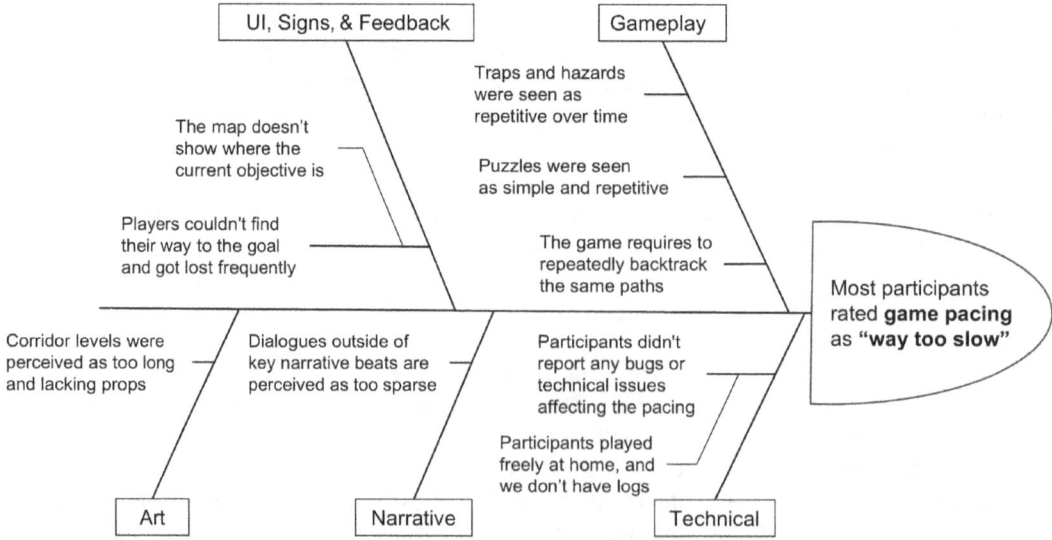

FIGURE 12.5 Example root-cause analysis for game pacing rating with the use of a fishbone diagram.

analysis will likely be part of most of our studies, we choose other analyses pragmatically, based on the study purpose, gathered data, and constraints like time and budget. Certainly, conducting these analyses in a structured way gives us a higher chance to gather deeper and less biased insights, but if it's not feasible, it's still helpful for us to keep in mind the key questions from each of them as we go through the data.

When we look at those selected analysis methods, it's also worth noting that we probably read through them with the implicit assumption that we had to perform them on our own, alone. Nothing could be further from the truth. If the team has the time and willingness to engage in analyzing results, we can involve them as well, at least it is worth suggesting it. Looking at it pragmatically, taking part in the results analysis deepens the understanding of the players' perspective and increases the sense of insights ownership, which in turn increases the chance of taking action based on them (i.e. resulting in better research impact ratio and stakeholder satisfaction). Another effect of this kind of joint analysis may be shortening the research turnaround time, as the time needed from the end of the research sessions to the start of work on the obtained insights can be effectively shortened (e.g. the team doesn't have to wait until we finish the final report, and in some cases, we may not need it after all). After all, cooking can bring people closer together.

TABLE 12.1
Summary of Selected Analysis Methods

Analysis Method	Purpose	Key Questions
Thematic analysis	Identify common themes and patterns that emerge from the behaviours and statements of our participants	What is recurring in the data? Are there any patterns emerging?
Differential analysis	Spot and compare differences across participant sub-groups	Who is experiencing what? What is the difference in player experience between participants who faced the issue and those who did not? What is the difference in player experience between participants who rated the game higher and those who rated it lower?
Temporal analysis	Trace how issues and strengths unfold over time	How do earlier events affect what happened next? How do the issues and strengths experienced by participants change over time?
Explanatory analysis	Uncover root causes behind observed issues or strengths	How do different things we observed during the session (e.g. the game, the participant, but also the environment) contribute to or cause the observed issues?

Annotation. [Own elaboration].

BOX 12.4   COULDN'T WE USE A MULTICOOKER INSTEAD?

Certainly, not all of us are fans of fine dining (or just don't have enough time for it), so why bother learning how to use different utensils when we can use a multicooker? Writing instructions, tasks, formulating questions, taking notes, and analyzing results of our study manually can seem like much effort. Especially when we have some handy tools at our disposal. We can use software that performs interview transcriptions, supports performing analyses such as thematic analysis, and so on. But those are rather typical kitchen aids. Then, we have a real multicooker in the form of AI, and there is not much I can do to stop you from using it to ease all the pain of the first attempts in conducting your studies. However, my belief is that doing things manually can be a worthwhile effort to get a deeper understanding of both the strengths and limitations of our work, and to better grasp what is crucial in the process. Preparing various study elements manually helps us develop the ability to clearly define goals, formulate unbiased questions, and design an effective study structure. As user researchers, we also want to remain reflective about what has to be done to fulfil the study purpose in a given context, how different tasks and questions connect to specific goals, and where there may be gaps or wrong assumptions in our own reasoning (which can be blindly replicated in prompts we feed AI with).

At the time of writing this paragraph, my experience is that AI tools can support our efforts, given that the specific tool doesn't raise legal or ethical concerns, and we know its potential limitations, like potential biases or risk of producing plainly wrong or made-up responses, the so-called hallucinations.

Generally, if we know what we want to achieve and how to do it, AI can support us in doing it more efficiently (e.g. write the draft of the research protocol yourself, understand the actual goals the study aims to achieve, and then – if you will – turn to AI for refinement and check it). If we don't know, we may just end up doing the wrong thing, but fast. So, use the utensils that best suit you, just try not to confuse the multicooker with the cook.

12.5   PRIORITIZING INSIGHTS

In perfect, though rarely occurring, conditions, the team will take all the insights and address everything that we managed to uncover. However, let's face the truth that not all insights are created equal, and the team will most likely choose only some of them to address, based on their perspective (e.g. taking into consideration creative vision and constraints like budget, time, or production priorities), so regardless of our best efforts, the team may simply disagree to take care of some things we find important for the game's success. And they have the right to do so.

It's better to be prepared by prioritizing insights beforehand and advocating for the most important ones in our reports and debriefs. We can also share the burden of prioritization with the team by addressing it during joint analyses, but this requires the team to have enough time and space in the production cycle (which is often not the case). Whether we have the opportunity to prioritize insights with the team or have to do it on our own, it's worth relying on some set of criteria that will help us decide on what's important to deliver better player experience, and ultimately for the game's success.

The good news is that, with strengths, most of the time it's enough for us to highlight that something stands out as a "good" thing rather than diving into the specific priority it has for the experience. **By highlighting strengths, we want the team to know that the game has succeeded at delivering the intended player experience, and that there are specific game elements worth preserving.** Having this information is important, as without it, the team can sometimes unintentionally remove the strength in the process of addressing issues. As strengths can typically be treated in a straightforward manner, we can focus our attention on issues, as they tend to be more complicated to prioritize. Let's start by looking at **some questions we can ask about the issue when trying to prioritize it**:

- **How difficult was it for the participant to overcome the issue? (Severity)**
  We consider the extent to which the issue disrupts the player's experience. Generally, issues that prevent participants from progressing through the game will be a greater concern to us than inconvenient, although manageable ones.
- **How often the issue appeared during the session? (Frequency)**
  We look at how often the issue was experienced during the session. Issues that occurred once will have lower priority than ones that occur multiple times during the session.

- **Are participants able to overcome the issue on their own when they encounter it again? (Persistency)**

  We check whether it's possible for participants to solve the problem on their own or find an effective workaround. We will want to solve first those problems for which the participants do not find effective workarounds.

- **Where in the game did the issue occur? (Location)**

  We look at whether the problem occurs on the "golden path" (i.e. the main path of the player's progression through the game) or rather concerns side content. Most often, we will prioritize the main content before we give more attention to working on things that are optional.

- **How much would fixing this issue improve the player experience? (Impact)**

  No matter how big or small the issue is, what matters most here is what will change for the player after the issue is successfully solved. Impact is not just the negative of severity, and can be treated more broadly, as a measure that encompasses severity, persistency, and location combined. The greater impact we expect, the higher priority we give to the issue.

- **How difficult or expensive is the issue to be fixed? (Effort)**

  Optionally, we can also look at how much effort the team requires to fix the issue. However, it is worth bearing in mind that we may often lack the appropriate technical knowledge to correctly assess the effort; hence, the assessment of this dimension will require consultation with the team.

Certainly, an attempt to prioritize issues based on a single dimension will rarely do the trick for us, but at the same time, we would need a separate priority list to use all those dimensions at once. However, we can simply start by assigning each issue a rating (e.g. high or low) for severity and frequency, and then create a matrix from that (Table 12.2).

It's a quick and dirty way to see where the team's attention is most needed. The problem is that the issues are not equal and regardless of severity or frequency, they will require different effort from the team to fix them. When we look at prioritization from the team's perspective, when considering the problem, they will often focus on assessing what the player experience will gain (impact) and what costs are associated with it (effort) (Table 12.3).

TABLE 12.2

Frequency and Severity Prioritization Matrix

	Frequency (Low)	Frequency (High)
Severity (low)	Low priority	Medium priority
Severity (high)	Medium priority	High priority

Annotation. [Own elaboration].

TABLE 12.3

Impact and Effort Prioritization Matrix

	Impact (Low)	Impact (High)
Effort (low)	Medium priority	High priority "low-hanging fruit"
Effort (high)	Low priority	High priority "big bet"

Annotation. [Own elaboration].

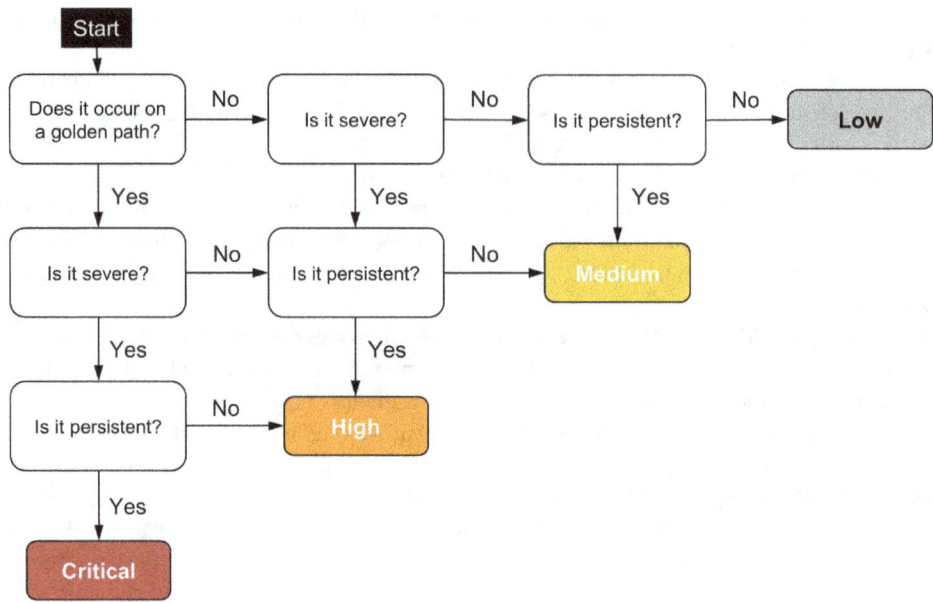

FIGURE 12.6 Decision tree for prioritizing issues. (Own elaboration based on Travis (2009).)

The obvious barrier to making a matrix based on impact and effort on our own is that rating Effort requires the participation of people from the team with the appropriate competencies to assess it. Therefore, we will more often use the impact and effort matrix as one of the final steps of joint analyses. However, the basic requirement for prioritization is the proper assessment of impact, which itself encompasses a few dimensions. To tackle this in a structured way, we can use David Travis's [2009] decision tree for prioritizing usability issues; with just a few minor adjustments, it can easily come to our aid in methodically assessing impact (Figure 12.6). Once we have assessed impact this way, we can assign priorities to issues, relying on other dimensions only in specific cases, and leaving effort assessment to the team.

Whether we prioritized insights with simple severity and frequency matrices or more elaborate approaches like decision trees, we have our priorities in place, and we can move on to composing our report and debriefing the team.

When analyzing results, we must remember the agreed key dates. If we notice we might miss deadlines, we inform stakeholders of potential risks and discuss with them how we intend to address them. We look for a solution that won't compromise the quality of the analysis and meets the team's needs. For instance, we check whether the report delivery date can simply be changed, or whether we need to arrange for additional delivery of top findings before the full report is ready, or we should limit the scope of our analyses. Therefore, during the analysis, we inform stakeholders via the study channel whether key dates agreed in the research protocol are at risk, or whether everything is going according to plan (which is also important information), and if necessary, we discuss any necessary changes to our approach.

12.6 CHAPTER SUMMARY

We begin creating individual bites of our dish, drawing on various cooking techniques. Our goal is to obtain insights (information that answers the questions: "What happened? Was it good or bad? Why did it happen? What can we do about it? What will happen if we don't do anything about it?") in the form of both issues and strengths. Knowing what we're looking for, we begin organizing and annotating the data, then we set our approach (deductive, inductive, or a mix of both), and move on to analysis. If applicable, we derive descriptive statistics, conduct basic nonparametric tests, and visualize the results to convey the right story for the study purpose. Next, we proceed with selected analyses (thematic, differential, temporal, and/or explanatory), while being mindful that the way we organize and analyze the data influences what kind of insights we can derive. With insights prepared, we move on to prioritization based on a simple severity and frequency or impact and effort matrices, or rely on more complex decision trees.

REFERENCES

Ishikawa, K. (1976). *Guide to Quality Control*. Asian Productivity Organization.

Ohno, T. (1988). Evolution of the Toyota production system. In T. Ohno (Ed.), *Toyota Production System: Beyond Large-Scale Production*. (pp. 17–44). Productivity Press.

Terry, G., Hayfield, N., Clarke, V., & Braun, V. (2017). Thematic analysis. In C. Willig & W. Stainton-Rogers (Eds.), *The SAGE Handbook of Qualitative Research in Psychology*. 2nd ed. (pp. 17–37). Sage Publications.

Travis, D. (2009). *How to Prioritise Usability Problems*. https://www.userfocus.co.uk/articles/prioritise.html

13 Composing and Serving the Dish
Reporting and Debriefing

So, we have the single bites that will make up our dish, but since the whole is a little more than the sum of its parts, we now have to compose them on the plate and then deliver them to our guests, while remembering that the way we serve it affects the taste.

13.1 PREPARING REPORT

When we start preparing a report, whether it's a full or just a top findings one, it's worth reminding ourselves that **our goal is to provide the team with actionable feedback on the strengths and issues of the game, to spark discussion that leads to specific design and business decisions and actions**. To have a better chance of achieving this goal, we need to pay some attention to the report structure. Let's start by focusing on the typical building blocks of a report, and then we will go through some sample types of structures for reporting insights.

13.1.1 REPORT STRUCTURE

Report building blocks aren't there for the sake of filling space (no one judges us by the number of words, but by their weight), and each of them has an appropriate function and typical place in the report structure.

13.1.1.1 Title Page

First, we want to orient the audience so they know exactly what they're looking at. To do this, we provide details like the game's codename, the test topic and method (e.g. "Combat - Component Playtest"), the build number or version of the game, the date the report was published, the author(s), and the peer reviewer (i.e. someone who read the report and gave us feedback before it was published, such as another researcher or someone in the studio who can be impartial about the study, such as a QA specialist who is not directly involved in the creation process).

13.1.1.2 Key Insights (a.k.a. Executive Summary)

This block is intended to provide an overview of what we learned during the study and offer concise answers to the design and business questions posed in the study purpose. For the sake of brevity, we summarize individual insights within broader categories and present the most important ones, divided into positives and negatives. To create this block efficiently, we write it as one of the last steps, after organizing the insights in the report. Key insights are especially useful for stakeholders who do not have time to go through the entire report or can serve as a strong introduction to capture the team's interest.

13.1.1.3 Study Purpose

We're basically including the essence of the section of the same name from the research protocol. We aim to provide a short recap of what we wanted to achieve with this study (e.g. specific input for design or business decisions, assessing risks) to set a clear interpretation frame for the team.

DOI: 10.1201/9781003501909-15

13.1.1.4   Methods and Tools

Again, our base is the research protocol section of the same name. Although we have carefully picked the method and prepared the tools, our stakeholders, in most cases, won't be interested in all the knowledge and finesse that went into the process. Our aim is to be transparent on how we conducted the study, using just a few words or sentences.

13.1.1.5   Participant Profile

We want to provide context for interpreting the report by explaining who is represented in the insights. The content and scope of this block depends on the information we gathered during recruitment and warm-up, so we might end up saying that "8 people participated in the study, all of whom played at least one of the competitor games", but it could just as easily take more elaborate form of a table listing various participant characteristics (e.g. competitor and reference games played, genre preferences, demographic information). The purpose of the participant profile block is to set expectations and remind the report recipient that the study represents a sample of specific people from the target audience, not the entire audience.

13.1.1.6   Study Limitations

Some say that a well-written report speaks for itself. And while I deeply believe in this, at the same time, even if the team doesn't contest our results, they can still misinterpret them or draw hasty conclusions. Therefore, in order to better set the team's expectations regarding the insights in the report and deepen their understanding, it is worth for us to clearly articulate what cannot be derived from the insights and where the interpretation is limited (e.g. because of methods used, sample size, participant profile, study setting). As we mentioned earlier, with most of the methods listed in this book, the basic limitation is that, based on a single study, we cannot generalize results to the whole target audience (note that, it's another way of saying that we're more focused on finding holes in player experience and less on seeing how many players fall into them). In general, to determine the most relevant limitations, we can ask ourselves, "If we would change <potential limitation> in a study, would it influence or even flip the results?" (e.g. If we would invite left-handed participants, would they face the same issues or more of them?). Although the study limitations block may be seen as optional in user research reports, my experience suggests that it can help us build the team's trust in results, and give a greater chance that they will receive the message we wanted to convey.

13.1.1.7   Prioritization

We want to keep transparency and clarity throughout the report, and let the report recipient know that prioritization was made from our perspective and may not be perfect. We provide a short information on how we prioritized insights in the report.

13.1.1.8   Insights

Here, we present the findings and insights that we identified during the results analysis. We present insights in the format described in Chapter 12, and illustrate them with supporting materials such as screenshots, participant quotes, links to specific moments in the session recordings (if available), and/or results of the numerical data analyses and their visualizations. The general rule of thumb is to put one insight per page (or presentation slide) to keep the report clear and readable. However, if we have a bit more time, we can consider putting related insights on one page. The key is to assess whether this will support the team's understanding and not negatively affect the readability of the report. As the insights structuring can take varied forms, we will take a closer look at it in a separate section in this chapter.

13.1.1.9   Next Steps

In this block, we suggest actionable steps the team can take to improve the player experience based on the most crucial insights and share identified follow-up research opportunities. These may include studies aimed at addressing remaining or newly emerged questions or countering the limitations identified in the current study. On the other hand, we can elaborate this block during the debrief session, as we will have additional design and business context stemming from discussion and stakeholder reactions to insights. We may also propose running a workshop to collaboratively define next steps and actions based on the insights, but this may depend on the team's time and preferences (e.g. some prefer to reflect on the insights independently). In the end, this block's main aim is to plan and call to specific actions based on the delivered insights.

13.1.1.10   Closing Page

Instead of only writing "Thank You" on the report's last page, we additionally include our contact and links to supporting materials (e.g. full session recordings, survey data) so the team can easily access them when the need arises.

Most of the report building blocks have a relatively stable structure, although they may differ in form between researchers (e.g. some researchers prefer to place the key insights "in plus" first or on the same page as the key insights "in minus"), and can be combined in different ways (e.g. there is nothing bad in combining study purpose, methods and tools, and participant profile on one page). We simply need to decide what will be best to reach the stakeholders with our message in a given circumstance. To provide you with a scaffolding you could adapt for writing your own reports, you will find the document "GURCB_01_010101- book - Full Report - template" on the book's website. Both the full report and top findings share many common elements, but the latter contains them in a shortened and condensed version (e.g. there is no elaborate info on study purpose, participant profile, methods and tools, or study limitations for brevity and prioritization is simplified, as new insights may still emerge, and existing ones may change in the process).

13.1.2   ORGANIZING INSIGHTS IN THE REPORT

It is worth noting that the way we structure insights in the report may significantly differ depending on the study purpose, the analyses performed, but also the preferences of the stakeholders and organizational maturity of the studio. At the same time, just as the analyses performed influence the insights we obtain, the way we organize insights can influence how they are received and acted on by the team. As the insights are the core part of our report and will take up most of the space, we will now spend some time on the selected approaches to organizing them.

13.1.2.1   "The Good vs the Bad"

Basically, we divide the block with insights into two sections "positives", in which we list all the strengths and "negatives", in which we list all the issues. This is one of the most straightforward, but also quick ways to organize insights, in which the strengths of the players' experience can be well heard by the team. However, it has obvious drawbacks. With this approach, we can easily lose nuance and relations between insights and oversimplify them, so we rely on it when time is of the essence (e.g. when we have to deliver preliminary findings).

13.1.2.2   Priority

This approach assumes that at the beginning of the insights block, we will find the highest priority insights, and the further we go, the lower the priority we will find. The advantage is again simplicity, but also focusing the team's attention on addressing the most pressing issues. The risk is that lower priority issues can slip under the team's radar, and similarly to "the good vs the bad", we can easily lose nuance and relations between insights. This approach works well in situations where time is limited and the team places a lot of emphasis on quickly prioritizing the most important issues (e.g. right after release, when the game starts receiving negative reviews).

13.1.2.3   Components or Themes

We can organize insights into broader categories, typically ones that reflect either the main topics that emerged during the research or specific game components. The single section of insights contains insights assigned to a single theme (e.g. Issues with the tutorial; Player navigation on levels) or, alternatively, insights assigned to a specific component (e.g. gameplay, art, narrative, UI). Organizing insights by game components can work well in more structured teams where responsibilities for various game elements are clearly defined (a situation more common in larger studios than in smaller ones). On the other hand, organizing insights by themes can help the team to better understand and empathize with participants' perspectives. Regardless of whether we organize by themes or components, we will face similar drawbacks. Insights may span multiple components or refer to several themes, which may make them hard to confidently assign to just one category (although we can use additional tags to highlight other categories the insight applies to). Furthermore, dividing insights by categories brings the risk of fragmenting insights that are part of a broader issue.

13.1.2.4   Journey-Based

With this approach, we organize insights chronologically as they appeared during the session. The advantage of this approach is mirroring how participants interact with the assets we prepared for the study. This often provides a narrative structure, which can be used to build a better understanding and empathy for the participants' ups and downs. It works well in structured studies involving tasks or those aimed at assessing player experiences with a semi-linear progression (e.g. game divided into levels). It is much more difficult to apply this approach to less structured studies and to open-world or sandbox games, where player journeys can vary significantly, as identifying a common sequence of events across participants without losing meaning or nuance can be time-consuming.

BOX 13.1   WHAT TO DO IF THE DISH IS TOO SALTY?

The general rule of thumb in most kitchens is that if there is too much salt in your dish, you can try to counterbalance it with sugar. Maybe we can get away with it when it comes to soup, but this is not a good way to proceed when it comes to presenting research results in the reports.

While most of our methods focus on uncovering even minor issues in the player experience, it's equally important to highlight situations when core game elements, mechanics, or systems worked as intended or even exceeded expectations. However, let's not force ourselves to look for strengths just for the sake of making reports seem more balanced or less dreadful. As we've already mentioned, providing insights isn't about making someone feel good or bad about their job. Rather, our goal is to stimulate action and catalyze informed decision-making within the team to improve player experience. If we care about team motivation and morale (and it's a good sign when we do), there are better, though a bit more demanding, ways to support them. Let's take a look at a few of them:

- Clarify your agenda – We clearly communicate that we are evaluating the player experience, not the team's performance. We want to acknowledge that the team is probably aware of some issues, and emphasize that we aim to provide the most complete picture of the experience "as is" to make it easier to navigate to the intended "to be" state. We can do this on various occasions, such as a casual chat, a kick-off meeting, or a debrief, but we can also include it directly in the report under study limitations. This way, we can reduce potential team defensiveness and encourage more open dialogue around issues.

- Point out common patterns – We can also signal that it's natural to observe fluctuations in type, number, and severity of issues during the production cycle. As we go through the production cycle phases, we may observe that together with the team's goals changing, our focus on research also shifts. From exploring more general themes in the conception phase, through assessing specific core elements and systems in pre-production, to checking how those elements interact together in delivering the whole experience in the production phase. As a side effect, the team may feel swamped with issues at times when we move from one phase to another. If that's the case, put them at ease by emphasizing that these issue influxes often stem from a change in objectives or reflect changes the game has had to undergo (e.g. redesign of the core system due to a pivot). At the same time, we can highlight that we're in the right time to address those issues.
- Capitalize on existing strengths – In the report, we can spot opportunities for showing how identified strengths can be further capitalized, and organize insights accordingly. For instance, if the team has implemented a good practice successfully in one place, we can first showcase this strength, then point out specific issues where a similar approach could be applied. This way, we highlight what works well, but also help the team see how existing strengths can inform future solutions.

It's worth remembering that there's nothing wrong with mixing these structures in our reports, and in fact, we'll combine them to get the best understanding of the insights and the best chance for the team to act on them. For instance, we can organize insights in the report by components, and use "the good vs. the bad" structuring within each section, and in the end, give a short summary of the player's story by placing all insights on a timeline. However, we must take into account that giving a multi-layered structure to a report takes time, so it is worth measuring our strength over intentions (e.g. in the case of a study whose results determine the payment for a milestone, we may want to mix several ways of organizing insights, but in the case of a quick usability test on menu screens, we may decide on the quick and proven "the good vs. the bad").

13.1.3 POLISHING AND SHARING THE REPORT

You may have heard about the custom in some aristocratic households where, before serving a dish to guests, someone else first tastes it to check for poison. Well, it may be history, but we can allow ourselves a similar luxury to spare our team from potential indigestion.

As we approach report completion, we can take one additional step, namely, conduct a peer review. Since, in this book, we're considering small- and medium-sized studios, we'll rarely have the opportunity to bring another user researcher on board to review the report and provide feedback. However, user research isn't the only discipline that supports the team and pays close attention to detail. If our team has a QA specialist (or we have other trusted team members), we can ask them to read the report before it's shared with the rest of the team. When sharing the report draft with this person, we have to clarify that the aim is to check for obvious errors or misinterpretations and ensure that the content is understood as we intended. The feedback received will allow us to improve the report quality, but it can also be a good opportunity to develop our communication skills.

With the report finalized and polished after peer review, we can now share it with our stakeholders. We typically do it at least a day before the planned debrief session to give stakeholders time to review the report and come prepared for a productive discussion. We can deliver the report (or link to it) via the study channel, together with a reminder about the upcoming debrief (which we agreed on earlier within the research protocol under the key dates section), to confirm or adjust the meeting time if necessary.

13.2 CONDUCTING DEBRIEF

We've submitted the report to the team and might conclude that our work on the study is over. Well, sometimes this might be the case (e.g. when working as a freelancer), but generally, it's worth ensuring that the most important themes from the study resonate as intended, and that the team has the opportunity to develop a shared understanding of the insights and plan further steps. Debriefing is the closing meeting of the study, providing such an opportunity.

13.2.1 DEBRIEFING FORMATS

While we've mentioned the basic goals of debriefing, we have to tailor its format to the team's characteristics, needs, and constraints. So let's take a closer look at how we can conduct a debriefing and what to expect. We can organize debriefing approaches from those that require the least effort but also offer the fewest opportunities for team engagement, to those that, while demanding more effort, can be highly engaging for the team.

13.2.1.1 Lecture-Like

In this format, we present the report with minimal interaction or discussion with the team. We ask the team to take notes with questions and comments or post them in the chat during the report presentation (e.g. if we're debriefing remotely). Then, after the report is presented, we move on to answering questions and discussing comments. This format is good for ensuring a structured and coherent message, or when we need to systematize the knowledge gained from the study (e.g. because some team members didn't have the opportunity to read the report or the study was relatively large and complex). A significant disadvantage is significantly less room for discussion, which would foster a better and deeper understanding of the insights provided, and potentially lower team engagement. However, from the user researcher's perspective, this format allows for better control of meeting time and is also less burdensome than other formats.

13.2.1.2 Presentation with Discussion

This is one of the most frequently chosen forms of debriefing, in which we conduct a moderated discussion with team members while presenting the insights. We aim to clarify the information in the report, address the team's concerns, and encourage active participation, asking questions, and sharing thoughts (a good practice in this regard is to prepare warm-up questions, such as "What surprised you most?" or "Do any of the insights raise concerns?"). Managing the meeting time can be somewhat challenging at the beginning of our endeavours, and we may need to prepare a presentation that summarizes the key content of the report.

13.2.1.3 Workshop

In a workshop format, we assume that the team will be familiar with the insights, so we have to communicate this clearly to stakeholders before the meeting, so they come prepared. To conduct the workshop, we may also need additional materials (in the form of a digital or physical board, sticky notes, markers, and pens) and preparations (preparing tasks and activities for the team; writing down the insights on the physical or digital sticky notes, so we could use them as a starting point). During the workshop, we guide the team through various activities and tasks we prepared. For instance, we may want to proceed sequentially through activities such as selecting issues, generating solutions, and prioritizing them. We first ask workshop participants to individually list the most important issues identified in the research, and then discuss them as a group. We then proceed to individually generate solutions to the selected issues, which we then regroup and discuss together. Finally, we ask workshop participants to individually prioritize each problem based on a common criterion (e.g. effort), and later discuss the prioritizations in a group to identify the "low-hanging fruits" and necessary, but more demanding solutions. Finally, we agree with stakeholders on which issues they will look at first and what the next steps will be. To ensure we can manage the workshop, we allocate a specific time for each activity and task, which we communicate to workshop participants (e.g. "For the next 10 minutes, we will generate solutions for 'x'"). Workshop format can help us engage the team and build shared responsibility for creating and implementing solutions to issues. Obvious challenges can include the time required to prepare the workshop, the need for the team to allocate more time, and facilitation skills on our behalf (i.e. supporting the group in collaboration, focus, and achieving goals during the workshop).

Certainly, we have to communicate and agree with stakeholders what form of debriefing we propose in a given study, so they know what to expect. While workshops may be tempting due to the potential for high participant engagement, they aren't always necessary to achieve the desired outcome. We would rather choose the debriefing format based on our needs and constraints. Sometimes a lecture-style format isn't as bad as it may seem, especially when we have limited time or aren't yet comfortable with more dynamic forms of group work. Regardless of which form we choose, each one can increase our chances of stimulating action and catalyzing informed decision-making. Of course, we may sometimes need to modify the format to better suit our needs. For instance, instead of a full workshop, we may conduct a presentation with a discussion, which is summed up with a prioritization activity.

13.2.2 Attitude during Debriefing

We outlined several key characteristics of a user researcher and our relationship with the team when discussing our role in Chapter 3. We mentioned the importance of striving to be reliable, transparent, communicative, empathetic, proactive, flexible, and patient. While these qualities are important throughout all our research endeavours, during debrief, they may be put to the test. **No matter how hard we've planned the study, how well we performed it, or how clearly we've reported insights, the debrief is the time when rubber hits the road, and the study becomes a real thing for stakeholders**. When we discuss insights with people whose work is directly impacted by them, emotions may run high. That's why our attitude and communication style can have a strong influence on how insights are received and acted on by the team. It's not just about what we present and suggest but how we do it and respond to the team's concerns.

In such circumstances, stakeholders may raise challenging questions or even critical comments. And basically, most of the time, this isn't a sign of our failure or their resistance; it's rather a sign that they care about the game from their own perspective. So rather than "defend" the insights we prepared (if we correctly reflected the participants' player experience, there is nothing to defend), let's focus on fostering the team's understanding, and taking an open stance to their questions and comments, and sometimes even say, "That's a great point. Let's improve this next time". To not sound vague or moralizing, let's go through some examples on how we can approach typical situations during debrief.

13.2.2.1 We're Not Sure about Making This. Isn't This Too Few Players?

This is a commonly vocalized concern, especially for the type of research we discuss in this book. It may stem from the notion that research involving many participants is more reliable. However, as we already know, our answer boils down to the type of questions we were asking in the study purpose. If we were looking for a reliable answer to the questions "to what extent" or "how often" something is an issue, it's actually fair to say that to check our initial interpretations, we need further research (or analytics data) to obtain a larger sample. However, if we used the methods as intended (e.g. to identify issues and understand their causes), we can dispel doubts in several ways. For instance, "That's an important question. Our goal in this type of study wasn't to formulate statistically representative claims, but to find recurring patterns in player behaviour and statements, as well as to gain a deeper understanding of their causes. In this context, a small number of diverse participants is standard and appropriate practice". Depending on our situation and the results, we might add, "We observed that the issue affected all/most of our participants", and end on an actionable note like "It can be worthwhile to compare our assumptions with analytical data", or "We will monitor whether this issue appears in subsequent studies. If so, this may be a clear signal to revisit the matter and resolve it".

13.2.2.2   Why Didn't You Include "x"?

This concern may reflect a valid gap in the study, or a misunderstanding of the scope we agreed on in the research protocol. In the place of "x", we can hear things such as specific features, parts of the game, or even a specific player group. Whatever the case, it's good to refer to the research protocol and point to the study purpose and participant profile agreed there. In most of our studies, we will have to make some trade-offs between the desired scope and our constraints (budget, time, or access to participants). As a result, some features or groups may be intentionally excluded (not because they were unimportant, but because other things were more urgent for making design or business decisions at the time). It is worth acknowledging it and offering some path forward, "Thank you for sharing this observation. For this study, we intentionally focused on <feature(s) or player group(s)>, as defined in the research protocol. We decided to follow that direction, as we see it as having the best cost-impact ratio based on the most pressing questions at the time, as well as our time and budget constraints, and access to participants. At the same time I understand the value of exploring <feature(s) or player group(s)>. If there's a specific decision you need to make or question you want to ask, let's consider them in future studies".

13.2.2.3   Why Didn't You Ask about "y"?

Even with the scope agreed and well understood, it's rather common for new questions to pop up just when we ended working on a study, or when the stakeholders had some time to think about the insights in the light of their changing priorities and perceived risks. Certainly, jointly defined research protocol and active communication with our stakeholders throughout the study will mitigate this to some extent. However, even when everything was done in the best possible way, some questions may still emerge. In such situations, there is no need to worry, but we would rather focus on whether the raised question will help stakeholders make some decisions or alleviate risks. If yes, we might say, "Thank you for raising this topic. This study focused on <shortly on our study purpose>, but I understand it's a vital topic to explore, and let's consider including it in future studies to fill in blind spots". If the raised question seems like a basic miss during study preparation, we can treat it as a chance to improve, and add "This is also a good example of how helpful it is to collaboratively define the research protocol from the beginning. Let's ensure that we have more space for it next time".

Certainly, we can be asked about the multitude of other things (e.g. What would you recommend based on your perspective? How sure are you about "z"? Wouldn't a better explanation be "t" instead of what you wrote in the report?), and the most straightforward approach is to **stay calm and open minded, rely on facts and favour a simple, yet complete interpretation of the gathered data**. After answering the most vital questions and comments and agreeing on next steps for us and the team to take, we can close the debrief meeting and signal that we will ask for feedback on the study to improve our practices (e.g. we can write a message to stakeholders or meet with them individually and use rose-bud-thorn technique we discussed in Chapter 3 to get some structured answers).

Fortunately enough, as one of the next steps, we will have another study topic to dive into, so we can go back to the third step (i.e. Chapter 6) of this basic recipe and repeat the steps in the process. However, to better tailor this basic recipe to various occasions and inspire own endeavours, in Part 3 we have a list of selected recipes within the production cycle.

13.3   CHAPTER SUMMARY

We need to arrange everything on a plate and serve it to our guests, remembering that presentation affects taste. Regardless of whether we are creating a full report or a top findings one, each has a specific structure that we should adapt to the needs and constraints of a given study (e.g. combining some sections for brevity). With a report prepared, we can ask one of the team members to perform a peer review to ensure the report conveys the message we intend. Finally, we send the report to the team and schedule a debriefing, the format of which we agree with the team based on the type of study and needs. The debriefing can take the lecture-like form, a presentation with discussion, a workshop, or a combination of them, depending on what best supports the team in understanding the insights and making decisions and taking actions. During debriefing, we adopt an open attitude, respond to the team's questions and concerns, relying on facts and a simple yet comprehensive interpretation of the collected data. After the debriefing, we ask the team for feedback to improve our practices (e.g. using the rose-bud-thorn technique) and return to the third step of this recipe (i.e. Chapter 6) with the next research topic.

13.4   FURTHER READING

Below you will find two books that complement the material we've covered in Chapters 4–13:

Games User Research (2018) Edited by Anders Drachen, Pejman Mirza-Babaei, and Lennart Nacke

- In a nutshell: Another perspective on what, when, and how to conduct user research for video games.
- Description: This book is a thorough and comprehensive overview of game user research topics, which can provide you with additional knowledge and perspective on methods, good practices, and the challenges we face as researchers. That said, some of the methods, approaches, and tools discussed in this book are more applicable to larger studios, so if you work in a smaller studio or as a freelancer, you may need to adapt or scale them down to fit your reality. Nevertheless, this book can provide you with a deeper understanding of the breadth of the discipline.

Game Analytics: Maximizing the Value of Player Data (2013) Edited by Magy Seif El-Nasr, Anders Drachen, and Alessandro Canossa

- In a nutshell: The other side of analyzing the player experience.
- Description: This book offers a comprehensive and clear introduction to collecting, analyzing, and using data in games. While our primary tools will be interviews, tasks, and surveys, understanding the language and possibilities offered by data analytics will help you improve your research practices and prepare yourself to work hand in hand with data analysts and scientists alike. While some chapters assume a bit more technical foundations or focus on larger organizational settings, this book still provides essential insights for working with analytics. You don't have to become a data analyst yourself, but it's useful to understand the other side of the coin.

Part 3

A Recipe List – Selected Methods within the Production Cycle

This part describes ten research methods, along with examples of their application in the development cycle of various games developed by teams of 5 to 20 people. Each method is a modification of the ten-step process we discussed in Part 2. Sticking with the cooking metaphor, each method is presented in a separate chapter as a recipe, so before diving into each one, let's take a look at their general structure:

- Nutritional value – To what extent it answers selected questions on gameplay experience (Do players like what they see or hear? Do players understand it and know how to use it? Do players engage in it? Do players want to continue?).
- Prep time – The time required for conducting a study from kick-off to debrief. We should treat times provided in recipes as approximates. The actual time it will take to conduct the study may vary depending on many factors (e.g. the pace at which the team delivers assets and their quality; whether or not we have participant recruitment process in place, or the challenges we encounter during it).
- Pots and essentials – Here, we find the assets we will need to conduct the research, as well as the number of participants to obtain a good balance between the costs incurred and the insights gained.
- Steps in the process – What should we pay attention to during each step of the research process?
- Tips – Additional elements worth considering when conducting a given type of study.
- Variations – Other forms in which a given study occurs.
- Ways to spoil the dish – Some risks and errors when using the method.
- Serving example – An example of applying the method.

As with all recipes in cookbooks, they are not set in stone, and each of us can prepare dishes based on them in slightly different ways. Treat them more as guidelines that can be further adapted to your needs and possibilities.

DOI: 10.1201/9781003501909-16

14 Competitor Analysis

When the creative vision is just taking shape, it's important to understand what alternative titles with similar aims have already been done and how players experienced them. Our team probably has a one-of-a-kind idea about the game, but many systems that will accompany it were already explored by other studios. In such a reality, there is no need to waste time and budget on reinventing the wheel. It's better to save them for what will be truly unique to the game team is trying to make. With competitor analysis, we want to explore competitor or reference titles to uncover actionable insights, and inform the team's business and design decisions early on in the production cycle, by answering questions like:

- How do various components among competitor and reference games compare to our game and what stands out?
- What opportunities do we find for our game in the context of other games available in the market?

14.1 RECIPE

Prep Time
- Approx. 5–7 days

Pots and Essentials
- Three to five selected competitor and/or reference games
- This recipe doesn't require participants

Nutritional Value

Do players like what they see or hear?	++
Do players understand it and know how to use it?	++
Do players engage in it?	++
Do players want to continue?	+

Typical serving time: Conception

14.1.1 Utensils

- Spreadsheet (e.g. Google Sheets, Microsoft Excel) and/or board with sticky notes (e.g. physical or digital one like Miro).
- Recording software (e.g. OBS) for video clips of specific interactions or flows, visualizing the insights.

14.1.2 Steps in the Process

I. During the kick-off meeting, agree on games to be analyzed, and define the study purpose. Discuss whether the focus is on selected game components, specific gameplay experience layer like usability or a more general overview of the player experience, and agree on data sources (e.g. player and/or expert reviews, forum and social media threads, let's play streams).
II. Play each game within a given time-box (e.g. first 2–3 hours) to familiarize yourself with the experience offered and gain context for later analysis.
III. (Optional) Conduct expert analysis, especially when the scope is focused on specific layers such as usability (more on it in Chapter 16).

DOI: 10.1201/9781003501909-17

IV. Search and pre-select specific data (e.g. search for and list "let's plays" to watch, save bookmarks with expert reviews to read, scrape player reviews). Next, gather and organize data from selected sources. If you decide to watch "let's play" videos, approach them like unmoderated sessions to observe player behaviour and to better understand nuance in statements made in reviews.

V. Conduct thematic analysis for each game and derive first insights. Next, conduct differential analysis to compare insights within a single title, and check which insights are shared among titles. First, you can use store filters to get a basic understanding of sentiment and to compare insights within a single title (e.g. compare 1-star vs. 5-star reviews). Next, create a table with insights recorded in rows (this will help you structure your report), and then mark in the subsequent columns which titles a given insight applies to.

VI. Prepare the report (use quotes, annotated screenshots, or video clips to illustrate insights) and conduct a debrief.

14.1.3 Tips

- Certainly, we can decide to analyze more than five titles and/or rely on all possible data sources, but bear in mind the constraints and potential saturation of results (i.e. we will still gain new information, but less and less with each additional title).
- While performing differential analysis, we may spot sub-groups of players focusing on different aspects of the experience (e.g. among 5-star reviews, we see that some of them concentrate on physics, and others are more revolving around narrative), which may provide us with a better understanding of potential player segments in the target audience.
- If we're analyzing a specific element or component (e.g. player onboarding), on top of thematic analysis, we can perform temporal analysis to better understand the evolution of the experience in time.
- Most of the time, we'll have to analyze a lot of data (e.g. hundreds, if not thousands of player reviews), which has its pros and cons:
  - We can supplement individual insights with the percentage of reviews that mention them to identify the most frequent ones.
  - If we have limited time, we can decide to reduce the amount of data to be analyzed. For instance, we can select 200 reviews for each title that meet certain criteria (e.g. reviews considered helpful by at least five people, and reflecting the overall positive-to-negative ratio of all reviews). However, we have to bear in mind that this will be a limitation to our analysis (e.g. we risk omitting less popular reviews containing valuable insights).
  - This is one of the rare occasions where AI solutions can be considered particularly useful. To make the most of it, one approach is to manually analyze a selected subset of reviews in a similar fashion to the approach described in the previous point, and later use AI to process the rest of the data, providing it with the same category set and definitions. However, we don't forget to check AI results with the actual data to avoid nasty surprises in the form of hallucinations or incorrect categorizations.

14.1.4 Variations

- Comparing the same titles on various platforms (e.g. console vs. PC) to spot platform-specific design solutions or patterns.
- At later phases of the production cycle, when the team has more specific questions (e.g. We want to better understand the tactics available or used by players during encounters on arenas), we may want to conduct shorter competitor analysis focused on answering the question or even organize a playtest to explore those aspects of the reference or competitor titles to derive more precise insights for our game.

14.1.5 Ways to Spoil the Dish

- We may think we've pinpointed that now we know which strengths to emulate and issues to fix in our game, but analyzing only well-received or commercially successful titles is leaving us prone to survivorship bias (i.e. overfocusing on titles that succeeded hides which strengths truly mattered and which issues can be fatal). To counter this, we may want to include lower-rated games to broaden our perspective, and surface overlooked issues and challenges to reduce guesswork. Does it mean we shouldn't perform competitor analysis based only on well-received titles? Of course, not! However, if we decide to perform it that way, we have to mind the limitations when deriving insights out of it.

14.2 SERVING EXAMPLE

During the conception phase for the game codenamed *Freedom Pilot*, we analyzed five selected titles (three competitors and two reference titles) as presented in Figure 14.1. This involved playing each title for approximately 2 hours to become familiar with it. Based on the time and budget constraints, we decided to base our analysis on player reviews posted on store pages (depending on the platform, this was Steam or Meta Quest).

First, we collected and organized player reviews. We excluded reviews of less than five words, such as "Cool game" or "This game sucks", which didn't provide information about the reasoning behind the review. Instead, we focused on longer comments, where players elaborated more on their impressions and opinions. Relying on the RGD approach and core pillars of the planned game, we created a list of 15 categories into which we assigned fragments of statements during thematic analysis (a single statement could be classified into multiple categories), and colour-coded them for sentiment we recognized (e.g. red for issues). We used an additional 16th "other" category, to which we assigned statements that might have some value, but didn't fit into any of the pre-defined categories. After the first round of categorization, we re-examined the responses that fell into the "other" category and, based on this, separated three additional categories (Figure 14.2).

After summarizing the individual categories and dividing statements into specific insights, we then proceeded to differential analysis to see which issues and strengths were common across all analyzed games and which appeared only in some of them. As a result, we marked in the report which games a given insight applies to (Figure 14.3).

ANALYSED GAMES

Table. 0. Analysed reference and competitor games.

Characteristic		Game				
Title		Warplanes: WWI Fighters	Warplanes: Battles over Pacific	Ultrawings 2	Ace Combat 7: Skies Unknown	Project Wingman
Type		Competitor	Competitor	Competitor	Reference	Reference
Abbreviation		W-WWI	W-BoP	U2	AC7	PW
VR Platforms		PC-VR, Quest	PC-VR, Quest, Pico	PC-VR, Quest, Pico	PSVR	PC-VR, PSVR2 (pending)
Release date	Steam	4 III 2021	26 I 2023 (VR only)	27 X 2022 (VR only)	31 I 2019 (PC only)	1 XII 2020 (PC-VR)
	Meta	29 VII 2021 (App Lab)	11 VIII 2022 (App Lab)	3 II 2022	-	-
Overall rating	Steam	91% (347 rating) PC + VR	83% (113 ratings) VR only	79% (91 ratings) VR only	87% (27743 ratings) PC only	94% (11302 ratings) PC + VR
	Meta	92% (3268 ratings)	89% (1114 ratings)	86% (693 ratings)	-	-

4/76

FIGURE 14.1 Report page with basic information about the games selected for analysis. (Courtesy of Gamedust.)

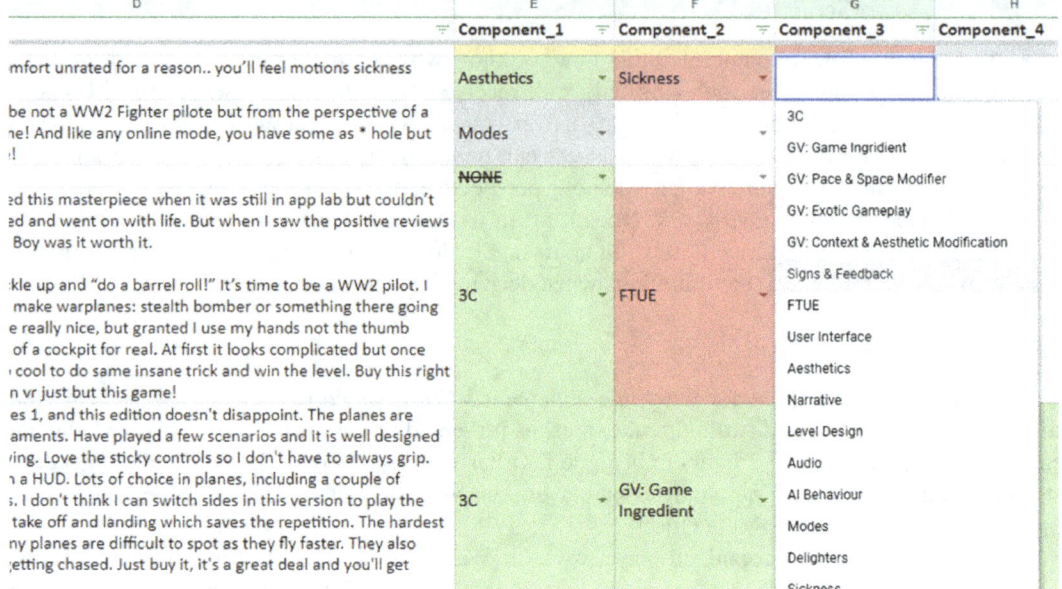

FIGURE 14.2 Excerpt from spreadsheet used to gather and analyze the data from player reviews. (Courtesy of Gamedust.)

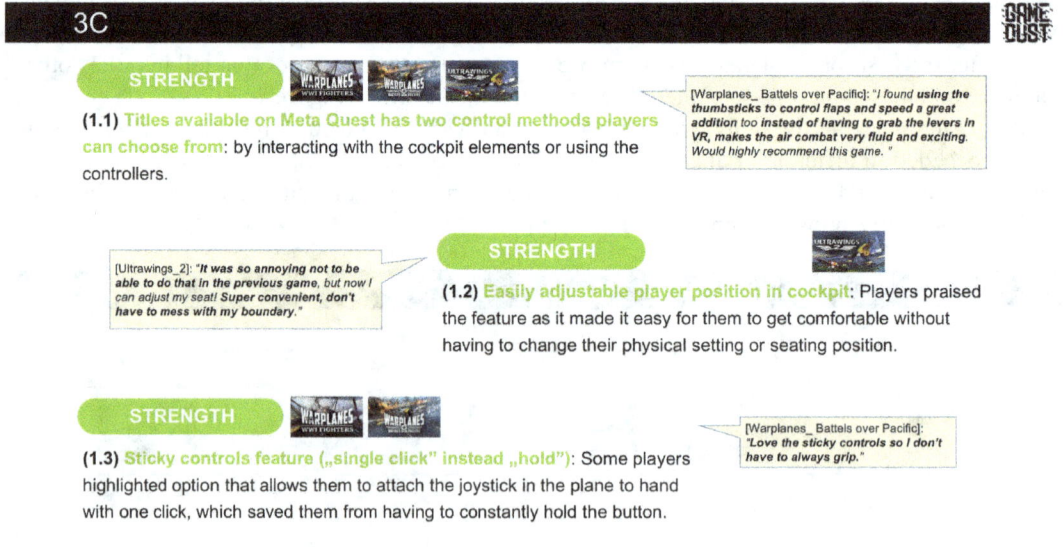

FIGURE 14.3 Report page with insights, including the competitor games they apply to. (Courtesy of Gamedust.)

Even though the analysis had the limitation of being focused only on successful titles, it helped identify the features and solutions of competitors that are worth relying on in the planned game, as well as those that are better to ignore to avoid falling into costly dead ends. On the production level, it acted as a reference to better define the game's scope and potential risks down the road. A welcome side effect was spotting topics of interest for future studies, as well as planning workshops for selected game elements (e.g. design workshop on the HUD discussed in Chapter 17).

15 Concept Test

The conception phase is the time in the production cycle when the high-level creative direction is most of the time not firmly established. To test and present various emerging ideas, the team often creates a variety of assets, such as concept art, narrative fragments, and even playable prototypes. Still, the team may often rely on their gut feeling when evaluating those assets. However, even the most original ideas can benefit from a second pair of eyes. Concept testing provides us with the opportunity to check if the ideas the team is so excited about resonate with our potential players as well. Certainly, we are not aiming to put a seal of approval on every idea or asset, but to spot red flags in critical elements of the emerging creative vision, before pursuing a specific direction consumes too much budget or time. With concept tests, we want to use the emerging ideas and assets to understand:

- What feelings and thoughts does this game (or its concept) evoke in players?
- Which ideas and aspects of the game resonate most with our target audience?
- Is the player's fantasy interesting for the players? What would it have to be to be engaging?

15.1 RECIPE

Prep Time
- Approx. 1–2 weeks

Pots and Essentials
- Selected early assets (e.g. from story premise and game world outline, through sketches and concept art, to working prototypes demonstrating mechanics)
- 6–12 participants

Nutritional Value

Do players like what they see or hear?	+++
Do players understand it and know how to use it?	–
Do players engage in it?	–
Do players want to continue?	–

Typical serving time: Conception phase

15.1.1 Utensils

- Interview and/or survey.
- Recording software (e.g. OBS) to capture sessions.
- Spreadsheet (e.g. Google Sheets, Microsoft Excel) and/or board with sticky notes (e.g. physical or digital one like Miro).

15.1.2 Steps in the Process

I. During the kick-off meeting, agree on elements that are most critical to realizing the creative vision, what the unknowns and the most pressing concerns are, to flesh out the study purpose. Discuss whether the focus is on specific game elements like the main plot and characters, layers like the art direction, the overall game concept, or a combination of these.

II. Gather the required assets and combine them into a digestible and structured format (e.g. it can be a presentation, but also a narrated recording of a prototype walkthrough). Generally, don't overdo assets presentation to avoid distorting how they're perceived, as your aim is to clearly communicate ideas, not to sell them.

DOI: 10.1201/9781003501909-18

III. Based on the study purpose, adapt methods and tools, and decide on study structure (e.g. first, present assets to the participants in more detail and then discuss them during the interview or decide to perform an interview intertwined with the presentation of assets, or decide to conduct a survey). Next, prepare an interview or survey (or both) relying mostly on general, open-ended questions to explore participants' reactions to assets (e.g. "What do you think this game is about?", "What comes to your mind after reading this fragment of the story?"). Write instructions and prepare the moderator guide based on the methods and tools prepared.

IV. Recruit participants.

V. Conduct sessions.

VI. Conduct a thematic analysis to understand what was clear and what was unclear about the concept, what seemed exciting and what was off-putting to participants, and what emotions and expectations (e.g. hopes or fears) the concept evoked in them. Depending on the study purpose and time available, you may also want to conduct a more structured differential analysis.

VII. Prepare the report (use quotes and annotated assets to illustrate insights) and conduct a debrief.

15.1.3 Tips

- We don't need to have production-quality assets. Even the hand-drawn sketches or basic plot descriptions can provide us with the required information.
- If there are several concept versions discussed by the team, we can still assess them all in one study to support more informed decision-making. For example, we can ask participants to arrange the concepts in order from the one that best fits the provided criteria to the one that least fits it. Then, we can ask them for the reasons behind the ordering.
- It's a moderated study that can be conducted effectively both on-site and remote, depending on what you agree with the team. However, if our time or budget is limited, an unmoderated version (e.g. relying on survey format for both presentation and questions) can provide us with quick and dirty insights.
- If we have to introduce the overall game concept, which is still vague, we can use comparisons used by the team (e.g. "This game is like X meets Y") and check how participants respond to those references.
- It is worth asking participants to describe the game in their own words (e.g. How would you describe this game to your friend?) to understand how clear the overall concept is.
- In this book, we focused our attention on moderating individual sessions. However, this recipe can be run either individually or with small participant groups. If we're new to group formats, we can consider sessions run in so-called dyads (two participants) or triads (three participants). These are much easier to moderate than typical Focus Group Interviews with 8–12 participants, while still offering some view into how players build on each other's thoughts or uncover nuances that might not surface in individual sessions.

15.1.4 Variations

- We mentioned recorded prototype walkthroughs as assets. Certainly, if we have playable prototypes, we can include them among the tested assets and let participants play them themselves to better grasp the concept, and discuss their reactions afterwards.
- When we plan to involve the target audience in refining the concept or its aspects (e.g. world-building), the concept test can be used as a warm-up before the co-design workshop (more on it in Chapter 17).

15.1.5 WAYS TO SPOIL THE DISH

- Preparing and selecting assets can be tricky. We don't want to swamp players with too much material or vague ideas, because they may struggle to give meaningful answers. As a rule of thumb, it's better for us to focus on keeping clarity while presenting assets rather than on their completeness. If participants felt confused, it should be because of the concept, not our delivery of it.
- We may easily misinterpret polite remarks as real excitement. Participants may say that something is "cool" or even "awesome", because they don't want to hurt our feelings or just because of the sheer opportunity of seeing a game at such an early stage. To protect ourselves against this, we can rely on active listening techniques (e.g. clarifying), and checking participants' understanding. In general, it's better for us and the team to hear "I don't get it" now than to discover it in the midst of the production phase.

15.2 SERVING EXAMPLE

For the game codenamed *Freedom Pilot*, we conducted a concept test focused on evaluating three competing art concepts for one of the game's main characters. Each concept was developed to represent a strong female lead, aligned with the narrative direction and character dossier prepared by the Lead Designer. The study was requested to mitigate the risk of biased representation of the female character stemming from the production team's composition (at the time, the production team consisted entirely of men). The study purpose was to check which of the proposed art concepts best captured the intended character traits, and on a more basic level, whether these traits actually reflected a strong female character.

This study was a rare occasion when we decided to invite participants based on socio-demographic criteria. We recruited only women to provide a potential counterweight to the team's perspective on the assets created. Due to limited budget and time, we relied on friends and family for recruitment, and instead of interviews, we opted for a survey with questions inspired by a review of resources on the representation of strong female characters in games, film, and literature. To minimize presentation bias, we also agreed with the team that the art concepts needed to be delivered in a similar format and quality (e.g. each character was presented in the same poses and profiles on the grey background).

To give participants some context, we first shared a short description of the game concept. And later showed all three concepts and asked participants to order them from the one that represents the strong female character best to the one that does it least, and provide their rationale for the ordering (Figure 15.1).

Next, we asked more detailed questions about each character's perceived traits, and later provided a character dossier describing the main character's backstory and motivations for participants to read and to share their thoughts on how well it described a strong female character. Later, we again showed three art concepts and asked which one best resonated with the provided dossier. We designed a study structure in that way to replicate the process of meeting new people, from first impressions of someone (watching visual assets), through learning new facts about them (reading character dossier), to developing a certain attitude (rewatching visual assets). This way, we wanted to see which character would be most consistent and which would give designers the opportunity to surprise players by challenging some of their initial impressions.

We performed thematic analysis to categorize participant responses, and supplemented it with differential analysis to highlight differences in perceived character traits and assess how consistently each concept aligned with the dossier (Figure 15.2). What's interesting, and obvious in hindsight, is that specific design elements (e.g. costume detailing, accessories, and facial expression) contributed to the evaluation of the character's traits.

Concept arts

Below are some concept arts featuring characters from the game.
Please review them before answering the questions below.

In your opinion, Do any of the above characters accurately represent a strong   *
female character?

Try to justify your choice by describing:
- why you chose a particular character.
- why you rejected other characters.

It may be that none or all of the characters represent a strong female character in your
opinion. In such a situation, try to describe the specific elements that influenced your
choice.

Your answer

FIGURE 15.1 Survey fragment with character concept arts and an open-ended question. (Courtesy of Gamedust.)

MATCH BETWEEN CONCEPTS AND CHARACTER DESCRIPTION

(3.3) Learning the character dossier most often changed the perception of concept art #1:
Although concept art #1 itself was perceived as too strong, hostile, and stereotypical in the beginning, after learning the dossier, some participants started to see it from different perspective (e.g. rather than hostile and stereotypical, concept art #1 started to be perceived as sad and hardened by experience). Importantly, two other concepts didn't see such shifts in participants perception, with concept #2 perceived as most closely matching the dossier, while concept #3 was considered too young and delicate to fit the description.

Interestingly, the character description changed my perception of the concepts. Now my favourite character is #1

#1 - mature [...] after reading the description, I also see that she isn't hostile, just sad and deeply experienced. [...] #2 is a "fierce" warrior, although she lack a shred of empathy, and #3 is too delicate and young for the experiences described in the description.

'Character #2 seems like the perfect candidate, as I argued in the question above [she knows who she is and what she wants]. The second best candidate is character #1 because she seems sharp and fierce, which is a likely expression with such a background. Character #3 is too delicate. Of course, she could be someone with a similar family history, but [...] Character #3 seems too submissive..'

After reading the character description, I decided to choose Mary #1 as my choice. [...]

21/24

FIGURE 15.2 Report page with a finding on the match between concept arts and character dossier. (Courtesy of Gamedust.)

We have to note that the study was a compromise between the cost and effect, and had a number of limitations, such as the reliance on friends and family, and the use of a questionnaire instead of an interview (e.g. the inability to ask live follow-up questions on certain topics in participants' statements), to name two. At the same time, even under constraints at the time, it still provided the team with a better understanding about which concept features best conveyed the intended character traits, and revealed a need for small but vital tweaks of the character's backstory to represent it as intended. Insights gathered also helped to support early alignment between team members focused on different game components (e.g. art, gameplay, narrative) while flagging areas requiring further iteration.

16 Expert Analysis

In pre-production, the team is busy translating concepts into concrete assets to determine how the game should be made together with the scope, budget, and time needed. As new assets are created, there isn't always time or opportunity to take a step back from work and reflect on it. In such circumstances, relatively obvious issues with gameplay experience can often be overlooked or downplayed, as the game "is not ready". Studies with participants are generally preferred, but aren't always the most pragmatic or cost-effective choice in early pre-production (e.g. when we're dealing with unstable builds and frequent shifts in feature or system design). During analysis, we rely on established knowledge and good practices to quickly identify issues, especially those in accessibility and usability layers, and those that can carry on to the production phase, where they can be much more difficult or costly to fix. With expert analysis, we want to inform the team's decisions and reduce the risk of future rework by answering questions like:

- Do selected design solutions introduce barriers to entry for players?
- Is the interface clear and provides the information players need at a given moment?
- Can basic interactions be performed effectively and efficiently, and are they consistent with genre expectations?

16.1 RECIPE

Prep Time
- Approx. 1–3 days

Pots and Essentials
- Assets like game builds, interactive prototypes, and interface mock-ups
- This recipe doesn't require participants

Nutritional Value

Do players like what they see or hear?	–
Do players understand it and know how to use it?	+++
Do players engage in it?	+
Do players want to continue?	–

Typical serving time: Pre-production

16.1.1 UTENSILS

- Recording software (e.g. OBS) to capture your walkthroughs.
- Spreadsheet (e.g. Google Sheets, Microsoft Excel) and/or board with sticky notes (e.g. physical or digital one like Miro).

16.1.2 STEPS IN THE PROCESS

I. During the kick-off meeting, agree on the scope for analysis (e.g. it could be an interface for a specific game system, evaluating player onboarding or analyzing gameplay with focus on accessibility and usability).

II. Walkthrough the available assets. Aim to best understand the design intent behind the specific solutions (e.g. What the team is trying to achieve? What assumptions they made?). You can go through the assets while thinking aloud, and record your session to capture initial impressions and reactions. During your walkthrough, focus on things such as:
- Clarity (e.g. Are game objectives clearly communicated by the game?).
- Feedback (e.g. Does the game respond to player actions in a meaningful way? Are consequences of those actions apparent?).

DOI: 10.1201/9781003501909-19

- Efficiency and Effectiveness (e.g. Can core actions be performed smoothly with the desired outcome?).
- Consistency (e.g. Are naming conventions, button placement, visual metaphors, or interactions coherent across the game?).
- Cognitive load (e.g. Does the game provide the player with too much information at a time, such as complicated instructions, unclear symbols, conflicting feedback?).
- Accessibility (e.g. Are there potential barriers to entry present in the experience?).

III. Do another walkthrough of the assets relying on existing knowledge in the form of:
- Frameworks (e.g. RGD we discussed in Chapter 1 or APX [AbleGamers Foundation 2022]).
- Guidelines (e.g. Xbox Accessibility Guidelines [Microsoft 2023], BBC Subtitle Guidelines [BBC 2022]).
- Theory (e.g. Self-Determination Theory (SDT) and (game)Flow discussed in Chapter 2).

IV. Conduct thematic analysis focusing on the accessibility and usability layers of the experience, and derive first insights. If feasible (e.g. when evaluating player onboarding), conduct temporal analysis to spot points where the process under consideration breaks.

V. Prepare the report (use annotated screenshots or video clips to illustrate insights) and conduct a debrief.

16.1.3 Tips

- You can optionally support yourself with existing metrics (e.g. checking contrast ratio of selected element against background with contrast checkers; probing text difficulty with Flesch Kincaid Grade Level), but use them as guidance, not the final evaluation. For instance, a 3:1 contrast ratio may not be sufficient for most players to see something clearly, as the visibility of an element also depends on things such as its placement and size.
- We can also rely on heuristic sets (e.g. general ones like Nielsen's Heuristics [2024] or more specific ones like Game Usability Heuristics [Desurvire & Wiberg 2009]), but some of them may be too general for our purposes or impossible to reliably assess during expert analysis (e.g. "The game uses humour well").
- Don't guess the player reactions and issues, but highlight potential risks and areas that need further evaluation through studies with participants. An expected side effect of expert analysis is that it allows us to identify potential areas for research further in the production cycle.
- Expert analysis is a good first step for us to better understand the game and its creative vision, spot known issues and violations of good practices, and prepare for future studies with participants. After all, if we remove known accessibility and usability issues now, we free future participants to get deeper into the experience, creating space for deriving more in-depth insights.

16.1.4 Variations

- Accessibility review – Accessibility is a vast and complex topic (in larger teams, we may find dedicated specialist working in that discipline), so it's worthwhile to conduct expert analysis with scope focused mainly on assessing potential barriers in the experience (i.e. cognitive, auditory, vision, hearing, or emotional which can be situational, temporal, or permanent in nature). The rule of thumb is to do it early in the pre-production, so insights have better chances to be applied while designing various features, and not be considered as a costly afterthought in production.

- Health check – Some teams benefit from running expert analysis on a regular basis during pre-production to early production to check assets and generate questions before planned studies with players. These analyses are usually smaller in scope to stay cost-effective.

16.1.5   WAYS TO SPOIL THE DISH

- We all have our own tastes (e.g. "I love games with rich narrative"), so it can be tempting to broaden the scope of an analysis to areas beyond our expertise, perhaps by pointing out what we feel is lacking in the game mechanics, narrative, or art. But it's not our role! With expert analysis, we focus on the accessibility and usability layers of the experience, and staying reliable by doing what we agreed to do, and not doing what we didn't agree on.
- Evaluating based on our own preferences or guessing player reactions (e.g. "This will be too difficult for players") can steer us into serving unfair criticism (or praise, when the thing under consideration matches our preferences). To avoid falling into the abyss of subjective opinions and arbitrary evaluations, we stay grounded in the existing knowledge and what the game is trying to achieve. Remember that the expert analysis is also a tool for generating questions to be explored later with players. For instance, it's normal to have doubts on difficulty, especially in pre-production, but doubt it's not an insight to be acted on immediately. It can act as a potential prompt to check it with players, later in the production cycle.
- Literally applying existing knowledge (e.g. guidelines or theories) without considering genre specificity or design intention. For instance, if we point at the lack of elaborate player onboarding in roguelike where learning by doing is at the core of the experience, the team may doubt our general understanding of what they're trying to achieve. Recall what we said in Chapter 12: the analysis to be valuable has to be based both on what is observed and the information we have on the game, tailored to the specific context. We aim to figure out what the team is trying to achieve, and if we have doubts, it's always worthwhile to clarify it with them.

16.2   SERVING EXAMPLE

Expert analyses we conduct will focus on accessibility and usability layers, but their scope doesn't need to be confined to interface elements or strictly to what's explicitly outlined in established guidelines. In many cases, it's valuable to broaden our perspective and apply the same perspective to less obvious elements of the game.

While working on the publisher's side on the racing game *Sunrise GP* (a Nintendo Switch title developed by a five-person team, Garage 5), we supported the development team by conducting regular health checks throughout the production cycle to help prioritize design improvements and plan necessary studies within the available budget. During one of our pre-production health checks, we started by evaluating interface elements on the mock-ups prepared by the team to get rid of typical accessibility and usability issues (Figure 16.1).

Besides mock-ups, we received a game build with one track to look for potential issues with the interface and interactions. At the same time, we knew based on documentation and discussions with the team that one of their goals was to make maps more appealing by placing distinctive Points of Interest (POIs) such as a viaduct with a passing train or harbour cranes carrying crates. So, we paid additional attention to these elements during analysis. It turned out that some POIs were partially or fully hidden by surrounding geometry or appeared too briefly due to their placement on track, making them unlikely to be noticed by players (Figure 16.2). In other words, while we weren't guessing whether players may like POIs or not, we identified concrete issues in the current team's approach to using them within level design.

(G)UI ELEMENTS: MENU SCREENS

SERIOUS

(1.1) Low readability of key interface elements in the menu screens: The game doesn't consistently use adequate contrast between the background and key information. Buttons either have no background or have semi-transparent backgrounds [1]. Additionally, labels in tables and on buttons are placed against a non-uniform background, reducing their readability [2]. Overall, this makes the interface less readable.

SUGGESTIONS:
- To increase interface readability, consider a solid, dark background for the buttons.
- For the icons for the gamepad/Joy-Con buttons, consider placing them on a black background with a white outline.

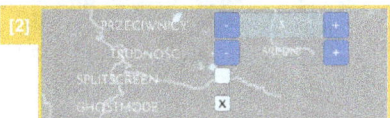

5/20

FIGURE 16.1 Report page with example usability issue. (Courtesy of Gamedust.)

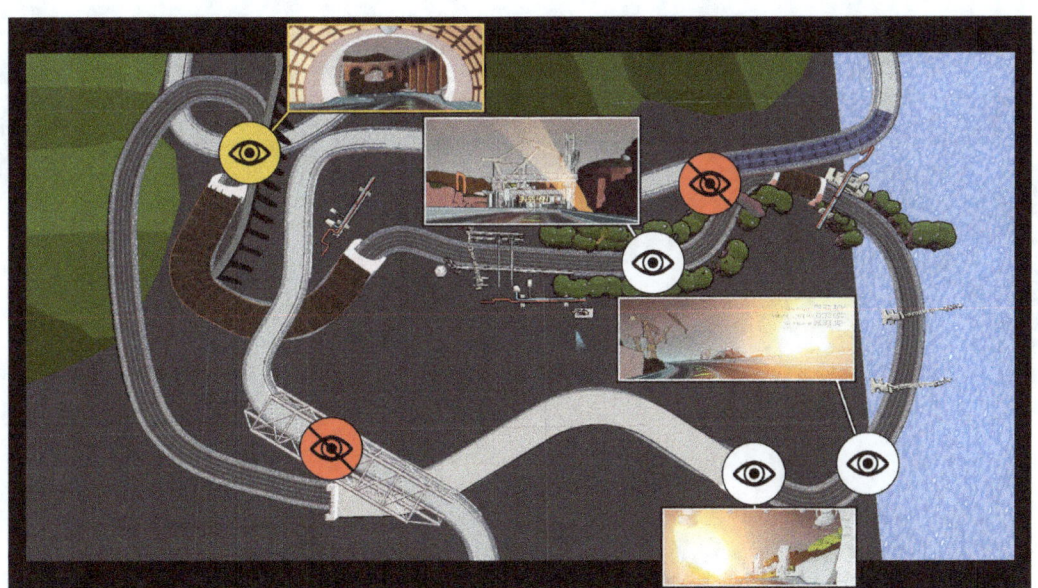

FIGURE 16.2 Top-down view of the track with annotated Points of Interest, including their visibility. (Courtesy of Gamedust.)

The analysis informed the team's approach to level design of other tracks, and solved a few issues for conducting effective studies (i.e. basically, if participants can't see POIs, they can't evaluate them). Generally, while expert analysis is commonly applied to traditional UI elements (e.g. buttons, menus, dialog boxes) and interactions, we can thoughtfully extend it to other game elements and components without losing focus on accessibility and usability.

REFERENCES

AbleGamers Foundation (2022). *Accessible Player Experiences (APX)*. https://accessible.games/accessible-player-experiences/

BBC (2022). *BBC Subtitle Guidelines*. https://www.bbc.co.uk/accessibility/forproducts/guides/subtitles/

Desurvire, H., & Wiberg, C. (2009). Game usability heuristics (PLAY) for evaluating and designing better games: The next iteration. In *Online Communities and Social Computing. OCSC 2009. Lecture Notes in Computer Science* (vol. 5621, pp. 557–566).

Nielsen, J. (2024). *10 Heuristics for User Interface Design*. Nielsen Norman Group. https://www.nngroup.com/articles/ten-usability-heuristics/

Microsoft (2023). *Xbox Accessibility Guidelines*. https://learn.microsoft.com/en-us/gaming/accessibility/guidelines

17 (Co)design Workshop

During the conception phase, the team answered the question "What game do we want to make?", and now, during the pre-production phase, focus is turned to "How should we make it?". Instead of waiting for each discipline in the team to tackle design challenges in isolation, we can catalyze alignment by inviting stakeholders (and optionally players or external experts) to flesh out solutions collaboratively. (Co)design workshops provide us with a structured format to discuss ideas and iterate on solutions, while taking into consideration constraints and opportunities that might stay hidden in individual work. By bringing together diverse perspectives, the team can faster resolve project discussions and develop a more coherent approach to realizing a creative vision, saving both time and budget. With co-design workshops, we want to explore:

- What are the critical goals and constraints for this game element?
- Which requirements are vital for realizing the creative vision and delivering the best player experience?
- Which solution best balances creative vision and player needs with technical feasibility, budget, and time constraints?

17.1   RECIPE

Prep Time
- Approx. 2–3 days

Pots and Essentials
- Early sketches, mock-ups, or prototypes of the target game element
- Three to ten participants. The number of participants varies, as it can be just key disciplines responsible for designing and implementing specific elements (e.g. art, game design, narrative, and programming), but we may want to invite perspectives external to the team (e.g. players or domain experts)

Nutritional Value

Do players like what they see or hear?	++
Do players understand it and know how to use it?	++
Do players engage in it?	+
Do players want to continue?	–

Typical serving time: Pre-production

17.1.1   UTENSILS

- Workshop plan.
- Recording software (e.g. OBS) to capture workshop session.
- Board with sticky notes (e.g. physical or digital one like Miro).

17.1.2   STEPS IN THE PROCESS

I. During the kick-off meeting, agree on elements to focus on during the workshop (e.g. HUD layout) and people that should be involved in the workshop session, because of their impact on developing solutions and knowledge on constraints (e.g. team members) or using the solution (e.g. players) or bringing specific knowledge (e.g. domain experts).

DOI: 10.1201/9781003501909-20

II. Gather existing sketches or prototypes and other relevant reference assets (e.g. competitor HUD screenshots), as well as the results of previous research and analysis (if applicable).

III. Based on an agreed purpose, prepare a workshop structure and plan. Although workshops can be planned for a whole day or even longer sprint, in a smaller team, it's good to start from more rapid sessions to address the most pressing or discussed topics, ensure a good cost-to-effect ratio, and build buy-in for this method. Our workshop plan might look like this:

- Warm-up (15 minutes): Discuss the workshop purpose, its main topics, and summarize what is already known.
- Setting goals (15 minutes): List, discuss, and agree on the player goals (based on creative vision and prepared assets) to be supported by elements under consideration.
- Individual solutions (15 minutes): Participants draft their own ideas and solutions.
- Group Walkthrough (20 minutes): Each participant shares their solution.
- Break (10 minutes).
- Synthesize (15 minutes): Discuss common patterns, surfacing constraints and opportunities, and flag divergent proposals.
- Prioritization (20 minutes): Discuss the strongest directions within existing constraints worth pursuing further.
- Next steps (10 minutes): Discuss actions to be taken after workshop (e.g. who prototypes what, and how the team will proceed with it).

IV. Invite team members and/or recruit external participants. Distribute the workshop plan together with an assets package to participants at least 1 day before the workshop, so they can come prepared.

V. Conduct the workshop, with the aim to iterate quickly rather than polishing solutions. Make sure the team doesn't stray into side topics by using techniques discussed in Chapter 11 or prompts like "How might we approach <specific constraint, creative or player experience goal>?" to keep discussion aligned with the workshop purpose. When discussing solutions, take note of which ideas address player goals within constraints.

VI. Prepare and share the short workshop summary with addressed player goals, and the proposed solutions, together with the trade-offs made, open questions, unresolved discussions, and agreed next steps.

17.1.3 TIPS

- We set time-boxes for activities during the workshop to prevent time overruns, and for sessions longer than 60–90 minutes, we plan short breaks and activities unrelated to workshop purpose to keep participants focused and engaged.
- It's easy to find creative solutions if we invite only team members dealing exclusively with design and art, but to root those solutions in the technical and business realities of the game, having programmers and producers on board is invaluable.

17.1.4 VARIATIONS

- Generally, we focused on a workshop setting where we invited team members only. However, we can conduct workshops with a wide range of participants, depending on a purpose, we may want to additionally invite domain experts (e.g. when working on a game world set in a specific historical period, we can invite historians; when trying to figure out barriers our players may face and how to ease them, we may want to turn to accessibility advocates and experts) or players (e.g. certainly when we think of accessibility, we can also invite players facing specific barriers to better understand their lived experiences; when working on a sequel, we may want to invite those who played previous entry, to check whether the creative vision for the next entry is not alienating them).

- When it comes to workshop format, we can opt to mix participant groups together in one session (e.g. team members with players or domain experts) or keep them separate. For instance, we can conduct the workshop session in two parts. In the first one, the team works on ideas and comes up with solutions, and in the second part (taking place on the same or the other day), these solutions are discussed and evaluated with players.

17.1.5 WAYS TO SPOIL THE DISH

- Skipping the preparation may seem like saving time, but it often leads to spending even more time to agree on what we know and why we're in the workshop, instead of working on solutions. Generally, we provide participants with materials in advance to provide them with the context necessary to effectively participate in the workshop session.
- When someone takes over the discussion, quieter or more junior team members may be less willing to share their perspectives, which results in working on a limited number of ideas or reinforcing existing biases. To ensure that every voice is heard, we ask quieter participants to share their thoughts, modify speaking order in discussions, or intertwine group and individual activities.
- Some participants may focus too much on polishing sketches or solution drafts, which consumes energy needed to pursue other directions, and may prompt sticking too early to a single idea (because it's polished). On such occasions, it's worth reminding participants that we want to focus our energy on exploring ideas and solutions, rather than on production-quality deliverables.

17.2 SERVING EXAMPLE

For the game codenamed *Freedom Pilot*, we conducted a series of rapid design workshops focused on developing cockpit and HUD elements for the player's aircraft. The workshops were scheduled early in pre-production to flesh out ideas that could be implemented in a prototype prior to an upcoming 3C component playtest (3C standing for Character, Control, and Camera). The aim was to ensure that solutions adopted in HUD didn't hinder players' ability to understand what was happening with the aircraft or control it.

The first workshop was conducted with the Lead Game Designer and Art Director to agree on the creative and player goals for the cockpit and HUD, and then explore solutions together before committing time to implementation. Workshop materials included selected pages of the competitor analysis report (see Chapter 14), and a sketch made by the Lead Game Designer presenting the information he wanted to convey to the players (Figure 17.1).

The first workshop session focused on aligning around the player goals and creative constraints, and listing information perceived as necessary for the players to efficiently and effectively control the aircraft. We ended up agreeing that the art team will prepare non-interactive interface mock-ups to see in what form and where to place specific elements in the game (Figure 17.2). We also decided that the next session will be the right time to invite members of the programming team to better understand what are the technical constraints and possibilities.

In the second workshop, we discussed and refined the prepared mock-up with the Art Director sketching specific solutions in real time. Once most cockpit and HUD elements were agreed on, the discussion turned to player awareness of allies' and opponents' positioning. The team discussed a radar solution with additional spatial indicators (e.g. directional arrows). The Art Director considered the radar less consistent with the game's historical period, but the Lead Game Designer deemed it essential to meet player goals. Having the Programmer present in the workshop helped to quickly settle the discussion. While both options had their pros and cons, implementing a radar would require significant development effort, and at that point, we didn't have enough insight (e.g. from playtests) to justify it. Given programming team capacity and priorities, the radar concept was shelved in favour of the lighter solution for the game

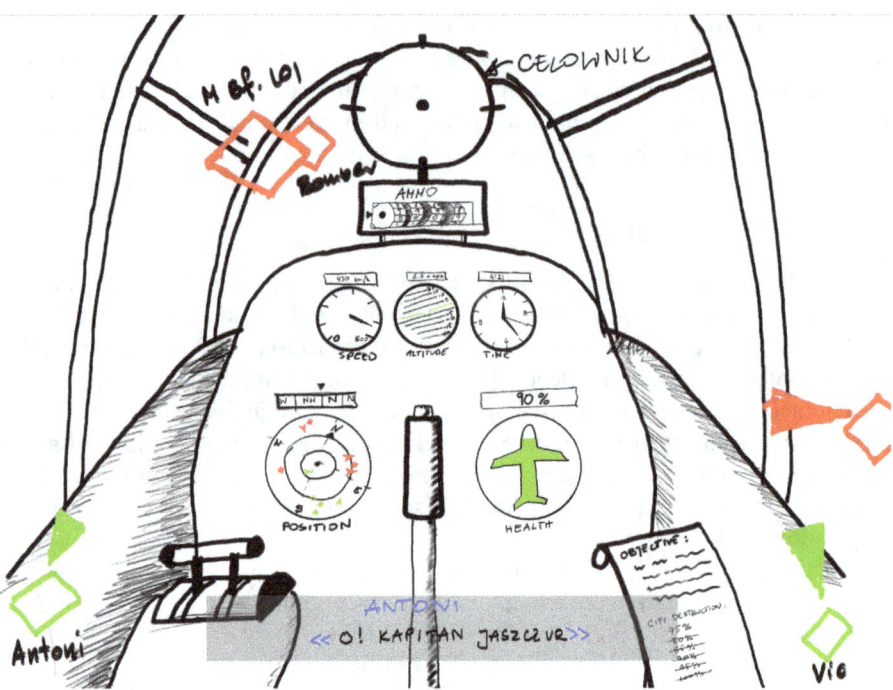

FIGURE 17.1 A hand-drawn sketch of an airplane cockpit with highlighted information that the player should have access to. (Courtesy of Gamedust.)

FIGURE 17.2 Non-interactive interface mock-up implemented in the game engine. (Courtesy of Gamedust.)

prototype. The next steps included revising a mock-up to reflect the decisions made by the team, and agreeing on steps specific team members have to make to prepare assets required for implementation (Figure 17.3).

FIGURE 17.3   Revised interactive interface mock-up in the prototype. (Courtesy of Gamedust.)

Design workshops allowed the team to quickly find feasible and desirable solutions while bringing together design intent with technical constraints. The solutions agreed during workshops had team support, allowing them to confidently implement the first version of the cockpit and HUD interface in the game prototype, as well as come up with more detailed questions for component playtest planned further in the production cycle.

18 Team Play Session (or Review)

It happens that the team creating the game shares various materials among themselves (e.g. assets such as graphics, sounds, but also prototypes). The spontaneous feedback that appears from other team members can be a good source of information and a first test of the early iterations of created things. However, it often happens that this feedback is undirected and lacks enough structure to draw actionable conclusions from it (after all, the answer to the question "what do you think?" or "how do you like it?" gives a lot of room to manoeuvre), it's also rarely written down, which makes it difficult to return to selected threads. One of the solutions that can support the team in improving the quality of feedback provided to each other is to propose the framework for giving feedback (e.g. by sharing good practices or even templates) and support in organizing team play sessions (i.e. a designated time during which the team or part of it, plays and provides feedback on the game or its selected elements) or supporting team reviews (i.e. structured way of providing feedback to assets like concept art, narrative beats). When supporting team play sessions or reviews, we help to answer a few basic questions:

- What do you want feedback on?
- What are your key questions?
- What kind of feedback is most needed by you right now?

18.1 RECIPE

Prep Time
- Approx. 1–3 days

Pots and Essentials
- Assets that team member(s) is working on
- Team members as participants (possibly coming from varied disciplines)

Nutritional Value

Do players like what they see or hear?	+
Do players understand it and know how to use it?	+
Do players engage in it?	+
Do players want to continue?	–

Typical serving time: Pre-production, production

18.1.1 UTENSILS

- Survey or interview questions.

18.1.2 STEPS IN THE PROCESS

I. Whether you initiate the discussion or have a team member approach you directly, offer support in obtaining more structured and useful feedback. You don't have to organize a formal kick-off meeting, but you can secure time to discuss what kind of feedback will be useful to make progress with the given asset. Then, prepare questions together and choose an appropriate format (e.g. a short survey to be published with the asset). In the end, agree on where and how the questions and assets will be published by the team member (e.g. on which internal messaging channel), and the deadline for interested team members to respond.

II. Monitor the responses and support team member(s) in results interpretation. Ensure the team discusses the results and determines which feedback will be addressed.

DOI: 10.1201/9781003501909-21

18.1.3 TIPS

- This method has an "egg and chicken" problem built into it. It requires the studio's organizational maturity, which allows team members to take time and space to reflect on created assets from a player experience perspective. At the same time, it helps to develop organizational maturity by fostering a culture of open feedback and reflecting on one's work. Especially, before it's introduced to the team, it's worth agreeing with the stakeholder responsible for time and budgeting of the team's work (e.g. producer) to allocate time for team members to provide each other with feedback. While discussing the introduction of the method to studio practice, it's worth highlighting that:
  - Feedback on early and non-finished assets is better than late validation of things that are considered "ready".
  - It's not an exercise in assessing someone's performance, but an opportunity to discuss work in progress to better iterate on it.
  - All disciplines should be encouraged to share feedback, as varied perspectives help to uncover more valuable information.
  - All disciplines should be encouraged to share their work, whether it's a single concept art or a more elaborate mechanic or system, to detect potential issues and solve them on the spot.
  - Last but not least, team play sessions or reviews don't replace player feedback; they're just an additional step before we invite players.
- While preparing questions, we still want to leave room for general comments or unsolicited feedback to not miss potentially valuable information, and to keep team members engaged by letting them know they're heard.

18.1.4 VARIATIONS

- Team play sessions or reviews are more of a snack than a full dish. They're aimed at building a mindset in the team to seek feedback and iterate based on it before we run studies with participants (not instead). In the recipe we discussed, the simplest form of structuring team feedback in a review format, which has a small risk of disrupting teamwork (e.g. it's voluntary to provide feedback), while fostering more informed decision-making. However, depending on the needs and possibilities, we can support organizing more elaborate play sessions where the whole team is supposed to participate (e.g. between milestones, so the team has a chance to reflect on the gameplay experience in its current state and what still needs to be done to achieve the milestone goals).

18.1.5 WAYS TO SPOIL THE DISH

- We have to watch out for team members weaponizing gathered insights, especially if they're at odds with insights we gathered based on studies with players. First, play sessions and reviews are not the first choice for teams, where we spotted some of the misconceptions about user research still alive (e.g. "We do not need you – we are the players!" discussed in Chapter 3), or where the team has little to no experience working with insights gathered from studies with players. Before introducing the method, consider the studio's organizational maturity. Second, we have to acknowledge that teams' and players' perspectives may differ, and frame the method as a step towards studies with players, not as a standalone study. Third, we don't assume from the start that our player-derived insights are right (remember, we can rarely be sure we're right, and there's always a chance we're wrong). Take a closer look at what exactly is at odds and try to understand the reasons for it.

- When we don't have clear questions we want to find answers for, we can get a lot of information that may be valuable, but might as well miss the point, making the sessions and reviews less productive.
- Even if we have clear questions in an appropriate format, the team may fall into the trap of reducing sessions or reviews to a "likes and dislikes" fest. Our responsibility is to ensure that the team doesn't try to "act like players", but evaluate assets based on their domain knowledge together with how well those assets support intended player experience (e.g. defined by creative vision, core pillars).
- While most of us will focus on supporting and preparing appropriate questions, if we don't monitor and support how the team analyzes gathered data, we can end up with a method that invites harmful misinterpretations. And even if we help to derive proper insights, if they don't lead to decisions or actions, the method can quickly lose its credibility.

18.2   SERVING EXAMPLE

Introducing and using team play sessions or reviews is more of a process rather than a one-off study, and can be tricky. To support your endeavours on the book's website, you will find the template "GURCB_01_010101- book – play session readme and survey - template". I used it with some teams to support them in self-defining what they want to ask, and how to ask it to gather more structured and useful feedback, focusing on monitoring how they use it, and supporting them only when necessary. While using the template, remember to first consider the studio's maturity level and potential misconceptions that may still linger in the team (described in Chapter 3). Next, agree on the necessary requirements and approach with your stakeholders (e.g. allocated time, supporting open feedback, treating it as a step towards research with participants, not the standalone study) and tailor the template to your needs.

In my experience, team play sessions and reviews helped to spot and solve some of the issues early in the process, leaving more room for gathering deeper insights from players. They also led to discussions more focused on realising creative vision, or about the creative vision itself, still leaving room for spotting unobvious ideas and solutions. However, it worked well primarily in studios where the user research role was understood by stakeholders and where the insights derived from studies with players were already valued by the team and acted on.

19 Usability (Play)Test

As prototypes and builds featuring gameplay fragments or selected systems begin to emerge, the team is usually strongly focused on "how much fun the game is". However, even if the game mechanics and systems are clever and beautifully implemented, players may still get stuck, miss key mechanics, or misinterpret information given by the game, which effectively may prevent them from engaging in it. Usability (play)tests can help us spot those issues early, before they become costly to fix or too embedded in the gameplay experience to be easily changed. We simply follow the logic that we relied on in this book: first, we need to remove potential barriers to entry for players so that they can efficiently learn the rules of the game and use them to finally get engaged in it. With usability playtests, we want to observe players trying to play the game to understand:

- Do players understand and know how to perform what is expected from them by the game?
- Can players effectively and efficiently perform the actions required by the game?
- Where and why do players get stuck or confused by the game?

19.1 RECIPE

Prep Time
- Approx. 4–7 days

Pots and Essentials
- Game build or other prototype (e.g. core mechanic prototype, gym with specific system or component, gameplay fragment, but also an interactive interface mock-up)
- Five to eight participants

Nutritional Value

Do players like what they see or hear?	–
Do players understand it and know how to use it?	+++
Do players engage in it?	+
Do players want to continue?	–

Typical serving time: Pre-production, Production

19.1.1 UTENSILS

- Tasks, interview, and/or survey.
- Recording software (e.g. OBS) to capture sessions.
- Spreadsheet (e.g. Google Sheets, Microsoft Excel) and/or a board with sticky notes (e.g. physical or digital one like Miro).

19.1.2 STEPS IN THE PROCESS

I. During the kick-off meeting, agree on which of the game elements are most critical for players to understand and use efficiently and effectively in order to engage in the experience. With a focus on usability over game enjoyment, the discussion may include unknowns, risks, or concerns related to game elements such as UI, menu screens, interacting with core gameplay systems, but also player onboarding.
II. Gather the required assets and check if they are suitable to realize the study purpose (e.g. stable build with no critical bugs in the elements or systems under consideration).

DOI: 10.1201/9781003501909-22

III. Based on the study purpose, decide on and adapt methods and tools (e.g. whether it will be a moderated or unmoderated study, on-site, or remote). Flesh out the study structure with specific tasks for participants to complete, and additional interviews and/or surveys to gather robust data. Write instructions and prepare the moderator guide based on the prepared methods and tools.

IV. Recruit participants.

V. Conduct sessions.

VI. Conduct a thematic analysis to understand common themes and patterns that emerge from the behaviours and statements of your participants, with focus on misunderstood UI elements, unclear objectives or feedback provided by the game, and troublesome interactions. Next, perform differential analysis (especially if you invited specific player groups or participants had varied experiences with the same element). Additionally, you may want to conduct a more structured explanatory analysis to dig deeper into the root causes of observed issues and structure them better.

VII. Prepare the report (use quotes, annotated screenshots, and video clips to illustrate insights) and conduct a debrief.

19.1.3 Tips

- We have to remember that usability (play)testing isn't about whether players like the experience, but whether they can access, understand, and use what the game has to offer.
- Usability (play)tests can be easily adapted to the time and budget constraints we face. Observing participants as they perform specific tasks is vital, but if our resources are very limited, we can trade-off surveys or interviews to make the study feasible.
- Especially in smaller studios, we will rarely have access to gym builds to explore systems in relative isolation. If that's the case, we look for places within gameplay that provide us with structure to perform required tasks (e.g. a selected room, part of the map, or level with various environmental elements allowing us to check how the specific mechanics are experienced).
- Usability playtests focus on tasks, but don't be fooled into thinking we need to always define them on our own. Often, the game itself assigns specific tasks to players (e.g. player onboarding), so we may ask participants to play freely and focus on observing what will happen. Especially later in the production cycle, we will have more opportunities to rely on tasks defined by the game (e.g. when playtesting onboarding in the production phase) rather than writing them from scratch on our own.
- If a participant fails to notice or understand something (e.g. core mechanic or where to click in the interface), don't assume they were "unfocused", but look for situations where the game didn't direct their attention clearly enough.

19.1.4 Variations

- Narrative usability – This variation focuses on early evaluation of the narrative's usability layer. Instead of asking participants to play something, the tasks include reading fragments of a story or character descriptions (often paired with art assets), and asking them questions, checking their understanding (e.g. What is this story about? What are the main character's motivations? What will happen next?) to see what needs to be changed or further clarified.
- RITE (Rapid Iterative Testing and Evaluation) – Instead of running sessions with five to eight participants and then analyzing all gathered data, RITE focuses on a continuous cycle of playtesting and adjusting design. Typically. one cycle includes conducting a research session with one participant, deriving preliminary insights, and making adjustments to the design before inviting the next participant. We repeat cycles to the point when we get stable

and satisfactory results. RITE is particularly effective when we need to quickly refine specific elements, but it requires a high level of engagement from the team, as someone has to constantly decide on and make the required changes between the sessions.

19.1.5   WAYS TO SPOIL THE DISH

- Certainly, we want to be empathetic towards participants, but over-instructing them defeats the point. We have to patiently observe them struggle or misinterpret things in the game to uncover usability issues.
- We have to watch out for suggesting a team to make surface-level fixes to the discovered issue (e.g. suggesting adding tooltips, tutorial popups) without first checking for the issue's root causes. For instance, if we discovered that participants were confused by the way the inventory interface was structured, adding tooltips or guiding players through each inventory element would likely mask rather than solve the issue, as these solutions don't address the root cause related to the interface layout.

19.2   SERVING EXAMPLE

In the late pre-production for *Best Forklift Operator*, we conducted a usability playtest of the interface mock-ups and player onboarding, focusing on how players learn and use basic mechanics and complete early objectives. As an optional addition, we decided to evaluate the game's messaging clarity and accuracy on its Steam page.

Study sessions started with a brief introduction and warm-up, after which each participant was invited to complete tasks on the interface mock-ups, commenting aloud on their actions and thoughts. Next, participants were invited to play through the game's onboarding mission, again commenting aloud on their actions and thoughts. After completing the mission, each participant completed a survey about their experiences and participated in a short interview. After the interview, participants were asked to review the game's Steam page and assess the extent to which the content there

MISSING FEEDBACK

SERIOUS

(2.6) Participants lacked clear, unambiguous, and immediate feedback and signs on specific activities and events during the game:

- No visual feedback and signs when turning on/off the reverse gear caused participants to go in a different direction than intended (currently there is only audio feedback).
- No visual feedback when forklift collided with something leaving participants unsure whether they have hit something or not (currently there is collision counter in the HUD and short audio feedback on collision).
- No warnings that the time for objective is running out.

P03: *I would emphasize the collisions themselves more. Maybe a 'splash' on the screen showing the direction of the collision? [...] **There was information about the number of collisions, but the moment of collision itself was poorly emphasized. With the counter reading "4," I was convinced I had only "2" collisions.***

P02 during timed objective: ***Ugh... I ran out of time? That's not cool.***

10/39

FIGURE 19.1   Report page with insight into the feedback provided by the game. (Courtesy of Gamedust.)

matched what they experienced during gameplay. Each session lasted about 120 minutes, was run remotely via Google Meet and recorded with OBS.

We conducted a thematic analysis to categorize observations and participant statements, and then supplemented this with a temporal analysis to see if there were interrelationships between the issues. The analysis revealed a group of thematically related usability issues, so they were presented together for brevity of the report (Figure 19.1). As this was the first study for the game, we put additional emphasis on providing suggestions with examples to support the team in getting traction in addressing identified issues (Figure 19.2).

Overall, the study provided insights into what worked well in player onboarding, and what is still missing to ensure players can learn the rules and basic mechanics efficiently and effectively, as well as discovered more general and persistent issues (e.g. missing feedback during basic activities). It also provided information on how to improve the interface before implementation, making it clearer and more understandable, as well as provided some hints on improving messaging on the game's Steam page.

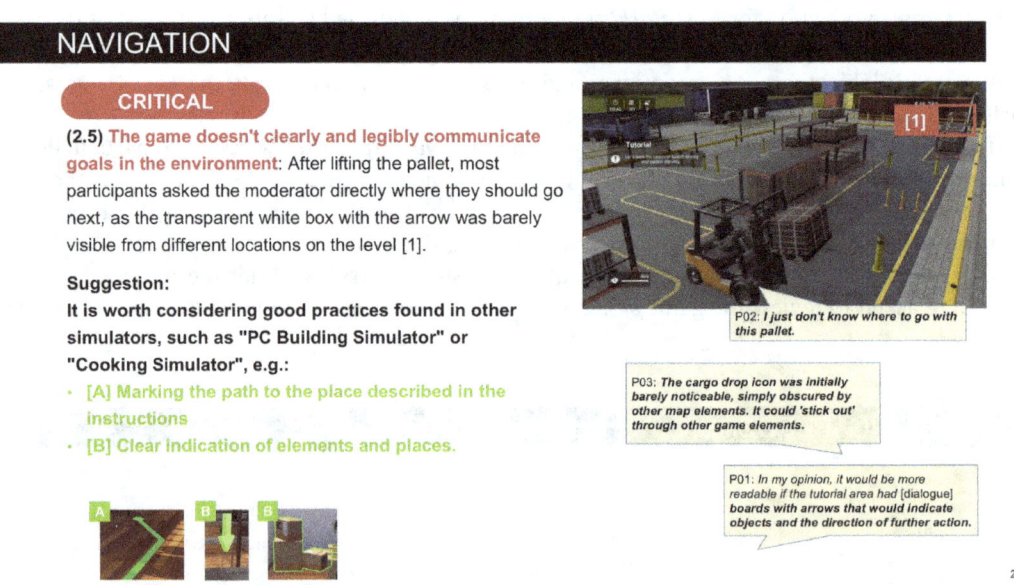

FIGURE 19.2   Report page with insight into game clarity in communicating goals. (Courtesy of Gamedust.)

20 Component Playtest

While the team works on the core game systems and their supporting elements like art, narrative, and audio during pre-production, we want to check whether all these elements are likely to work together as intended before everything is fully integrated. With component playtests, we are in the middle ground between usability and experience playtests, as our focus is wider than if the players understand and know how to use something, but we limit the breadth of our attention to engagement with the specific game systems that are core to the intended player experience. Our aim is to identify design mismatches, assess how individual assets support or hinder the player experience, and spot potential risks in combining various elements that worked well in isolation. With component playtests, we want to understand:

- Is the core game system experienced as intended, both in isolation and within the context of other game elements?
- Do gameplay, narrative, audio, or art assets elements support or hinder the intended experience for the corresponding game system?

20.1 RECIPE

Prep Time
- Approx. 7–10 days

Pots and Essentials
- Various assets representing selected game components or systems (ranging from game builds with gyms and gameplay fragments, to narrative beats, visuals, sounds, and music)
- Five to eight participants

Nutritional Value

Do players like what they see or hear?	+
Do players understand it and know how to use it?	++
Do players engage in it?	++
Do players want to continue?	–

Typical serving time: Pre-production, production

20.1.1 Utensils

- Tasks, interview, and/or survey.
- Recording software (e.g. OBS) to capture sessions.
- Spreadsheet (e.g. Google Sheets, Microsoft Excel) and/or a board with sticky notes (e.g. physical or digital one like Miro).

20.1.2 Steps in the Process

I. During the kick-off meeting, agree on which elements of the component or system under consideration are critical for gameplay experience (e.g. Do we consider observing gameplay within the gym build or gameplay fragment or both? What non-playable assets such as art, audio, or narrative elements are vital for the component we want to check?).

II. Gather the required assets and check if they are suitable to realize the study purpose. Apart from build stability and debug options, ensure that all assets are presented in a way to limit potential bias (e.g. art assets are presented against neutral backgrounds or the gym build has codenames for elements such as items or NPCs instead of actual in-game names reflecting the specific characteristics).

DOI: 10.1201/9781003501909-23

III. Based on the study's purpose, select and adapt methods and tools. In most cases, this will be a moderated study, conducted on-site or remotely. One of the biggest challenges may be the study's structure, which will allow for accommodating diverse techniques and reliably examining various assets. Typically, you'll examine gameplay in the test section, while non-playable assets will be examined in the pre-test or post-test sections. However, it all depends on the study's purpose (e.g. if you're examining the clarity of the element function based on form, you'll do it before gameplay, but if you want to assess the impressions left by that element, you'll do it after gameplay). Having decided on the study structure, flesh out specific tasks (if applicable), interviews, and/or surveys to gather robust data. Then, write instructions and prepare the moderator guide.

IV. Recruit participants.

V. Conduct sessions.

VI. Conduct a thematic analysis to understand common themes and patterns that emerge from the behaviours and statements of your participants. As a next step, perform explanatory analysis to capture how various elements contribute to the issues and strengths you discovered. Depending on the time available, you may want to conduct a more structured differential analysis (especially if you invited specific player groups or had participants had varied experiences with the same elements).

VII. Prepare the report (use quotes, annotated screenshots, non-playable assets, and video clips to illustrate insights) and conduct a debrief.

20.1.3 TIPS

- What constitutes a core game system can vary from studio to studio, and from game to game. To avoid confusion, we ask stakeholders (and check available documentation) which systems are most crucial to building the intended player experience within the core pillars or the broader creative vision and player fantasy (e.g. Which game systems are critical to realizing the fantasy of being a flying ace?). We then look at which elements are vital to fully experience that system (e.g. if we're working on a racing game and plan to explore the driving system, we'll also want to examine the available car models, their art, the sounds they make).

- Especially in smaller studios, we will rarely have access to gym builds to explore systems in relative isolation. If that's the case, we look for places within gameplay that provide us with structure to perform required tasks (e.g. a selected room, parts of the map, or a level with various environmental elements allowing us to check how the specific mechanics are experienced).

- When fleshing out study structure, we can rely on how things are about to be presented in the actual player experience (e.g. typically players see game trailers before they play, so we will ask them to watch video in pre-test to check their expectations, and ask them to play the game within test; many times players first have to notice something before they interact with it, so in most cases, we check character models before gameplay) while taking into account specific questions we want to find answers for (e.g. if we want to capture discrepancies between what participants experienced in the game, and what was communicated within game trailer, we first ask them to play in test and then to watch a video in post-test; in a horror game, we may first let the participants experience jump scare within gameplay, and in a post-test check if this element triggers a specific experience when looked closed to).

- Designing the right study structure for component playtest can be tricky at times. More than in other study types, the role of a pilot study can be critical in spotting potential weaknesses in study structure, such as those resulting from the order of presenting various assets (e.g. participants could read the function of opponents not because of the clear form, but because they had earlier watched the video presenting those opponents in action).

As a matter of additional self-check after sessions, we can conduct basic temporal analysis to verify our interpretation of the causes for the identified issues and strengths.

- By default, we focused on research for single-player games, where a single participant interacts with the various assets. However, if we're dealing with a game that offers multiplayer mode (whether online or local, such as couch co-op), we can run single sessions with multiple participants (e.g. in dyads or triads). We can conduct separate playtests for single-player and multiplayer modes, or we can conduct half the sessions with one participant and the other half with a few participants. However, we must remember to adapt methods and tools and update the moderator guide accordingly, invite more participants, and secure the necessary equipment.

20.1.4 VARIATIONS

Component playtest is variation in itself, as it combines elements of usability (paly)test and experience playtest.

20.1.5 WAYS TO SPOIL THE DISH

- Component playtests represent a hybrid study in which we may playtest a breadth of assets, so the most basic way to get ourselves into trouble with it is by defining scope too broadly. We have to watch out for situations in which we're asked to find answers for mutually exclusive questions or tendencies to packing every element in a single step of the study structure (e.g. trying to assess game trailers, character art together with narrative beats and sounds in pre-test), as those are clear signals that we should agree on priorities first (e.g. which of those elements are most critical to make design and/or business decision or assess risks). Discussion on priorities and scope may even be a prompt for us to conduct a study with a simpler structure first, such as a usability playtest.

20.2 SERVING EXAMPLE

For serving example, follow the "Bite of practice" sections in Part 2.

21 Experience Playtest

As various game systems and other components get combined by the team and start to constitute an integrated whole in late pre-production and throughout the production phase, we smoothly start to shift our focus from the usability layer to the experience layer. Even though the team might have already addressed major barriers to entry and critical problems with understanding and using various game mechanics, we still need to check if there are issues that prevent players from engaging in the experience. During experience playtests, whether they last 2–3 hours (i.e. first impressions playtest) or over a dozen or so hours (i.e. extended playtest), we want to observe players freely playing the game and their emotional reactions to experience "as is" to inform changes needed to reach the "to be" state defined in creative vision. With experience playtests, we want to understand:

- Which moments during the gameplay resonate most with the participants and which put them off?
- How do the audio, art, and narrative, among other elements, contribute to the overall gameplay experience?
- How do players perceive the game's difficulty, length, pacing, and progression?

21.1 RECIPE

Prep Time
- Approx. 2–3 weeks

Pots and Essentials
- Game build with gameplay fragment
- 16–32 participants

Nutritional Value

Do players like what they see or hear?	++
Do players understand it and know how to use it?	+
Do players engage in it?	+++
Do players want to continue?	+

Typical serving time: Production

21.1.1 UTENSILS

- Survey(s) and Interview.
- Spreadsheet (e.g. Google Sheets, Microsoft Excel) and/or a board with sticky notes (e.g. physical or digital one like Miro).

21.1.2 STEPS IN THE PROCESS

I. During the kick-off meeting, agree on general questions on experience (e.g. What is the most frustrating/favourite moment or aspect of experience with the game? What is the most memorable moment in the experience? How is the difficulty level/pacing/length/game progression perceived?). With a focus on intended experience, the discussion may include risks or concerns related to specific game aspects that may be worth exploring within the study. For instance, you may ask only general questions on how art/narrative/audio/etc., resonates with players, but you may also want to supplement it with additional information on specifics (e.g. Whether players perceive environments as sufficiently varied/big/believable/etc.? How does the final boss battle feel? Does it evoke intended emotions?).

DOI: 10.1201/9781003501909-24

II. Gather the required assets and check if they are suitable to realize the study purpose. Confirm with the team the stability of the game build and whether all critical errors that may block participants' progression in the game are resolved. Check debug options as well as the ability to hide them and call them out on demand to prevent accidental use by participants (e.g. relying only on the debug console commands).

III. Based on the study's purpose, select and adapt methods and tools. In most cases, this will be an unmoderated study, conducted on-site or remotely. When it comes to the study structure for the shorter experience playtest sessions, participants will typically play the game freely during the test section, and you will conduct a survey and/or interview in the post-test. With longer ones, however, you have more things to take care of, as you may want to rely on multiple surveys for participants to complete during the session (e.g. giving participants survey to complete each time they reach major narrative point or finish specific missions/maps/levels) within test section, and (optionally) decide to perform interview in the post-test. Having decided on the study structure, prepare a survey(s) and an interview if you decide to include it. Then, write instructions and prepare the moderator guide based on the prepared methods and tools.

IV. Recruit participants.

V. Conduct sessions.

VI. Conduct a thematic analysis to understand common themes and patterns that emerge from the behaviours and statements of your participants. As a next step, perform differential analysis to spot general changes in experience during gameplay (e.g. changes in ratings for difficulty/pacing/length between experience bits). While performing differential analysis, you may spot sub-groups of players focusing on different aspects of the experience (e.g. narrative-driven or gameplay-driven), which may provide you with some hints on how to tailor the experience to their taste (or provide options to customize it). Depending on the time available, you may want to conduct structured temporal analysis to better structure insights in time and spot related ones and/or explanatory analysis to capture how various elements contribute to issues and strengths you discovered or explain changes in ratings throughout the gameplay.

VII. Prepare the report (use quotes, annotated screenshots, and video clips to illustrate insights) and conduct a debrief.

21.1.3 TIPS

- Conducting experience playtests requires the arrangement of a place and equipment to invite multiple participants to play the game. However, besides arranging a multi-seat lab setting, we have other not mutually exclusive options at our disposal:
  - We can start with small sessions over weekends.

    Experience playtests require a relatively significant number of participants to reliably evaluate the gameplay experience. Conducting individual research sessions most of the time will be inefficient, and conducting them in a group format will require a properly arranged place and, more importantly, equipment (e.g. multiple computers with game builds configured to record gameplay). One solution is to conduct experience playtests over weekends, when the team is not working (hopefully), and we can more freely use the place and equipment in the studio. Arranging and preparing even four to five seats can allow for making study feasible, and conducting it in a reasonable amount of time.
  - If possible, we can conduct sessions remotely.

    Remote format can offer us more flexibility, with a known cost (e.g. access to the build must be easily assigned and revoked) and risk (e.g. we must consider the risk of leaks). Options such as "breakout rooms" (dividing participants into separate virtual rooms) during remote sessions give us the possibility to consider them in a group format. To manage such a remote group session, it's worth starting by inviting a smaller number of participants (e.g. three to four), and only gradually increasing the number once we become comfortable with "hopping between virtual rooms".

- We can also rely on solutions specific to the distribution platform.
  Built-in features like Steam Playtest allow us to easily provide access to the game. However, they often rely on passive data collection, so we still have to manage participants to provide us with gameplay recordings, filling in surveys to gather required information, etc.
- If our budget allows, we can use external game testing platforms.
  External services such as PlaytestCloud, Antidote, or UserTesting for games can help us overcome the logistical constraints of conducting experience playtests, so they may be an alternative worth considering.
- With multiple surveys during the session, we have to control for their length, as well as stability of some questions across surveys (e.g. we may ask for experience/difficulty/pacing/length rating in each survey to later compare them across experience bits; we may want to ask for most memorable moments in each bit). At the same time, we may want to change questions on elements specific to the experience bit (e.g. asking about specific narrative events).
- We don't always need to test the game from the beginning. Sometimes the team's goals and perceived risks will revolve around specific parts of the experience. For example, if the focus is on what players will experience in the mid- or late-game, we might start the study with a player onboarding (either in-game or provided by us), then skip selected experience bits (e.g. missions/levels) and provide participants with necessary information about what happened during those skipped bits (e.g. in the story and mechanics that have been introduced). Next, we ask participants to start playing the game from the experience bit we need to assess.

21.1.4 Variations

We mentioned three basic variations based on the length of the gameplay being studied:

- First impressions playtest for assessing gameplay experience within the first 2–3 hours of gameplay.
- Extended playtest to assess gameplay experience over several hours of gameplay.
- Playthrough playtest for assessing gameplay experience within the whole game, start to finish.

21.1.5 Ways to Spoil the Dish

- Game builds with bugs, whether minor or critical, can always cause difficulties during a research session and later analysis, but these are more evident when research is conducted in a group format. When we have to divide our attention among multiple participants at once, additional technical issues can make sessions hard to manage.
- Another problem with bugged game builds is that experience playtests focus on how players engage in the game, and biases stemming from bugs can be harder to spot in this layer of gameplay experience than in the usability and accessibility layer.
- Certainly, we might be tempted to evaluate fine details of the gameplay experience, especially in extended playtests, but asking too many questions, too often, or making them too specific may be counterproductive, as participants can get tired of filling in surveys and less focused on providing meaningful information.

21.2 SERVING EXAMPLE

While the team working on *Yupitergrad 2* was approaching the vertical slice milestone, marking the end of the pre-production phase, we decided to conduct an experience playtest to check how the gameplay offered in the game build reflected the experience intended by the team. The aim of the playtest was to assess general experience with a gameplay fragment representing the opening part of the game. We wanted to check how gameplay, art, and basic narrative elements are experienced by the players to inform further design efforts.

Sessions started with an introduction and warm-up. As the tutorial wasn't implemented, participants were provided with information on the control scheme and asked to familiarize

EQUIPMENT PRESENTATION

STRENGTH

(2.6) The way the equipment was presented in the game was very positively received by participants: Participants emphasized that the equipment complements the rest of the game's visuals and (in the case of the Minigun and Nozzles) clearly presents its function. The equipment swap animation was also perceived as highly satisfying. It's also worth noting that the way equipment is presented in the game environment (before being acquired by the player) was similarly perceived as highly satisfying.

P01: *That's pretty nice with the stuff coming out, so you can totally... you totally understand what you are doing. If the nozzles were on the backpack you wouldn't know, you can control it sideways. That's a pretty neat feature.*

P01: *It looks red, it looks pretty cool. And it have a nice crosshair now. Yeah, that's cool.*

P02: *I like the way it looks like it's cartoonish, it's slightly goofy, but it matches the design of the thing, so you have this plunger with the machingun attached – so yeah, I like it, it looks great.*

P04: *It looks pretty impressive, that gatling gun.*

17/60

FIGURE 21.1 Report page with insight into equipment presentation. (Courtesy of Gamedust.)

ACQUIRING NEW EQUIPMENT

SERIOUS

(2.7) Some participants pointed out that acquiring new equipment is not properly communicated and highlighted by the game: While the presentation of equipment was perceived as highly satisfying by all, acquiring new equipment proved somewhat of a disappointment for some participants. Some participants even emphasized that acquiring new equipment was one of bigger disappointments, as the entire situation was not accompanied by the game's recognition of the moment when the player achieved something.

P03 on biggest disappointment: *I got a new gadget, but it didn't give me the "wow" effect", I didn't even really know how to use it and what it gave me. [...] Just getting that item was quite disappointing for me. In most games, as a player, I'm used to that "wow" effect, like in the old ones, you know... Zelda, where there was this big thing that I got, in Mario, where even that stupid mushroom would escape from you, you'd just take it and have some effect, that something happened, or I don't even know, in games like Diablo, which is a completely different story, but suddenly you dropped a legendary item that has a different color, a different sound, it seemed to drop a bit differently, like there was a "wow" and something was behind it... here I have this impression, okay, there was something shiny and I flew through it and absolutely nothing, like there was no animation, like something popping up, like, you know, I actually notice something, that something is happening, or some kind of system, like on this HUD, some robot saying that something has been installed there, a new mechanism for something, I just flew through it - there were stars, there are no stars*

18/60

FIGURE 21.2 Report page with insight into acquiring new equipment. (Courtesy of Gamedust.)

themselves with it in the opening level of the game build. Then, participants were invited to play freely through a gameplay fragment representing the opening part of the game. Although sessions were moderated, we didn't ask participants to think aloud during gameplay, as we wanted to capture their experience closer to one they would have at home, together with less biased perceptions of difficulty and pacing. After completing the gameplay fragment, participants completed a survey about their experiences and participated in a post-test interview. Each session lasted approximately 180–210 minutes.

After sessions, we conducted a thematic analysis to categorize observations and participant statements. Then, we conducted a temporal analysis to see how experience evolved in time, and if there were interrelationships between the issues (Figures 21.1 and 21.2).

Overall, the study provided the team with insights that informed future iterations of specific game elements. Besides gathering a more general view on experience "as is", the study also revealed still existing usability issues preventing players from fully engaging in the experience.

22 Diary Study

As the game starts to constitute an integrated whole during the mid-late production phase, we increasingly want to consider not only how this integrated whole is experienced by players once, but also how that experience changes over time. While single research sessions may give us valid reasons for optimism, we still don't know whether players will become bored or find that something is missing in the experience after repeated exposure. Similarly, players may be sufficiently engaged for one or two sessions, only to not engage in the third one and abandon the game entirely. To uncover these types of insights, we may need to observe players beyond a single session with the game. A diary study aims to capture how gameplay experience changes over time, giving us the perspective of days or weeks. What's equally important is that it gives us additional perspective on how the game is played within the context of participants' daily lives, which cannot be fully captured with other methods. With diary studies, we want to understand:

- How does the player experience change from session to session? What are the ups and downs?
- What keeps players coming back, and what pushes them away?
- What supports the intended experience, what subtracts from it, and what's missing in the long run?

22.1 RECIPE

Prep Time
- Approx. 2–4 weeks (or longer)

Pots and Essentials
- Game build that has reached at least alpha milestone or later (i.e. feature-complete, and playable start to finish)
- 8–12 participants

Nutritional Value

Do players like what they see or hear?	+
Do players understand it and know how to use it?	+
Do players engage in it?	+++
Do players want to continue?	+++

Typical serving time: Production, post-production

22.1.1 UTENSILS

- Participant guide.
- Pre-test interview (also called intro interview).
- Survey(s).
- Post-test interview (also called follow-up or outro interview).
- Spreadsheet (e.g. Google Sheets, Microsoft Excel) and/or a board with sticky notes (e.g. physical or digital one like Miro).

22.1.2 STEPS IN THE PROCESS

I. During the kick-off meeting, agree on what will be observed within gameplay experience over an extended period (e.g. What elements become tiresome or boring after repeated exposure? What issues have a persisting impact on the experience, and which ones fade with time? How does the experience of the narrative change as the story progresses?

DOI: 10.1201/9781003501909-25

How does the perception of pace and difficulty change over time?). In general, the discussion may include unknowns, risks, or concerns related to how the experience unfolds over time. The other topic to discuss is how often you want to ask participants to share entries in their diary. Typically, participants are asked to complete a survey at a specific point in time (e.g. daily in the evenings) or after a specific event (e.g. immediately after a session with a game or after accomplishing a specific game objective/reaching level "x" of their character/finishing chapter "y" in the narrative).

II. Gather the required assets and check if they are suitable to realize the study purpose (e.g. game build with no critical bugs, stable across days with a working save system).

III. Based on an agreed purpose, decide on methods and tools (e.g. obviously the study will be conducted remotely), and flesh out the study structure. It's a bit more complex, as a diary study spans over multiple days and sessions with the game.

- The study begins with an intro session. The format used in this book includes an intro, a warm-up, and a pre-test interview. This is a relatively short session where you brief participants and provide them with onboarding materials (e.g. participant guide) explaining how and when to complete their diary entries.
- For the test, create a basic structure for a diary (usually in the form of a survey) that participants will complete (e.g. every evening) over a specified period.
- Conduct outro session (covering post-test and wrap-up), for which you will prepare an interview summarizing participant's experiences with the game and aimed at providing you with a better understanding of themes captured in the surveys.

IV. Recruit participants.

V. Sessions last for many days, which requires constant monitoring of what is happening and analyzing the incoming diary entries, so we'll discuss conducting sessions and analysis steps together:

- Conduct intro sessions with participants and share participant guides with them.
- Monitor responses throughout the specified period, while staying in contact with participants (e.g. via Discord or messaging app) to answer any questions, helping solve technical issues, and sending reminders about performing planned activities (i.e. entry in the diary). Conduct a thematic analysis (e.g. daily when you asked participants to provide an entry daily) to understand common themes and patterns that emerge from the participants' statements. Having at least a few entries for each participant adds temporal analysis to check how those themes and patterns in experience evolve over time (look for ups and downs, as well as situations when nothing changes). Prepare a daily top findings report and discuss it with the team.
- After the specified period (or when the participant abandoned the experience), conduct outro interviews to fill in gaps in your understanding and clarify ambiguous entries. In the end, conduct another round of thematic and temporal analysis to sum up the whole experience participants had with the game. Depending on the time available, you may also want to conduct a more structured explanatory analysis.

VI. Prepare the report focusing on changes over time instead of only isolated insights (use quotes, annotated screenshots, as well as player journey maps) and conduct a debrief.

22.1.3 Tips

- The obvious requirement for a diary study is to make the game available for players to play at their homes, which raises concerns about potential leaks when the game is not released yet. Certainly, we ask participants to read and sign an NDA, but during the intro session, it's still worth sensitizing them that leaks (e.g. sharing screenshots or gameplay recordings publicly) can undermine the team's efforts and negatively impact the perception of the game in the making.

- It's worth asking participants to supplement their diary entries with additional materials to gain a more complete understanding of their experiences. For instance, we might ask participants to document their experiences by sending us screenshots of something that stood out for them (either positively or negatively).
- Diary studies are one of the stark examples of how data analytics and user research can cooperate to deliver a more complete picture of the player experiences for deeper insights. We combine diary entries with analytical data (if available), to track things such as when and how often players interact with a specific mechanics and features (e.g. What they are over or underusing?), or how they progress in the game (e.g. How long it takes for them to reach specific levels? How often and where do they fail?).
- We simply don't wait with analysis till the last day, but perform it on an ongoing basis, so as not to be overwhelmed with data.
- The advantage of diary studies is that they give us the possibility to see how the game experience fits into the participants' daily lives. At the same time, they are long enough that we simply can't anticipate all the important themes that will emerge. That's why we leave room for more general or free comments on the experience in our surveys, and aren't afraid to adapt them on the go (e.g. by adding specific questions based on the results of ongoing analysis to better capture emerging themes and patterns).
- To make monitoring and communication with participants a bit easier for us, we brief them during the intro session and provide them with the same information in written format (participant guide), so they can refer to it later. In the participant guide, we include the information typically covered in the moderator guide (e.g. what participants are expected to do, how the data will be used, what the remuneration is) together with answers to typical questions participants may have, such as:
    - What to do if I have questions? (e.g. if questions or difficulties arise during the game, write to us via Discord).
    - What to do if I can't or don't know how to proceed in the game?
    - What to do if I no longer want to continue playing? (e.g. If for whatever reason you don't want to keep playing, that's okay. Just remember to write to us via Discord. We will want to understand what happened, so we will ask you to answer a few short questions. Your answers will help us improve the game for other players in the future).
    - What to do if I forgot to submit a survey within the specified timeframe? (e.g. We will send you reminders to complete the survey. However, if for any reason you are unable to complete it within the specified timeframe, please complete it at the first opportunity before your next session).
    - What to do if I play shorter than expected (e.g. less than 60 min/day)? (e.g. It's still okay, just remember to write down how long you played and fill in the survey).

22.1.4 Variations

As we already mentioned, a diary study can follow different structures depending on how and when participants fill the diary. Participants can provide entries at a specific point in time or after a specific event, and these entries can be provided in a more or less structured way (ranging from closed-ended questions in a survey, through interviews, to session recordings and participant notes taken while playing). The approach presented in this recipe is on the more structured end of the spectrum to better control whether we have covered all the questions the team might have, while still leaving some room for spontaneous feedback. At the same time, there is nothing stopping us from opting for session recordings and unstructured participant notes if that would ensure that the collected data better reflect how the experience naturally unfolds over time and keeps participant effort at a reasonable level. However, we have to bear in mind that this may require more time to analyze, and some topics may not arise spontaneously.

22.1.5 Ways to Spoil the Dish

- If we require participants to complete long and complex surveys or provide a variety of materials that require additional effort (e.g. recordings of sessions with comments), we may obtain low-quality data or a relatively higher number of participants resigning from the study before the end. We must strive for a balance between the scope and thoroughness of the study and participant engagement. If participants disengage during the study, the reasons should be found in the experience, not the methods used.
- Skipping outro sessions for participants who resigned is a good way to lose vital insights for the game's success (or lack thereof). Although it may be at times difficult to reach participants who have simply lost interest in continuing to play, the effort is usually worth it. For instance, by reducing the potential for survivorship bias in our analysis (focusing on participants who stayed engaged throughout the study may hide which strengths truly mattered and which issues hindered the experience). One of the solutions to have a greater chance of capturing thoughts of participants who disengaged with the experience is providing part of the remuneration based on going through the outro interview, instead of the completion of the whole study.

22.2 SERVING EXAMPLE

During late production of *Yupitergrad 2*, when the game constituted an integrated whole and we had already explored specific experience bits in separation, we decided to conduct a diary study. The aim of the study was to assess how the gameplay experience changes over a longer period, with a focus on perceived difficulty, gameplay length, and pacing. Based on the estimated game length, we decided to monitor the experience in the diary format for 1 week.

Participants were invited to a study in which, after intro session conducted via Discord and receiving participant guides, they were asked to play the game at their own pace for 7 days, playing at least 60 minutes each day, and completing daily surveys. At the end of the study, participants completed another survey about their overall experience with the game. Eight participants took part in the study, three of whom finished the game. It's worth noting that none of the participants abandoned the study, but this may have been due to the short study period, rather than their engagement in the gameplay experience.

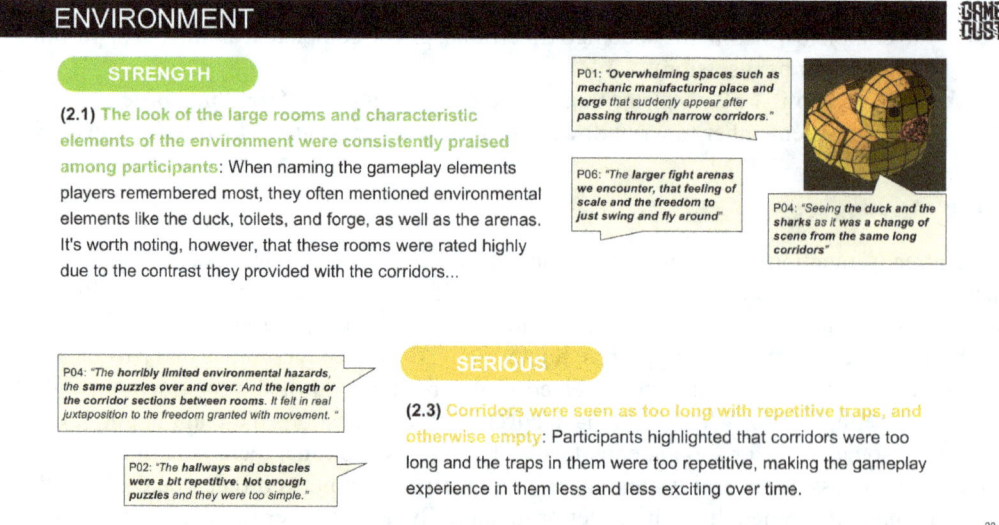

FIGURE 22.1 Report page with insights into the game environment. (Courtesy of Gamedust.)

During the study, the team, together with the user researcher, conducted a thematic analysis to categorize observations and participant statements on a daily basis, and then supplemented this with a temporal analysis to see how identified issues and strengths changed over time. The analysis revealed both issues and strengths that were prevalent throughout the experience with the game (Figure 22.1).

As we didn't have analytics to precisely check various information on sessions (e.g. length of sessions, fulfilling objectives, explored areas, number of deaths on specific levels), we had to rely on participants' self-reporting their session length together with the objective they ended their session on. Even with this limitation, we were still able to perform differential analysis to spot main areas during gameplay where experience was far from the design intent (Figure 22.2). The observed changes during the game experience, as well as participants' responses to the open-ended survey questions, informed a more formal explanatory analysis conducted later.

Overall, the study provided insights into what was engaging throughout the gameplay experience, and what became dull and repetitive after repeated interaction. Even with the limited precision, we also gathered hints on experience bits that needed to be prioritized and acted upon by the team to limit the risk of disengaging players (e.g. focusing first on slow-paced player onboarding, and later on abrupt game final).

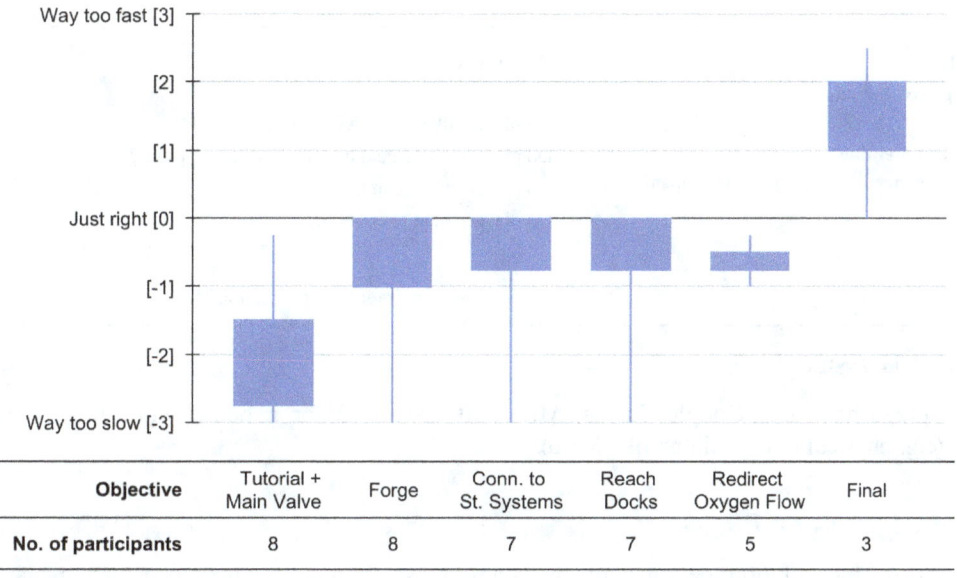

Objective	Tutorial + Main Valve	Forge	Conn. to St. Systems	Reach Docks	Redirect Oxygen Flow	Final
No. of participants	8	8	7	7	5	3

FIGURE 22.2 Participants' survey responses into game pacing across sessions visualized in box plots. (Courtesy of Gamedust.)

23 Review Analysis

Once a game is out in the wild and starts to generate interest from players and experts, at some point, they will start to share their opinions in the form of reviews, let's plays, requests for support, or posts in community spaces. We could certainly say that the rest of the team is most likely reading this information as well, so why bother? Since we are not the actual creators invested emotionally in specific ideas (and release can be a very emotional time during the production cycle), we can provide a more structured view of what is happening to prevent selective use of information or misinterpretation based on preconceptions. However, it requires us to act fast, to provide information on what the most urgent and frequently reported issues are, so that they can be rationally prioritized with the team. With review analysis, we want to understand:

- What are the most severe and frequent issues?
- How do player and/or expert experiences align with the intended design?

23.1 RECIPE

Prep Time
- Approx. 1–3 days

Pots and Essentials
- This recipe doesn't require participants

Nutritional Value

Do players like what they see or hear?	++
Do players understand it and know how to use it?	+
Do players engage in it?	+
Do players want to continue?	+

Typical serving time: Post-production

23.1.1 UTENSILS

- Spreadsheet (e.g. Google Sheets, Microsoft Excel) and/or a board with sticky notes (e.g. physical or digital one like Miro).

23.1.2 STEPS IN THE PROCESS

I. During the kick-off meeting, agree on data sources to be analyzed (e.g. focus first on player or expert reviews, let's play streams, and add forum and social media threads if feasible).

II. Search and pre-select specific data (e.g. search for and list "let's plays" to watch, save bookmarks with expert reviews to read, scrape player reviews). Next, gather and organize data from selected sources. If you decide to watch "let's play" streams, approach them like unmoderated sessions to observe player behaviour, and to better understand nuance in statements made in reviews.

III. Conduct thematic analysis and derive first insights. Next, conduct differential analysis to compare insights, and check which insights are shared among sources (e.g. between experts and players). You can also filter sources for sentiment (e.g. compare positive vs. negative reviews). Next, create a table with insights discovered in rows (this will help you structure your report), and then mark in the subsequent columns from which sources a given insight comes from.

IV. Prepare a brief report (use quotes, links to sources like expert reviews, let's plays fragments to illustrate insights) focused on prioritization and conduct the debrief.

DOI: 10.1201/9781003501909-26

23.1.3 Tips

- Doing review analysis effectively requires us to collaborate with the team members responsible for marketing, community management, or relations with the media (e.g. press outlets, influencers). After all, they are the ones who monitor and react to the information generated by players and experts, so they can point us to the most impactful sources that need to be analyzed first, and we may even conduct analysis jointly for better and faster effect.
- If you have more time, look into the negative space to see what's missing in the reviews (e.g. What key elements of the creative vision aren't highlighted in the reviews?).

23.1.4 Variations

- The recipe focuses on rapid review analysis, providing the initial insights needed for more rational decision-making (especially in crisis situations). If the game's situation in the post-production phase is favourable or we have more time to react, a more in-depth analysis of various sources can provide input for planning subsequent game updates.
- There are other occasions before the release, where review analysis can come in handy. For instance, when an early game demo is released, or when marketing team members organize game previews or silent reviews (e.g. sending the game to expert reviewers for review, which will not be publicly available). While the insights may be limited because people are sensitized to the fact that the game they're (pre-)reviewing isn't finished and may change before release, it is still worth supporting it for more actionable insights (e.g. proposing questions to be asked to pre-reviewers).

23.1.5 Ways to Spoil the Dish

- Analyzing every mention of the game we can find thoroughly might make sense in the long term, but right after release, it's crucial to act fast so the team can quickly adapt their actions, especially when the initial outlook is relatively bleak.

23.2 SERVING EXAMPLE

We typically conduct a review analysis after a game's release. However, release doesn't necessarily mean the game has gone through a full production cycle. A game can be released earlier, for example, in an Early Access format (where the game will evolve based on player impressions and feedback) or by releasing a demo version before the full release.

While working on the publisher's side on adventure-puzzle game *Rooms of Realities* (VR title developed by a team of several people from the Bluekey Games studio), we conducted such a review analysis shortly after the demo's release to have more structured view on the first impressions about gameplay and various features in the game together with expectations about the full game, while the game was still in pre-production phase. The basic assumption was to quickly deliver insights to the team to adapt their priorities and inform their immediate actions.

First, together with the marketing team, we scanned for sources with mentions about the game. Then, we collected and organized player reviews and comments on the game from the community, players' discussions on product page forums, as well as listed articles about the game, and influencer reviews. We then conducted thematic analysis for each source (i.e. players, journalists, influencers) to spot strengths and issues. Next, we performed differential analysis to see which insights were common across all sources and which appeared only in some of them. It turned out that perceptions on the game from various sources were coherent, so we proceeded to combine insights and write a report in a short top findings format (Figure 23.1).

0.1 PUZZLES

+ The difficulty level of the puzzles was rated as "just right"
At the same time there were no negative comments on difficulty identified during the analyzed period.

- *"**The puzzles** are particularly **well balanced** and interesting"* - Influencer
- *"**The difficulty level of the puzzles is just right**"* - Influencer
- *"You had to think and I liked that too"* - Influencer
- *"**Some puzzles are harder than others and that's great!**"* - Player
- *"I thought **the difficulties of the puzzles was about right**"* - Player

— People struggled solving the last puzzle in the demo with the battering ram, as it wasn't clear what interaction they should perform and that the same interaction had to be performed simultaneously by all players.

- *"I still **don't really understand the last puzzle** but those in my party got me through it"* - Player
- *"For the final puzzle, even though **I knew which item I was suppose to use**, it wasn't clear to me *how* to use it. I'm still not entirely sure what I was *supposed* to do with it - crank it repeatedly? Hold it down? Time the pulls for when the red light illuminates? Not really sure. **Unfortunately, it made for a somewhat anticlimactic end**."* - Player

? The hint system helped to find puzzle pieces, but players expected that it would also support better understanding on what to do next or how to do it.

- *"I think you'll have to add some kind of a riddle system, **the current one helps with choosing the right objects, but doesn't help with what to do with them, or what order you need need to use them.**"* - Player
- *"**My one mild critique would be the hint system**. Am I right that holding Y basically "sweeps" the room and highlights any items that you have to interact with in order to solve the level? **Including items you've already used and that are no longer relevant?** I think that could use some improvement."* - Player

4/10

FIGURE 23.1 Report page with insights into puzzles. (Courtesy of Gamedust.)

This rapid study delivered input for prioritization of further work on the game, as well as highlighted areas and specific features of the game that were experienced as intended, as well as uncovered those that still needed more attention and effort.

Index

For Product Safety Concerns and Information please contact our EU
representative GPSR@taylorandfrancis.com
Taylor & Francis Verlag GmbH, Kaufingerstraße 24, 80331 München, Germany